I0157350

The Promise of Dualism

An Introduction to Dualist Theory

Alistair J. Sinclair Ph.D.

AP
Almostic

Almostic Publications
2015

Published by

Almostic Publications

Glasgow

ISBN 978-0-9574044-3-4

© 2014 Alistair J. Sinclair

The right of Alistair J. Sinclair to be identified as the author of this book has been asserted by him in accordance with sections 77 & 78 of the Copyright and Patents Act of 1988

To the memory of Sir Graham and Mary Hills

Then can I drown an eye, unused to flow,
For precious friends hid in death's dateless night.
Shakespeare, *Sonnet XXX.*

Contents

Book One – Introductory

Part One – The Ubiquity of Duality

Part Two – The Nature of the Dualist View

Part Three – The Humanist Consensus

Part Four – Applying Dualist Studies

V

Book Two – Expository

Part Five – The Nature of Dualist Interaction

Part Six – The Emergence of Complexity by Dualist Interaction

Part Seven – The Development of Self by Dualist Interaction

Book Three – Exploratory

Part Eight – The Logic of Dualist Interaction

Part Nine – The Pursuit of Truth by Dualist Interaction

Foreword

"The future is dualist" is the message of this book. It argues that the future progress of humanity depends on the dualist viewpoint being adopted that takes account of both sides of an argument and corrects imbalances created by the application of extreme points of view. Most of the divisions causing conflict and war throughout the world have resulted from monist thinking which takes one side of an argument to extremes. However, moderation is not always the answer; dualism means finding the most practical, workable and humane way forward. Dualist theory deals with the problems arising from adopting this dualist viewpoint.

This book introduces dualist theory using excerpts from my published and unpublished writings on the subject. It is an exploratory text which does not yet form a complete or consistent system. Many arguments are repeated in different contexts. There may be superficial or contradictory passages but it is perhaps sufficient to show the range of the subject and the extent to which dualist theory can provide an alternative view of ourselves and our role in the universe. It is argued that the development of this theory can add to our knowledge and understanding of ourselves and give us more hope that we can overcome our problems and make a better future for life in general as well as humanity. The extent to which dualist theory has a promising future should be clear from this book.

The theory concerns the way that dualist interactions can be used to explain change, complexity and innovation in the universe, including how these interactions give us an insight into ourselves and our society. A dualist interaction is a one-to-one relationship between existents which is harmonious over a period of time and which leads to differences being created. These differences are caused by the respective interactions. Perhaps the most obvious example is a male-female relationship in which offspring are produced.

Dualist theory also addresses many of the flaws in human thinking that are currently causing problems throughout the world. It promises a better future if these flaws are overcome in the manner suggested in this book. The point is to show how reason can solve our problems. Our reasoning powers are not to be disparaged just because past ways of thinking are now failing us. We have the brains to solve our most pressing problems in the long term. It is a matter of improving our ways of thinking and this has always been the aim of philosophy, though it has lately been remiss in that regard. We must not allow past and present failures to make us despair of our future and resort to religion as the only way forward. The later Roman Empire took that path and it crippled civilisation by terminating intellectual progress. It took centuries to repair the damage caused, and even yet we are ignorant of much of the history, literature and achievements of the Roman Empire because so much was lost through religious bigotry. As things stand, an extreme religious mentality could easily prevail and make it a crime to be doubtful and uncertain of orthodox beliefs.

We are currently beset by extremism, fanaticism, fundamentalism and terrorism. This will continue indefinitely unless we win the battle of ideas, which can only proceed through philosophy. It is worrying that philosophy no longer commands the attention of the public as it did up to the 1960s. Philosophical movements such as the analytical and postmodern movements are now spent forces and a fresh, invigorating approach is needed to take philosophy out of its present malaise. Hopefully, dualist studies can help revive interest in philosophy. But it will do so only if it is successful in its practical applications many of which are outlined in this book.

The development of dualist theory has hitherto been delayed by the blinkered focus on the mind/body, mental/physical dualisms. Indeed, the spectre of Descartes has haunted the subject of dualism throughout the 20th century, spawning an ever-burgeoning and bewildering variety of distinctions and categories, both for and against dualism in the narrow Cartesian mind/body sense. These are discussed in section B of the *Introduction*. However, dualist theory can make progress when the notion of dualist interaction is applied rigorously so that the complex interactions that make consciousness possible can be better understood. This is the subject of part six on *The Emergence of Complexity by Dualist Interaction*.

The contents of this book include revised excerpts from two papers on dualism published in the journal *Essays in the Philosophy of Humanism*.[1] Much new material is included, especially in parts eight and nine on *The Logic of Dualist Interaction* and on *The Pursuit of Truth by Dualist Interaction* respectively. This compilation attempts to introduce dualist theory in an interesting way with as few technical terms as possible. It is provisional work-in-progress that indicates the promise of dualism as a philosophical system. It does not cover the whole content of dualist theory. There is only superficial coverage of its application to ethics, society, or the dualist development of complexity in the universe. The treatment of both logic and truth in this book is also cursory and superficial. This book is only a beginning.

---

[1] Namely, (1) "Dualism and Humanism," Vol. 19 (1), Spring-Summer 2011, pp. 41-56; and (2) "World War One and the Loss of the Humanist Consensus," Vol. 19 (2), Fall-Winter 2011, pp. 43-60.

Introduction

A. The all-embracing nature of dualist theory

Dualist theory concerns dualist[2] or one-to-one interactions and how these can explain many phenomena in nature and in our society that are inadequately accounted for by the sciences. It is a new approach to understanding better how the things change, become more or less complex, produce new properties or qualities, and other unusual features that the sciences account for, adequately of not, with their respective methodologies. The theory is applicable to every aspect of our existence and is all-embracing in the sense of giving us an additional way of looking at everything around us. Dualist theory is therefore a new and different way of viewing the phenomena already explicated by the sciences in their various ways. It adds to our armoury in the common battle for greater knowledge and understanding of what we are and what our place in the universe. In that respect, dualist theory overlaps but does not supersede existing sciences.

Dualist theory does not explain everything; any more than a science such as physics explains everything about us. It is an additional method of explaining our place in the universe. It complements logic, mathematics and science and provides new insights into these. This is because its approach is through the interactive nature of consciousness and its apprehension of abstractions through intuition and induction. It is another weapon in the armoury of human reason which we can use to combat ignorance and prejudice. It opens up a new field of view and illuminates many aspects of what it is to be human. It is therefore a new philosophical viewpoint that adds to our knowledge and, if implemented, it could change the minds of extremists and fanatics who are daily causing so much unnecessary harm and suffering across the globe.

Dualist interaction is a key notion in dualist theory. It implies a one-to-one relationship between two entities. This fluid relationship is the theory's fundamental unit, its 'atom' as it were, as the world can be interpreted in terms of it. For example, when a politician addresses a televised meeting, he or she is establishing one-to-one relationships with each one of the listeners who will make what they will of what is being said by the politician. Even those listening at home will be interacting with what is being said on a one-to-one basis. They may even be shouting 'rubbish!' in response! Similarly, a flock of birds flying in formation are able to do so by forming one-to-one relationships with each of their neighbours. Dualist interaction applies even more strikingly to atomic structures which depend on one-to-one relationships powered by strong or weak nuclear forces. Thus, dualist interaction can also be used to explain the one-to-one relationships by which we function as biological entities. There are complex

---

[2] The grammatical rule for the word 'dualist' adopted in this book is that it becomes 'dualistic' only as an end word or an adverb as in 'the approach was dualistic' or 'it was used dualistically'. But as an adjective the suffixes 'ic' or 'ical' can be omitted for the sake of euphony.

series of interrelationships by which the physical activity in us is complexified into the biological activity that makes us living beings. Understanding these interrelationships goes far beyond the traditional mind/body and mental/physical distinctions.

It is a matter of thinking about things in strict interactive terms. When a thought occurs to us we interact with it by considering it further. The thought itself was generated interactively by unconscious processes. These processes in their turn were produced interactively by the physical processes that underlie them. In this way, a continuous chain of dualist interactions can be established, all of which can be shown to be physically based. Any gaps in the chain are due to our lack of neurophysiological understanding of the processes and perhaps of the extent to which quantum phenomena are involved. In this way, the so-called 'ghost in the machine' is pensioned off into oblivion. We can now see ourselves as being part of the material world rather than absolutely distinct from it. Only degrees of internal material complexity are involved and not an occult spirituality.

Unfortunately, the development of a thorough-going dualist theory has been hindered by the absolute nature of Descartes' mind-body distinction. This distinction is embedded in our thinking and leads us to think what happens within us is fundamentally different from the physical events happening outside us. Positing mind and body as distinct things reifies them as Aristotelian substances with essences and properties. This reification has poisoned philosophical thinking ever since as is argued below. In interactive dualism, the mental and physical are not fundamentally different. Mental events are seen as complex forms of physical events. When interactive dualism is rigorously and consistently applied, categorical distinctions that divide mind from body and the mental from the physical are rendered obsolete. To put mind and body into absolutely distinct categories is *categorical thinking* characteristic of monist as opposed to dualist thinking.

In interactive dualism, words such as 'mind', 'mental', or 'soul' are merely occult things that can't be explained in physical terms. What they refer to is explicable in terms of dualist interactions that occur in the brain and central nervous system, and they are as just as physical as the dualist interactions anywhere in the body or in the outside world. There is no need for immaterial substances or anything that can't be explained scientifically in material terms. Our subjective experiences are entirely physical and the fact that we seem to experience pains and feelings inside ourselves is only a matter of perspective. These experiences result from dualist interactions involving the holistic self (see part seven on *The Development of Self by Dualist Interaction*) interacting with what occurs physically in the brain. If we cannot explain these experiences entirely in physical terms, that is due to the lack of neurophysiological understanding and not to the existence of a 'mind' distinct from the body.

Dualism has been disparaged by its association with Descartes' retrogressive 'method' based on the so-called 'real distinction' between mind and body.[3] In his 'Sixth Meditation' Descartes says that he has a distinct idea of himself as a thinking, non extended thing (*res cogitans, non extensa*) and a distinct idea of body as an extended, non-thinking thing (*res extensa, non cogitans*) and therefore he is really distinct from his body and can exist without it.[4] Clearly there is a religious motivation here as he believes this distinction is supported by scripture. Presumably he has in mind, for instance, the precepts of St. Paul when he says the following in his Notes:

> The fact that mind is in truth nothing other than a substance, or an entity really distinct from body, in actuality separable from it, and capable of existing apart and independently, is revealed to us in Holy Scripture, in many places. And thus what in the view of some, the study of nature leaves doubtful is already placed beyond all doubt for us through divine revelation in Scripture.[5]

No doubt Christianity and religion in general are responsible for making the distinction between mind and body seem both primary and absolute in our thinking. For the distinction is essential to the idea that the soul survives the death of the body. Descartes consolidated that viewpoint by making it central to his philosophical doctrines. However, dualist theory sweeps away the primacy of this distinction as is discussed in more detail in this book.

Thus, an interactive dualist theory is not the same as Cartesian dualism. Its broader base goes beyond the narrow perspective of Cartesian dualism. By developing the notion of dualist interaction we eliminate the mind/body, mental/physical distinctions. A much richer panoply of dualist interactions accounts for our consciousness and our subjectivity without denying their fundamental physicality.

There is a complex continuity between conscious activity and the physical activity that makes consciousness possible. What might be called 'the mind

---

[3] The phrase 'real distinction' appears in the title page of Descartes' *Meditations* and as a subtitle to the Sixth Meditation. It is discussed at length by Bernard Williams' book, *Descartes: The Project of Pure Enquiry*, (London: Penguin Books, 1978, ch. 4, pp. 102-129, and elsewhere.

[4] Cf. Descartes, 'Sixth Meditation' 78, in *Meditations on First Philosophy*, trans. J. Cottingham, (Cambridge, UK: Cambridge University Press, 1986), p.54. This book contains the Latin text and a translation from that text rather than from the usual French one. The relevant passages are as follows:

- Latin: *Certum est me a corpore meo revera esse distinctum, et absque illo posse existere.*

- French: *Il est certain que ce moi, c'est-à-dire, mon âme, par laquelle je suis ce que je suis, est entièrement et véritablement distincte de mon corps, et qu'elle peut être ou exister sans lui.*

- English: It is certain that I [that is, my soul by which I am what I am] am really distinct from my body, and can exist without it.

[5] Descartes, 'Notes Directed Against a Certain Programme' (1647), 343, in *Key Philosophical Writings*, trans. E. S. Haldane and G.R.T. Ross, ed. by E. Chávez-Arvizo, (Ware, Herts: Wordsworth Editions Ltd., 1997), p.339.

assumption' that leads thinkers to assume that an additional source of energy is required to explain the existence of mind, mental events and consciousness. Dualist theory eliminates the need for any mental or spiritual energy to explain what happens in the brain which enables physical activity to produce our subjective experiences. In this theory, consciousness is a highly complex form of physical activity, and its emergence through complex dualist interactions is described in that theory (see part six of this book in particular). Thus, dualist theory is entirely materialist and physicalist when it is developed in a systematic way around the notion of dualist interaction

B. The inadequacy of current views of the subject

As already mentioned, the systematic study of philosophical dualism has been hampered by the fashionable fixation on Descartes and his simplistic mind/body, mental/physical dichotomies. Philosophers usually Take these distinctions the starting point for their treatment of dualism. For example, Colin McGinn defines it as follows:

> Dualism is the doctrine that mental phenomena inhere in an immaterial substance which is utterly different from the material substance composing the body: just as physical states are qualifications of a certain kind of stuff, namely matter, so mental states are qualifications of a different kind of stuff, incorporeal in nature.[6]

D.M. Armstrong also takes the rigid mind/body view of dualism: "A Dualist theory is one that holds that mind and body are *distinct things*. For a Dualist a man is a compound object, a material thing – his body – somehow related to a non-material thing or things – his mind."[7] Armstrong distinguishes two forms of dualism: Cartesian dualism and bundle dualism, and he proceeds to dispose of both these viewpoints in his book.

Daniel Dennett similarly assumes that dualism must *ipso facto* involve a belief in a 'mind stuff' existing of itself somewhere or other; a view that is fundamentally unscientific:

> It is surely no accident that the few dualists to avow their views openly have all candidly and comfortably announced that they have no theory whatever of how the mind works – something, they insist, that is quite beyond human ken. There is the lurking suspicion that the most attractive feature of mind stuff is its promise of being so mysterious that it keeps science at bay forever. This fundamentally antiscientific stance of dualism is, to my mind, its most disqualifying feature, and is the reason why in this book I adopt the apparently dogmatic rule that dualism is to be avoided *at all costs*.[8]

---

[6] Colin McGinn, *The Character of Mind*, (Oxford: OUP, 1982), ch. 2, p. 22.
[7] David M. Armstrong, *A Materialist Theory of the Mind*, (1968 London: Routledge, 1993), section 1, p. 6.
[8] Daniel C. Dennett, *Consciousness Explained*, (London: Penguin Books, 1993). Part 1, section 2, p. 37.

Needless to say, the dualist theory outlined in this book is not unscientific, is not based on 'mind stuff',[9] and does indeed introduce a comprehensive theory of how the mind works in terms of dualist interactions. In trying consciously to avoid dualism, Dennett constantly falls into it without acknowledging it consciously. Indeed, his book is permeated throughout with the duality of interactive contrasts. For example:

- Section 8 of his book *Consciousness Explained* is headed "How Words Do Things With Us". If we do things with words and they in their turn do things with us then this implies that dualist interaction is going on between them and us.

- His 'Multiple Drafts' model involves 'editorial processing' of some sort.[10] An area somewhere in the brain must be doing this processing, therefore that area is interacting dualistically with given information to produce the drafts. Arguably, this model cannot be made to work convincingly without a system of dualist interactions underlying it.

- In several places, he refers to higher and lower order thoughts.[11] For example, I may think that I feel a pain in my foot and when I think about it, I am having a higher order thought about it. I may even think about what I thought of the pain when I am no longer conscious of it. But in all these thoughts about thoughts there are interactions going on between my feelings of pain and my thoughts about it. An infinite regress of thoughts about thoughts is avoided because we are moving through different contexts from the conscious level down to the unconscious level and then down the levels of brain chemistry, all of which are connected interactively. Thus, a more complete account of what is going on here is possible than in Dennett's use of 'folk psychology'.

McGinn's and Dennett's unsympathetic views of dualism typify the static, logical interpretation of it in which mental and physical 'substances' are logical categories that are rigidly applied to the furniture of mind and body. Dualism is thereby subjected to a logical analysis which perpetuates the rigidity between dualist oppositions. Our thinking is not allowed to be fluid and flexible in relation to our experiences in the truly dualist manner. It is trammelled up and stultified by artificial logical divisions. These views are therefore associated with word definitions and the logical boundaries between rigid categories. The following are examples of the approaches that are insufficient and superficial compared to dualist theory based on dualist interactions.

- In *predicative dualism* psychological or mentalist notions are not reducible to physical notions. The idea of water may be reduced to the physical notion H_2O. But feelings of love or despair cannot be readily

---

[9] With this so-called 'mind-stuff', Dennett is referring to John C. Eccles' contribution to *The Self and its Brain*, (1977 - London: Routledge, Kegan & Paul, 1986), written jointly with Karl Popper. However, Eccles is constrained in his account of the mind's workings by his need to adhere to Popper's view of 'Worlds 1, 2 and 3'. As the interrelationship between these hypostatised 'worlds' is obscure and underdeveloped, his 'dualist-interactionist hypothesis' is flawed and incomplete. (Cf. Eccles *op. cit.*, ch. E7, p. 374).

[10] Dennett, *op. cit.*, section 5, pp. 112-113.

[11] For example, *op. cit.*, section 10, p. 307.

reduced to physical terms that relate to events in the brain or nervous system. In interactive dualism, feelings are related to physical events by a concatenation of interactive events. The accuracy of the connections depends entirely on the extent of our knowledge of the relevant causal connections. In the way, dualist theory can be a stimulus to scientific research to fill up the gaps by the appropriate research.

- In *bundle dualism* the mind experiences a succession of non-physical particulars that are distinct from the body. These particulars are bundled together to form our perceptions of things. This kind of dualism is said to be derived from Hume's well known disavowal of his 'self':[12]

> For my part, when I enter most intimately into what I call *myself*, I always stumble upon some particular perception or other, or heat or cold, light or shade, love or hatred, pain or pleasure. I can never catch *myself* at any time without a perception, and never can observe anything but the perception.[13]

The idea of the self vanishes when all our personal experiences are reduced to an endless succession of perceptions. And the mind is distinct from the body in being composed of these bundled together 'perceptions' or direct experiences of the external world. This view has the difficulty of accounting for the independent existence of a reality that seems only to be confined to experiences in the mind. In dualist theory that independence is ensured by our conscious attention to these 'perceptions' so that we are interacting with them and constantly ensuring that they are distinct from our experience of them.

- In *property dualism* the mind has immaterial properties and the body has material properties. This is a stronger dualism than either predictive as bundle dualism as it states that the properties of the mind such as consciousness cannot be reduced to physical properties. The mind is then fundamentally immaterial and may be thought of as being survivable after death. Dualist theory dismisses this immaterialism as much as dismisses spiritualist views of the mind. Mental activity as such involves more complex dualist interactions than less complex physical activity in non-organic entities. We just have to work harder to work out the chain of complex dualist interactions that make mental activity fundamentally different from less complex physical activity. It is all physical in the end.

- In *substance dualism* the mind is a thinking substance. This is Descartes' mind-body dualism. The mind is considered to be more than just a collection of properties. It is an entirely different thing from the body and therefore a different substance. As already pointed out, this is often treated as the default dualism and it leads to dualism as a whole being rubbished. It is ruled out by the view that organic activity consists of more complex dualist

---

[12] Cf. Armstrong, *op. cit.*, section 2, p. 20.
[13] David Hume (1739), *A Treatise of Human Nature*, ed. Nidditch, (Oxford: Clarendon Press, 1989), Book I, Part IV, Section VI, p. 252.

interactions than non-organic activity. It is all a matter of degrees of physicality.

- *Parallelism* is the idea that mind and body work in parallel to each other but without any causal interaction between them. This is not only simplistic but seems also to violate common sense which suggests to us that mind and body work together, however mysteriously they are connected. Also as it rules out dualist interaction altogether, it does not have a place in dualist theory.

- *Epiphenomenalism* is a popular hobby horse with those disparaging dualism and it is easily dismissed. According to this view, mental events are caused by physical events, but mental events have no causal influence on the physical. This one way form of interaction is inadmissible in dualist theory. Innumerable two-way causal interactions make up consciousness and our subjective experiences. The latter are made possible by complex dualist interactions which are entirely physical in their origin and nature. By these means, we can explain why our consciousness seems to be distinct from our bodies. The distinction is of the same dualist order as the other dualist interactions by which our bodily organs function and co-operate to make us viable living beings. Consciousness is therefore the name we give to our subjective experiences that are equally physical but only more complex and holistic than the other dualist interactions that enable us to function effectively as organic entities. A different perspective is also involved.

All these types of dualism are derived from or related to the Cartesian mind/body distinction. As a result, there is no end to the types of dualism that may be distinguished. They are based on rigid logical analyses of the problem rather than based on dualist interactions as in the dualist theory being developed here. The resultant logical distinctions are legion and include not only those mentioned above but also interactionism, occasionalism, and non-reductive physicalism. One is expected to pick one or other of these positions and then argue for or against it. The only alternative is to invent yet more distinctions that add to the confusion instead of resolving it. For example, John Searle has an online paper entitled "Why I Am Not a Property Dualist" in which he argues that his view is a "biological naturalism" rather than a 'property dualism'.[14] In contrast, the dualist view replaces the outmoded mind/body distinction altogether with a complex web of dualist interactions that involve our relationships to the external world, as is argued in this book. Thus, such distinctions become insignificant when dualism is studied systematically in respect of all its complications.

C. The importance of dualist interaction

In dualist theory there are many types of 'dualism' of which the following are among the most important:

---

[14] See this Berkeley University site:
http://ist-socrates.berkeley.edu/~jsearle/132/PropertydualismFNL.doc

- *Physical dualism*. This type documents the dualisms implicit in the external world. And it replaces the specious Cartesian dualism of the mind/body and mental/physical. Everything that happens in the universe involves dualist interactions of one kind or another. This means that biological interactions are not different from any other types of dualist interaction in that they too are physical and take place in the material world. What dualist interactions of all kinds consist in is outlined in part five on *The Nature of Dualist Interaction*.

- *Biological dualism*. This dualism is a sub-division of physical dualism and deals with the complexity of biological entities which are wholly physical and whose processes are wholly physical. For example, the organism interacts dualistically with its environment in feeding and breathing; male and female interact dualistically to produce offspring, and so on.   Our understanding of biological dualism begins with the dualisms of quantum theory and describes how dualist interaction has resulted in increasing complexification in the material world. This complexification culminates in the complexity of conscious beings such as ourselves. The process of complexification is discussed in more detail in part six on *The Emergence of Dualist Interaction*.

- *Social dualism*. This in its turn is a sub-division of biological dualism. It concerns the interactions that make our society work for us. These include our interactions with the mass media when we read newspapers, watch television and use the internet. They also include our interactions with all the organisations that make society work. The milieu of social dualism is the sociosphere within which all our communicative interactions take place. The internet is only one part of the sociosphere's activity.

- *Political dualism*. This refers to those types of social interaction that are political and economic in their effect. It is about such dualisms as liberal/conservative, and capitalism/ socialism. Political dualism is particularly important to us because it is a source of so much conflict and enmity. Liberal-minded people often think of themselves as being opposed to conservative-minded people and *vice versa*. The future of the human race seems to depend on both sides understanding each other, and ultimately in everyone incorporating these dualist opposites in their own thinking about things. Parts two and three below deal with political dualism in more detail.

- *Personal dualism*. We are constantly interacting on a personal level with other people on a one-to-one basis. This is the dualism of personal relationships. Friendship of any kind involves dualist interactions in which we are giving something of ourselves to others and receiving something from them. This is an extraverted dualism as compared with the introverted existential dualism.

- *Existential dualism*. This is the dualism of 'I am nothing' and 'I am everything'. It is an adjunct of the 'all or nothing' mentality. We all feel from time to time that we are insignificant nonentities having no consequence in the greater scale of things. Equally, we might swing to the opposite extreme and feel that we are everything in the sense that we are consonant with the whole of existence. The dualist view helps to mitigate these opposing propensities by showing the strength of the middle view in which we think positively and productively about ourselves and the possibilities of life.

● *Causal dualism.* Whether a dualist interaction admits of causal explanation depends on the extent of our knowledge, the availability of evidence, the presence of witnesses or other means of verification or falsification. Recognising or observing a dualist interaction means that it potentially has a causal explanation but whether it can be established or formulated is not always certain. It is contingent on our making the efforts required to find and establish a causal basis for a dualist interaction. There is more on the dualist view of causation in sections 6 and 7 of part five on *The Nature of Dualist Interaction*.

All these dualisms take place within physical dualism. Physicality is the ultimate reality that contains all the others since all events take place within physical reality. The way in which these particular dualisms are interrelated is very roughly illustrated as follows:

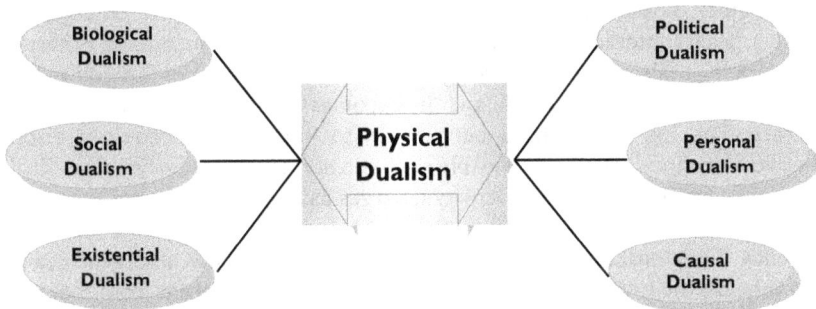

These dualisms, as well as countless others, are intimately linked together in an interactive manner. None of them can be categorically separated from the others. There is no clear dividing line between any of them because such dividing lines are inimical to the fluidity of dualist theory.

The dualist interaction is to process theory, what the atom is to physical theory. As the notion is fluid and flexible, it enables us to show how the complexity of both natural and biological processes has been built up over time through an unending succession of dualist interactions. This is shown in more detail in part six on *The Emergence of Complexity by Dualist Interaction*. The greater complexity of the biological processes makes the difference between life-forms and non-organic physical objects. It is argued in this book that the dualist interaction surpasses, for example. Leibniz's 'monad' is a way of showing how consciousness has emerged and developed in the universe. The monad should be discoverable in all matter but has never yet been distinguished in the manner described by Leibniz.[15] By contrast, the evidence of dualist interaction is ubiquitous and is shown by countless examples in this book.

Consciousness in particular is best understood in terms of dualist interactions, even though a full understanding of it may still elude us. In recognising dualist interactions outside ourselves, we also recognise them inside ourselves. We can then see that a complex feedback system is involved that makes consciousness possible. The relevance of dualist interactions to development of our inner being is dealt with in part six on *The Development of Self by Dualist Interaction* as well as subsequent sections. Dualist theory helps us to ascertain the extent of our ignorance about matters such as consciousness. Our conscious experience cannot yet be explained entirely in physical terms simply because we have yet to work out in detail the complex concatenations of dualist interactions that make consciousness possible. Simplistic mind/body relationships can be dismissed out of hand because they explain nothing and merely make the connection between them seem mysterious and unfathomable.

Moreover, dualist interaction helps us to understand better how consciousness emerged as a complex activity from less complex matter, and this is outlined below in part six on *The Emergence of Complexity by Dualist Interaction*. The theory is that mental activity is no more than physical activity experienced from an inner, holistic perspective. This theory means thinking of emergence as involving dualist interactions that add differences which do not exist otherwise. For example, a pile of sand is nothing more than a pile of sand. But add cement, aggregate, water and mix well and it becomes something different, namely, concrete. The ingredients have been made to interact to become a distinct, cohesive substance. Similarly, the physical activity of the brain involves dualist interactions from which mental activity emerges as something distinct to itself but still only consisting of physical activity. The dualist interactions make the difference. They enable us to explain in concrete terms how emergent qualities supervene on their constituents without being physically different from them.

Also to be explained is how dualist interactions occurring in the brain and central nervous system can somehow put us in touch with the realities of the external world. In dualist theory both the activity of both mind and brain is

---

[15] Leibniz (1714), *Monadology*, §33, as in *Philosophical* Writings, (London: J.M. Dent, 1990), p.184. Monads are an important part of Leibniz's metaphysics. Monads - from Greek *monas* "unit" - are essentially units of consciousness. They are the idealist's answer to materialism and provide an alternative way of looking at the universe instead of regarding it as full of material atoms and energy fields. Monads are basic substances that make up the universe but lack spatial extension and hence are immaterial. Each monad is a unique, indestructible, dynamic, soul-like entity whose properties are a function of its perceptions and appetites. Monads have no true causal relation with other monads. They all are perfectly synchronised with each other by God in a pre-established harmony. The objects of the material world are simply appearances of collections of monads. Since the monad of monads is God, this whole system is a set-up to bolster his arguments for the existence of God.

entirely physical and their unified interactivity organises their input and represents the outside world accurately for us. In a sense the outside world comes into our heads and we seem to be at one with the world. Yet we are also not the same as the outside world. The paradox of being both the same and not the same as the outside world is resolved by thinking in terms of dualist interactions. A constant succession of dualist interactions keeps us in touch with reality. What are treated as 'conflicts' between mental and physical accounts are here seen to be 'dualist interactions'. In this way, we can achieve insights into this problem that are not accessible to any other method of inquiry. All these matters are discussed in more detail in the part five on *The Nature of Dualist Interaction*.

Matter and life are both the products of dualist interaction so that there is no clear dividing line between these except in our thinking about them. The smooth transition from the one to the other is more readily explained in terms of dualist interactions than in strictly logical or mathematical terms. In dualist theory, our conceptual distinctions are hypothetically imposed on reality rather than logically imposed in a categorical, Kantian way. The latter makes them into rigid constructs instead of hypotheses which are representative of reality within limited contexts. Dualist theory thus aims to facilitate correct thinking instead of the rigid, categorical thinking that has dominated western thinking often to its disparagement.

D. What this book aims to do

It is argued here that life itself results from the build-up of internalised complexities accumulated over the 13.9 billion years of the universe's existence. Thus, the division between matter and life requires an understanding of the dualist interactions that have led to this accumulated complexity. According to this view, we need to understand the workings of the entire universe before we understand how our self-reflective consciousness came about, let alone reproduce it as 'artificial intelligence.' Thus, dualist theory seems to be the best way to understand properly our interactive relationship to the universe as a whole.

Dualist theory offers a new perspective on these matters. The complex interactions between things have hitherto been the preserve of the various sciences. They have explained them from causal, logical and mathematical points of view. Thus, for example, the interaction between ourselves and our bodies is examined by psychology, physiology and kindred sciences, and the strictly dualist interpretation is generally overlooked. The interaction between ourselves and society is studied by sociology, economics, anthropology and the like. The new perspective of dualist theory focuses on the dualist interactions themselves. It complements what these sciences are doing by accounting for their activities dualistically. For example, we can understand in concrete terms the attributes of hot and cold through the physics and chemistry of temperature, heat and thermodynamics. However, the same thing may be both hot and cold at the same time: what seems hot to one person may seem cold to another person.

This can be understood in terms of the differing interactions of each person; one of them may be in fevered state and be interacting differently with the said hot/cold object.   Moreover, the attributes of hot and cold form a dualist relationship; there can be no hot things without cold things with which to contrast them. Thus, the complex application of these attributes is only covered adequately in dualist theory. Similarly, there is a dualist contrast between the common sense view of a table as a solid object and the scientific view of it as mainly empty space. This apparent paradox is accounted for in dualist theory in terms of contextualisation and is discussed further in part eight on *The Logic of Dualist Interaction.*

Dualist theory is important in examining how we interact with the world we live in. There are benefits in reasoning dualistically. By such reasoning, we can make better sense of our place in the world. The dualist view helps us to get above the internecine divisions that plague our species and make us ashamed of ourselves. We learn to think of both sides of a dualist argument, instead of dwelling dogmatically in one point of view. Thus, the study of dualist theory is badly needed nowadays to remedy the flaws in people's reasoning that currently lead to wars, conflicts, enmity, murder and hatred. These flaws lead them to react in extreme ways to opposing opinions. They fail to understand or appreciate other people's ways of thinking and behaving. Dualist studies can help to correct this deficiency in their reasoning.

It is important to study and understand the nature of dualistic interaction for two further reasons. Firstly, it helps us to understand how our own thinking relates to existence and reality. The fact that we are constantly interacting with our environment is a starting point for making sense of this. Secondly, it helps us to understand ourselves better and this understanding helps us to build up our inner being which is an important aspect of dualist theory. 'Inner being' is what is more loosely called 'spirit' or 'willpower'. A strong inner being can make us the equal to everything that life throws at us, provided we come to terms with what this interaction consists in so that we can strengthen it. This is also discussed in part six on *The Emergence of Complexity by Dualist Interaction.*

The logic of dualist interaction outlined in part eight of this book is called a 'dynamic logic' to distinguish it from formal, deductive logic that can be used all too easily to prove the validity of absolutist viewpoints. It is dynamic in that it is concerned not with the form of words but their relation to specific situations in pursuit of our goals. It is interactive in relation to actual events. It gives accounts about what we do when we reason about things and it goes beyond simple reasoning based on the linear form of words used to express ourselves. These dynamic accounts are therefore more inclusive and comprehensive than syllogistic arguments or calculations in symbolic logic.

Dynamic logic broadens the scope of human reason by including deduction and induction in an interactive way. Both deductive analysis and inductive synthesis are included in the dynamic account. It combines internal coherence of argument with external correspondence to facts and evidence. At one extreme it accounts for intuition and inspiration in our reasoning, and at the other extreme it involves physical acts of doing things to verify or falsify conclusions. In this way, dynamic logic reconciles logical reasoning with scientific reasoning and it enables the various scientific methods to be examined and criticised by means of dynamic accounts. Mathematics can also be subjected to dynamic accounts and Gödel's incompleteness theorem is an example of a self-referential dynamic account of arithmetic principles. This puts Bertrand Russell's failed attempt to reduce mathematics to logic in its proper perspective since it arguably failed because it was too deductive and narrow in its scope.

One of the problems addressed by dynamic logic is *over-rationalisation*. Arguments are over-rationalised to the point that arguers believe their opinions to be absolutely true. For example, conspiracy theorists are absolutely convinced that conventional views are mistaken: for example, that JFK was killed by more than one person or that man has never walked on the moon. They can give logically consistent reasons for their beliefs and any evidence against these beliefs is argued away, one way or another. This over-rationalisation is the product of formal logic in which valid forms of arguments are sufficient to prove their truth. Dynamic logic deals with over-rationalisation, for example, with an intuitive *epochē* by which a break or suspension of judgment is achieved by seeing things from a higher perspective. This *epochē* reflects the need to suspend thought and criticise it. Failure to do this can lead to circular thinking that we cannot break out of, just like a computer caught in a loop that can't be broken without shutting it down. Thus, unless we cultivate the ability to distance ourselves from our viewpoints we are liable to enslaved by them instead of enlightened. Such a distancing helps us to criticise our thinking and not assume it to be gospel truth.

E. Dualist theory is anti-extremist

In the first place, the dualist view is anti-absolutist. The world is stricken with absolutist attitudes that stifle human progress. Currently we see absolutist regimes in countries such as North Korea that impose stability and sterility on their populace in an absolute manner. A polarisation of beliefs and opinions still persists throughout the world, and this is a perpetual source of unnecessary conflict. Dualist enmities are still evident in religion while Protestants hate Catholics, Muslims hate Jews, Hindus hate Muslims and the like. Still plaguing us are nationalist and racist antagonisms in which Scots hate English, Canadians hate Americans, Flemings hate Walloons, Norwegians hate Swedes, Serbs hate Croats, Ukrainians hate Russians, Chinese hate Japanese, Hutus hate Tutsis, and so on. The solution is not multi-culturalism but the monoculture of humanity as a whole, as I have argued in my e-book *The Future of Humanity: The Need to Believe in Humanity and its Future*. Such a monoculture ensures that religious and national identities are subsumed in the identity of the human race as a whole. In being a part of the whole, they are no longer isolated belief systems directly at loggerheads with similar belief systems. They have their own place in the scheme of things and need no longer fight for recognition and survival against rivals that are simply different from them. The dualist view reinforces this by ensuring that the rival viewpoints are taken account of and not demonised or treated as being inhuman.

Furthermore, the conflict and enmity between traditionalists and progressives is also world-wide. Countries in North Africa and the Middle East are in a state of ferment if not outright war because of enmity between these factions. Even the USA is ridden by conflict between liberals and conservatives not just among politicians but throughout the country. The dualist response is that no one can be absolutely and irrevocably either traditionalist or progressive in their outlook. There is a traditionalist lurking in every progressive and a progressive within every traditionalist. The aim of dualist theory is to bring these opposites to light so that everyone recognises the value of opposing views. The one does not need to do battle with the other in order to reach some understanding of the middle way or what has gone wrong in the imbalances and extremism in people's thinking.   In that way, the extremist view will become abhorrent and entirely avoidable.

When people deliberately take up opposing sides, this often leads to irreconcilable conflicts. We don't need politicians to take sides and argue opposing views to the extent of making them totally irreconcilable. This only increases conflict and confusion. It brings the political process into increasing disrepute. However, it is not simply a matter of compromise between opposing sides. It may mean correcting imbalances because we have gone from one extreme to another. There has to be a common understanding of this and the dualist view alone can provide this. For example, the bubble caused by excessive credit has resulted in an imbalance that threatens global finances unless it is corrected. These imbalances result from one point of view being applied absolutely and uncritically to excess. Recognising these excesses to the point of doing something about them requires a dualist viewpoint.

The dualist view is beneficial in preventing the polarisation of opposing and competing beliefs. Absolutism leads to such a polarisation. An absolutely certainty in their beliefs encourages opponents to go to war with each other to resolve their differences once and for all. This mentality is based on a monism that centres everything on one idea, one person, one religion, or one way of thinking. It is the antithesis of the dualist view which is more relativist than absolutist. According to the dualist view, nothing can be said to be absolutely the case. There is always the possibility of doubt and uncertainty. Dualist studies show that effective action is possible because of this doubt and uncertainty and not in spite of it. The long-term effectiveness of action depends on our taking account of all factors in a dualist manner whereas the short-term solutions of politicians are a response to media inspired crises.

Dualist studies are therefore needed to correct the faulty ways of thinking that lead us into extremism and absolutism in one direction or into error, doubt and confusion in the other direction. In other words, we must improve the tools of human reason if we are to survive as a species and think our way out of our problems without despairing of the future.

The dualist view is not popular at this time because it is not well understood. The dualist mentality is presumed to involve nothing but doubt and uncertainty. Dualists are thought to be neither one thing nor the other; they sit on the proverbial fence getting nowhere. But dualism is not necessarily about doubt and uncertainty. It is only the attitude of naïve dualists who don't know their own minds. They lack the inner development to make up their minds. At the other extreme of naïve dualism is absolute monism in which beliefs are held absolutely, rigidly and without question. The systematic dualist on the other hand has it all worked out: they know their own minds and what they can or cannot do in the world. They have a holistic view of things by considering the all the yeas and nays, pros and cons, advantages and disadvantages, strengths and weaknesses of the position to arrive at a conclusion, decision, choice, aim, goal, plan or whatever. This is discussed further in part two on *The Nature of the Dualist View*.

Finally, it is arguable that the future is dualist as far as philosophy is concerned. That is to say, a systematic development of the dualist view can ensure its future by giving it a new impetus and sense of direction. The dualist view is arguably an additional key to understanding ourselves and our place in the universe. Its further development will ensure that philosophy avoids stagnation and is no longer self-serving and useless to the public. In short, it takes the view that dualist interaction is a fundamental aspect of the workings of the universe, and that we are dualist beings who interact with ourselves and our environment on a one-to-one basis. When this view is applied consistently as a philosophical outlook, it provides us with new vistas and insights into the human condition.

Book One

Introductory

·

Part One
The Ubiquity of Duality

1. Duality is everywhere in the universe

Duality, in the sense of dualist contrasts such as left/right, is a fundamental part of the universe. The dualist view is that an understanding the nature of dualist interactions is a prerequisite to our scientific understanding of the universe. Therefore, dualist studies examine the dualist interactions which are found everywhere in the universe, life and society:

• *Universe.* The universe is replete with binary contrasts such as matter/anti-matter, positive/negative, left-handed/right-handed, existence/non-existence, active/passive, life/non-life, male/female, day/night and so on. The universe itself is very much a case of all or nothing. It came into existence to be something and it can only be something to itself. It interacts with itself so that the workings of the whole universe can be explained in terms of dualist interactions. For example, the four fundamental forces of electromagnetism, weak, strong and gravitation involve interactions between elementary particles. In the quantum field theory, the interactions between charged particles are shown in a dualist or one-to-one basis, as for example in Feynman diagrams (see the relevant Wikipedia articles on these matters). When one particle interacts with another, it interacts on a one-to-one basis, and wave/particles are produced which are evidence of that interaction. Such one-to-one interactions ensure that ever more complex entities are created in the universe. Life is the most complex product of these interactions so that all life springs from the workings of the universe as a whole. An important part of dualist studies gives a full account of these interactions and shows how complexity arises through constant dualist interaction over time.

• *Life.* Life-forms are dualist beings that interact with their environment to preserve their existence. As biological entities, we have internal workings that interact on a one-to-one basis with our external environment to keep us in harmony with it. We breathe in air and expel carbon dioxide. We imbibe food and water and expel liquid and matter accordingly. The metabolic processes inside us involve dualistic interactions that are markedly more diverse and complex than the activity in inorganic matter such as liquid and metal. As social beings we constantly interact with each other and with society and its institutions. Our thoughts are influenced by such interactions, and other people's thoughts are changed as a result of our interacting with them. What is inside us changes when we interrelate with what is outside us. This contrast between the internal and the external is inherently dualist.

• *Society.* Democratic politics often consists in an interaction between conservative and liberal elements of society. The present coalition government exemplifies how these elements can work together in a dualist fashion for the common good. Whether such a coalition can last the test of time remains to be seen. Dualist studies help to make sense of these interactions and may prevent the tendency to go to one extreme or the extreme by rationalising such tendencies. Both sides of any arguments need to be taken account of and an open, translucent political system depends on both sides getting a full hearing. Similarly, market economies are liable to go from one extreme to the other and are therefore better explained in terms of dualist interactions than by linear logical analysis which tends to exacerbate the extremes instead of moderating them. How the dualist view differs from linear logic is discussed in part eight on *The Logic of Dualist Interaction*.

• *Social Relationships*. Our relationships with each other are often dualistic. People get married or have partners on a one-to-one basis. It is natural for us to a *tête-à-tête* with another person during which we converse with them intimately and exclusively. For example, Plato's philosophy was expounded through dialogues between one person, chiefly Socrates, and another person on a one-to-one basis. When more than one person was involved, Socrates would turn successively to each one and deal with them individually.

These examples show the extent to which duality lies at the heart of things, and one of the primary tasks of dualist theory is to show that these contrasts can usually be explained and clarified in terms of dualist interactions. Dualist theory is therefore an important addition to our array of explanations of the universe and its workings. To that extent, it is an explanatory scientific theory that does not explain everything, though its primary development is inevitably philosophical (see my book, *What is Philosophy*, for more on the role of philosophy in furthering science).

2. The duality between good and evil in eastern thought

Zoroastrianism: Around the seventh century BCE, a pre-occupation with good and evil was widespread in eastern religion and philosophy. In Zoroastrianism, the creator *Ahura Mazda* is said to be all good, and no evil originates from him. Thus, good and evil have distinct sources, with evil (*druj*) trying to destroy the creation of Mazda (*asha*), and good trying to sustain it. The word *Ahura* means light and *Mazda* means wisdom. Thus *Ahura Mazda* is the lord of light and wisdom and the creator and upholder of Arta (truth). *Ahura Mazda* is therefore an omniscient and omnipotent god, who created a being called *Angra Mainyu*, the "evil spirit" who as the creator of evil will be destroyed according to the *frashokereti* (the destruction of evil). Zoroastrianism is often cited as an example of a dualistic religion in which the concentration of all that is good is around AHURA MAZDA, and all that is evil around ANGRA MAINYU. These two forces are at constant war and only at the end will good finally vanquish evil.[16]

The Vedas: In the Indian Vedic tradition the battle between good and evil also occurs between the families of the PANDAVAS and the KAURAVAS in

---

[16] Adapted from Wikipedia articles on this subject.

the   great epic poem, *Mahabharata*. Together, the *Pandava* brothers fought and prevailed in a great war against their cousins the   *Kauravas*, which came to be known as the Battle of Kurukshetra. The background of the celebrated *Bhagavad Gita* text is in this battle during which Krishna instructs Arjuna not to yield to degrading impotence and to fight his kin, for that was the only way to righteousness. He also reminded him that this was a war between righteousness and unrighteousness (*dharma* and *adharma*), and it was Arjuna's duty to slay anyone who supported the cause of unrighteousness, or sin.[17]

The duality of "yin-yang". The well-known Chinese dichotomy of yin-yang is inherently dualist but not exclusively so, as this extract from the Wikipedia article on the subject shows: "In Chinese philosophy, the concept of yin-yang which is often called "yin *and* yang", is used to describe how seemingly opposite or contrary forces are interconnected and interdependent in the natural world; and, how they give rise to each other as they interrelate to one another. Many natural dualities (such as female and male, dark and light, low and high, cold and hot, water and fire, life and death, and so on) are thought of as physical manifestations of the yin-yang concept. Yin and yang are actually complementary, and not opposing, forces, interacting to form a whole greater than either separate part; in effect, a dynamic system. Everything has both yin and yang aspects, (for instance shadow cannot exist without light). Either of the two major aspects may manifest more strongly in a particular object, depending on the criterion of the observation. The concept of yin and yang is often symbolised by various forms of the *Taijitu* symbol, for which it is probably best known in Western cultures. There is a perception (especially in the Western world) that yin and yang correspond to evil and good. However, in Taoist metaphysics, good-bad distinctions and other dichotomous moral judgments are perceptual, not real; so, yin-yang is an indivisible whole."

3. Duality in early Greek thought

The duality of the Orphic Religion. Dualism in Western thinking can be traced back at least to the Greek religion of Orpheus which may have been influenced by eastern religion.[18] The rites of the Orphic Cult involved purification of the soul as against the evils of the body; the aim being to achieve immortality for the soul. It may be the origin of the soul/body dichotomy in Western thought. Cornford puts it this way:

> Throughout the mystical systems inspired by Orphism, we shall find the fundamental contrast between the two principles of Light and Darkness, identified with Good and Evil. This cosmic dualism is the counterpart of the dualism in the nature of the soul; for, as always, *physis* and soul correspond, and are, indeed, identical in substance. The soul in its pure state consists of fire, like the divine stars from which it falls; in its impure state, throughout the period of reincarnation, its

---

[17] Cf. Juan Mascaró, *The Bhavagad Gita*, (London: Penguin, 1962), Introduction, p. 21f.

[18] Cf. John Burnet, *Early Greek Philosophy*, (4th edition 1930 – London: Adam & Charles Black, 1975), Ch. II, p.82.

substance is infected with the baser elements, and weighed down by the gross admixture of the flesh.[19]

There is also the Orphic tradition that refers to "the world as having started in the form of an egg. When it broke, Eros, the spirit of generation, emerged and, of the two halves of the egg, the upper now formed the sky and the lower the earth."[20] This duality of sky and earth is obviously fundamental to our thinking.

Pythagorean dualism. The dualist view is also to the work of Pythagorean philosophers such as Alcmaeon of Croton (c.500 BCE) who wrote: "Most human affairs are dual".[21] According to Aristotle, the Pythagoreans arranged their ten principles in two columns:[22]

Limited	*Unlimited*
Odd	Even
One	Many
Right	Left
Male	Female
Resting	Moving
Straight	Curved
Light	Darkness
Good	Bad
Square	Rectangular

However, the relationship between these dualist contrasts was never developed in a sufficiently systematic way to make them an important part of our thinking. Further development of this dualist view was impeded by later philosophers such as Plato and Aristotle and, as a result, a linear, monistic view of philosophy has predominated in western thinking down to the present day.

Plato was profoundly influenced by the ideas of Pythagorean philosophers as regards his views on mathematics and immortality, and there were signs that he was moving towards a dualist view of things in his later unpublished writings especially concerning the 'indefinite duo' (αoριστος δυας). Little is known or understood by us nowadays about Plato's dualist views. But Aristotle tells us that Plato differed from the Pythagoreans in separating the 'duo' and numbers in general from perceived objects. This was necessitated by his theory of forms and by his dialectic view of logic based on the definitions of words.[23]

---

[19] F. M. Cornford, *From Religion to Philosophy: A Study in the Origins of Western Speculation*, (1912 – Princeton: Princeton University Press,1991), Ch. VI, p. 197.

[20] W. K. Guthrie, *A History of Greek Philosophy*, (1962 - Cambridge: Cambridge University Press, 1980), Vol. One, Ch. III, p. 69

[21] Diogenes Laertius (c. 300 CE), *Lives and Opinions of Eminent Philosophers*, (Loeb Classical Library, 1980), Vol. II, Book VIII, Ch. 5, Alcmaeon, §83, p. 396. This quotation is also to be found in Aristotle's *Metaphysics*, as below.

[22] Aristotle, *Metaphysics*, Book I, Ch. 5, 986^a 22f.

[23] Aristotle, *op. cit.*, 987^b 23f.

Empedoclean dualism. Another Greek philosopher, Empedocles (c.484-c.424BCE) had a dualist view of the world which he saw in terms of Love (*Philotes*) and Strive (*Neikos*). There is a constant cycle in which things are brought together with Love and torn apart through Strife.

> These things never cease from continual shifting,
> At one time all coming together, through Love, into one,
> At another each borne apart form the others through Strife.[24]

This 'cosmic cycle' of Empedocles is very true of how unities come together as one entity and eventually, sooner or later, fall apart. This applies to material and biological entities, organisations, nations, empires and so on. It is noteworthy that this phenomenon is accountable more readily in dualist theory than in any other theoretical system, especially in those systems grounded entirely in logic and mathematics.

The duality of atoms and the void. Another dualism introduced by Greek philosophers was duality of the world being composed either of entities composed of atoms or of an emptiness within which things subsist. Little is known for certain about Leucippus who invented the theory of atoms and the void. He met Democritus (c.460-357BCE) presumably around 440BCE and Democritus developed the theory further in his voluminous writings. The void was seen not just as empty space but as a lack of the presence of atoms.[25] Everything consists of atoms which are too small to be seen with the naked eye. Their existence is inferred from the possibility of dividing things up into smaller and smaller pieces until the irreducible atom is reached. The Greek word *atomos* means uncut, not able to be cut or indivisible.[26] The theory is a stunning anticipation of modern atomic theory though we now know that even atoms are not solid but are also divisible. It was later adopted by Epicurus (341-271BCE) and his Roman disciple Lucretius gives us a very full account of how the theory explains the workings of nature in his *De Rerum Natura* (The Nature of Things). Its fundamental duality is expressed thus:

> In the first place, we have found that nature is twofold, consisting of
> two totally different things,
> matter and the space within which things happen.[27]

Atoms move through the void and therefore interact with it by replacing and overriding it. The theory is used to show how all the phenomena of nature consist of combinations and flows of atoms in relation to the void.

---

[24]G.S. Kirk and J.E. Raven, *The Presocratic Philosophers: A Critical History with a Selection of Texts*, (1957 - Cambridge: Cambridge University Press, 1969), Ch. XIV, pp. 326-327.

[25] Cf. Kirk and Raven, *op. cit.*, Ch. XVII, p.408.

[26] Cf. Liddell and Scott's *Greek-English Lexicon*, Abridged Edition, (1871 - Oxford: OUP, 1983), p. 113.

[27] Lucretius, (1st cent. BCE), *De Rerum Natura*, I, 504-505, translated by R.E. Latham, *On the Nature of the Universe*, (London: Penguin Books, 1994), p. 22:

> Principio quoniam duplex natura duarum
> dissimilis rerum longe constare repertast,
> corporis atque loci, res in quo quaeque geruntur.

4. The ubiquity of the dualist view in literature

The duality of Shakespeare's tragic heroes:

Many of Shakespeare's tragic heroes don't know the meaning of the word moderation. They have in common a capacity to lurch from one extreme to another. As Thomas Reid (1710-96) put it: "Extremes of all kinds ought to be avoided; yet men are prone to run into them; and, to shun one extreme, we often run into the contrary."[28] They lack the inner development that enables the systematic dualist to take a balanced view of the world and of what is to be done in it. The following 'heroes' all display this tendency to excess.

Macbeth begins the play "too full of the milk of human kindness" as his wife so deftly puts it.[29] He is not long in going to the other extreme of having no conscience at all about murdering the King without qualms while his wife goes mad with the blood on her hands. Macbeth goes so far off the rails that death is the only release from his unbalanced extremism.

Hamlet is a picture of inaction while he procrastinates and pretends to be mad. But when he gets going he doesn't know how or when to stop in his frenetic activity which results in the deaths of everyone including himself. He therefore vacillates dualistically between impotent passivity and manic hyperactivity, and clearly lacks the inner *nous* to find the correct and balanced way of dealing with his problems.

Coriolanus is incapable of moderating either his speech or his action. He is recklessly violent in his fighting, and is recklessly contemptuous of anyone who disagrees with him. When he is thrown out of Rome, he avenges the blows to his pride by offering his services to the very enemies he had just been murdering. But the pleading of his mother and wife leads him to betray his new 'friends' who understandably dispose of him. Clearly, he lacks any inner compass by which to guide his actions or his feelings.

Timon of Athens is the most extreme of them all. He lurches from placing absolute faith and trust on human beings to the other extreme of regarding them as utterly untrustworthy and contemptible. There is no middle way for him at all. He is rightly told: "The middle of humanity thou never knowest, but the extremity of both ends."[30] In other words, he is the ultimate monistic extremist, in the terms of this book.

Othello is a trusting innocent who is a hostage to fortune and a dupe to villains. He is not confident enough in himself to step back and see things as they are. He is easily persuaded by arguments founded on trumped up evidence that his wife and his friend are betraying him when they are not. He allows

---

[28] Thomas Reid, *Essays on the Active Powers of the Human Mind*, (1788), as in Sir William Hamilton's edition of *The Works of Thomas Reid D.D.* (Edinburgh 1895 - also Georg Ohms 1983), p. 635b.
[29] Shakespeare, *Macbeth*, Act I, Scene V, line 18.
[30] Shakespeare, *Timon of Athens*, Act IV, Scene III, lines 301-2.

words to become the reality and is incapable of suspending his judgment in a dualist way that would allow him to see things from a different and more correct perspective. He is unable to break out of the dogmatic cycle of thought that makes his wife's guilt seem absolute and beyond all doubt. A scintilla of dualist doubt would have made him step aside and think: "Hang on, is this really the case or not?" and act accordingly.

King Lear eventually loses it completely and is incapable of taking a balanced view of anything: "I will do such things – what they are, yet I know not; but they will be the terrors of the earth."[31] This is the sentiment of the unbalanced terrorist who wishes to stir up the world and press the restart button. He loses grasp of reality and instead of interacting with it, he becomes stuck in a solipsistic cycle of self-delusion.

Pope's *An Essay on Man* (1733):

An unusually direct and impressive expression of our duality is in Alexander Pope's outstanding poem, *An Essay on Man:*[32]

> Know then thyself, presume not God to scan,
> The proper study of mankind is Man.
> Placed on this isthmus of a middle state,
> A being darkly wise, and rudely great:
> With too much knowledge for the Sceptic side,
> With too much weakness for the Stoic's pride,
> He hangs between; in doubt to act or rest,
> In doubt to deem himself a God or Beast;
> In doubt his Mind or Body to prefer,
> Born but to die, and reasoning but to err;
> Alike in ignorance, his reason such,
> Whether he thinks too little or too much:
> Chaos of Thought and Passion all confused;
> Still by himself abused, or disabused;
> Created half to rise, and half to fall;
> Great lord of all things, yet prey to all,
> Sole judge of Truth, in endless Error hurled:
> The glory, jest, and riddle of the world!

This insightful poem beautifully encapsulates our dualist condition. We overlook the duality and ambiguity of our position at our peril. The more certain and confident that we are in our beliefs, the more likely that nemesis will follow our hubris. Duality is ubiquitous because we are dualist entities living in a universe and suspended between dualist extremes. The dualist view is the default view of the human condition because we are a medial species placed between the unimaginably large and the unimaginably small, between the huge macroscopic universe of astronomy and tiny microscopic universe of atomic particle theory. This medial position enables us to make sense of one extreme in relation to the

---

[31] Shakespeare, *King Lear*, Act II, Scene IV, lines 279-281.

[32] Alexander Pope (1688-1744), *An Essay on Man* (1733), Epistle II, lines 1-18.

other. The sphere of quantum physics is essential to our understanding the universe as a whole since it all began as an infinitely small singularity of some kind. In focusing on the universe at large, cosmologists have found strange phenomena such as dark matter and dark energy that need to be understood at the microscopic level of existence. Thus, in reconciling the immensely small with the enormously large, scientists go from one extreme to the other in their quest to understand the universe as a whole, and a dualist interaction between these two outlooks is involved. (There is more on our 'medial position' in my book entitled, *Sautonic Wisdom: What We Are Here To Do.*)

Buffon's *Homo Duplex*:

In his voluminous *Natural History*, Buffon (Georges Louis Leclerc, Comte de Buffon, 1707-1788). refers to *Homo Duplex*. The 'interior man' is double and contains two principles – the animal and the spiritual:

> *Homo Duplex.*The internal man is *double*. He is composed of two principles, different in their nature, and opposite in their action. The mind, or principle of all knowledge, wages perpetual war with the other principle, which is purely material. The first is a bright luminary, attended with calmness and serenity, the salutary source of science, of reason, and of wisdom. The other is a false light, which shines only in tempest and obscurity, an impetuous torrent, which involves in its train nothing but passion and error.
>
> The animal principle is first unfolded. As it is purely material, and consists in the duration of vibrations, and the renewal of impressions formed in the internal material sense, by objects analogous or opposite to our appetites, it begins to act, and to guide us, as soon as the body is capable of feeling pain or pleasure. The spiritual principle appears much later, and is only unfolded and brought to maturity by means of education: It is by the communication of others' thoughts alone that the child becomes a thinking and rational creature. Without this communication, it would be stupid or fantastical, according to the natural inactivity or activity of its internal material sense.[33]

This is clearly a Cartesian distinction in which mind is at war with the body to tame and civilise it. They are distinct principles whose actual existence in the mind or body is never clarified. Buffon therefore never gets out of the Cartesian frame of mind of thinking of these as substances having some sort of existence somewhere or other. Interestingly, the sociologist, Emile Durkheim was influenced by Buffon's distinction and he uses it in his book *The Elementary Forms of Religious Life*, where he says "that the notion of the person is the product of two factors."[34] But he stresses the individuality of the body as he sees 'the spiritual principle' as reflecting the spirit of the group or 'collective patrimony'. This is because he sympathises with Leibniz's difficult notion of the 'monad' that objectifies consciousness and thus makes a nonsense of our being individuals who think for ourselves and see things in ways that are entirely unique to ourselves

---

[33] Comte de Buffon, *Natural History, General and Particular*, (1749-1767 - Edinburgh: William Creech, 1780), Vol. III, 'A Dissertation on the Nature of Animals', p. 264.
[34] Emil Durkheim, *The Elementary Forms of Religious Life* trans. J.W. Swain, (1915 - London: Allen and Unwin, 1976), ch. VIII p. 270.

and therefore unpredictable. Only a thorough-going theory of dualist interaction is broad enough to account for our uniqueness in this way.

Fictional split personalities:

The Strange Case of Dr Jekyll and Mr. Hyde (1886).   Robert Louis Stevenson's famous tale reflects the duality of human nature, showing the contrasting good and bad of our natures. Nowadays, it is apparently called something like 'dissociative identity disorder'. Stevenson had previously written a play about the life of real life 'split personality', namely, Deacon Brodie, an 18th century Edinburgh councillor who was a respective citizen by day and a resourceful burglar by night. In *Jekyll and Hyde*, Stevenson takes this dissociation to its logical conclusion. His character Dr. Jekyll conducts experiments to find a drug that will separate what he calls the "primitive duality of man", that is to say, the "good and ill which divide and compound man's dual nature."[35] He succeeds all too brilliantly but in the course he looses control of the process and his evil side eventually predominates. Death is the only release from the extremes to which his experiment has taken him.

The Picture of Dorian Gray (1891). This also gives a dual picture of a man's character. Oscar Wilde admired the above work and gives his own slant to the good/evil dichotomy. Dorian Gray expresses the wish that his portrait should do the aging while he stated young. This wish is fulfilled and he is able to indulge himself with impunity, knowing that the ravages of time would be imposed on his portrait and not on himself. Each of his 'sins' disfigures the portrait. His behaviour is totally debauched over 18 years but he remains as young as ever. Eventually he tires of his wayward ways and desires 'a new life'. He expects to find that his portrait reflects this change of mind but it does not. He angrily plunges a knife into the portrait and kills himself in the process. The story explores the possibility that the 'bad' within us can be placed outside us while we remain 'good' within ourselves, but in the end perhaps it only reflects St. Paul's maxim: "The wages of sin are death."[36]

Jungian dualism:

In the psychology of Carl Gustav Jung (1875-1961) there are innumerable dualist contrasts that include the ego/unconscious, extravert/introvert and anima/animus contrasts:

Ego/Unconscious. Whereas Freud thought of the unconscious as containing repressed memories primarily from childhood, Jung saw it as constantly interacting with conscious ego. The unconscious is the source of individuality. It compensates for the deficiencies or excesses of the ego or self. This implies that dualist interactions are taking place, but Jung fails to exploit this to the detriment of his own arguments. Thus, he identifies the ego with the collective psyche,

---

[35] Robert Louis Stevenson, *The Strange Case of Dr. Jekyll and Mr. Hyde*, (1886 - London & Glasgow: Collins), 'Henry Jekyll's Full Statement of the Case', p. 202.

[36] St. Paul, *New Testament*, Epistle to the Romans, 6:23.

instead of arguing for an interaction between them that seems otherwise to be implied by his arguments.[37]

Extravert/introvert. Jung invented this distinction but he developed it in the form of categorical types. However, it cannot be the case that there is absolute distinction between the extraverted person who is sociable and out-going and the introverted person who is unsociable and keeps themselves to themselves. It is possible for people to change from one type to the other over a period of time or simply according to their mood or inclination. Jung does not make enough of this interplay between the extremes that tells us much about the human condition.[38]

Anima/animus. Jung proposed that the male unconscious possesses a feminine side called the 'anima' and the female unconscious possesses a masculine side called the 'animus'. These opposing sides are a source of creativity in both the male and female. "The animus corresponds to the paternal Logos" in the female and "the anima corresponds to the maternal Eros" in the male.[39] The anima and animus are themselves dualistic in having light and dark aspects. The one is life-giving and creative, and the other ossifies and can even destroy the personality. But this mystical, metaphysical treatment of the anima and animus really boils down to the common sense view that most of us have masculine and feminine attributes. We go through life balancing these propensities, and Jung's speculations seem to mystify than more than clarify the problems we face in our male/female confusions.

'I and Thou' dualism:

In his notable book, *I and Thou,* Martin Buber (1878-1965) gives us an explicitly dualist view of human nature. He begins his book thus:

> "To man the world is twofold, in accordance with his twofold attitude. The attitude of man is twofold, in accordance with the twofold nature of the primary words he speaks." [40]

In Buber's view, the primary words are the combined words 'I-Thou' and 'I-It'. He is therefore building up a view of human nature based on these dualist

---

[37] Carl G. Jung, 'The Relations Between the Ego and the Unconscious', *Two Essays on Analytical Psychology. Collected Works*, Vol. 7, Second Essay, § 202-295; Translated from *Die Beziehungen zwischen dem Ich und dem Unbewussen* (2nd ed. 1928, 1935), published by Rascher Verlag, Zurich. As in reproduced in *The Portable Jung*, (London: Penguin, 1978), edited by Joseph Campbell, translated by R.F.C. Hull, pp. 70--138.

[38] Carl G. Jung, *Psychological Types*, in *Collected Works*, Vol. 6, Part II, § 556-671. In *The Portable Jung, op. cit.*, pp. 178-269.

[39] Carl G. Jung, *Aion: Researches into the Phenomenology of the Self*, in *Collected Works*, Vol. 9, ii, § 1-42. As translated in The Portable Jung, *op. cit.*, p. 152.

[40] Martin Buber, *I and Thou*, translated by Ronald Gregor Smith, second edition, (1922 - Edinburgh: T. & T. Clark, 1959), Part One, p. 3:
> Die Welt ist dem Menschen zwiefältig nach seiner zwiefähigen Haltung. Die Haltung des Menschen ist zwiefältig nach der Zwiefalt der Grundworte, die er sprechen kann.
Martin Buber, *Ich und Du*, 1923, (Stuttgart: Philipp Reclam jun.), 1983, p,3.

relationships. In our interactions with the world, they are either of the 'I-Thou' nature or the 'I-It' nature. The first is a dialogue and the second a monologue. However, we can have 'I-Thou' relationships with plants, animals and inanimate objects when we make ourselves intimate with them. We also have 'I-It' relationships with people when we fail to appreciate them as individual and merely have a one-sided monologue with them. There is therefore an interaction between our 'I-Thou' and 'I-It' relationships as we oscillate between intimacy and formality in our relationships.

However, our 'I-Thou' relationship are transitory. Love never lasts forever, except in the case of one 'I-Thou' relationship, namely that with God. "Only one *Thou* never ceases to be *Thou* for us."[41] We may become remote from God but he can never desert us. "The Eternal *Thou* cannot by its nature become *It*."[42] Thus, there is an obvious religious motivation propping up Buber's book. It assumes the existence of God and is not helpful to those of us who have never had any conception of its existence.

Hofstadter's *Gödel, Escher, Bach* (1979):

Douglas R. Hofstadter's celebrated book is based on the notions of self-reference, recursion and 'strange loops'. Yet he fails completely to appreciate that dualist interaction is the simplest and most direct means of understanding such notions. He interprets everything through the prism of mathematical logic and is apparently incapable of stepping outside that paradigm. He uses categorical language in which he speaks of movement between different 'levels' in the brain, as if these levels occupied discrete places therein. This turns the brain into a kind of a pyramid with the ego at the top and its experiences ranged in layers below it.

"My belief is that the explanations of 'emergent' phenomena' in our brains – for instance, ideas, hopes, images, analogies, and finally consciousness and free will – are based on a kind of Strange Loop, an interaction between levels in which the top level reaches back down towards the bottom level and influences it, while at the same time itself being determined by the bottom level."[43]

The interaction is still one between fixed categories that exist in a particular place in the brain. In contrast the notion of dualist interaction is much more consonant with fluid neural networks moving around the brain and generating all the conscious and unconscious activity that characterises our so-called minds. .

Hofstadter's later book, *I am a Strange Loop* (2007), is more a literary than a philosophical work. He again fails to see that self-reference or the 'strange loop' involves dualist interaction. He remains firmly in the old Cartesian groove when he says that there is "the mysterious division of the *animate* world into two types of entity: *myself* and *others*."[44] This is categorical thinking that divides the world

---

[41] Buber, *I and Thou*, *op.cit.*, p. 99.

[42] *Op. cit.*, p. 112.

[43] Douglas R. Hofstadter, *Gödel, Escher Bach: An Eternal Golden Braid*, (London: Penguin Books, 1979), p. 709.

[44] Douglas R. Hofstadter, *I am a Strange Loop*, (New York: Basic Books, 2007), Epilogue, p. 358.

into chunks instead of seeing the dualist interconnections between things. The possibility of interaction between extremes is not countenanced. As a result, he is no clearer about what he means by 'strange loops'. In short, he is stuck in an eternal 'strange loop' reiterating the same idea *ad infinitum* without offering a systematic exposition of it that would take us forward instead of going round in circles.

Jonathan Haidt's *The Righteous Mind* (2012):

Haidt's book is on the right dualist lines but is a work of literature more than of rigorous philosophy. It is moreover based on the premise that people's genes make them either liberal or conservative in their outlook.[45] This is disproved by the fact that young liberals turn into old conservatives, and young libertines turn into old moralists. Young sinners can reform into old saints just as young saints can lapse into old sinners. The classic example is Dr. Johnson who was something of an anarchistic troublemaker when he was a young student at Oxford but became very conservative minded by the time Boswell knew him and began writing his biography.[46] As Haidt is a psychologist it is understandable that he would want to categorise people in absolute terms since that is what psychology does even though people may be no better for it.

In the book's closing chapter entitled "Can't We All Disagree More Constructively?" Haidt at last states the problem, namely, that there is an increasing polarisation in American politics that threatens its future stability. "There's been a decline in the number of people calling themselves centrists or moderates"[47] He ends his book by making vague suggestions that might have been the starting point of a book offering real solutions to the problem. The dualist view is that solution lies in education. People need to be taught from an early age that differing points of views are inevitable and that these views have to be understood from both sides. Only when we have these opposing views in our own thinking about things will we start to live constructively together instead of antagonistically.

5. The ubiquity of dualist contrasts

Political contrasts:

The workings of our complex society depend on a constant interplay between dualist contrasts such as the following:

Liberal	*Conservative*
Freedom	Security
Progress	Tradition
Nonconformity	Dependence
Self-Expression	Obedience

---

[45] Jonathan Haidt, *The Righteous Mind: Why Good People Are Divided by Politics and Religion*, (London: Allen Lane, Penguin Books, 2012), p. 312.
[46] Cf. James Boswell, *The Life of Dr. Johnson*, (1799 - London: Oxford University Press, 1966), 1729, *aetat.* 20, p. 54.
[47H] Haidt, *op. cit.*, ch. 12, p. 274.

It is important for us to see and understand opposing points of view with which we do not agree. The dualist view encourages us to take account of these viewpoints. Extreme left-wingers place excessive importance on left-wing, politically correct solutions and dismiss alternative views out of hand. They overlook the conservative view of things in favour of the progressive view. John Stuart Mill (1806-1873) noted these distinctions in his great work *On Liberty* in saying "that a party of order or stability, and a party of progress or reform, are both necessary elements of a healthy state of political life." And he goes on to say:

> "Each of these modes of thinking derives its utility from the deficiencies of the other; but it is in a great measure the opposition of the other that keeps each within the limits of reason and sanity. Unless opinions favourable to democracy and to aristocracy, to property and to equality, to co-operation and to competition, to luxury and to abstinence, to sociality and individuality, to liberty and discipline, and all the other standing antagonisms of practical life, are expressed with equal freedom, and enforced and defended with equal talent and energy, there is no chance of both elements obtaining their due; one scale is sure to go up, and the other down."[48]

It is therefore worth reiterating that to avoid its potential for extremism, humanity must be consciously dualist in its approach. This ensures its open-mindedness and tolerance which is reinforced by the dualist view. In so far as we are against prejudice, bigotry and narrow-mindedness of both the left and the right wings, we must also be dualists. If we are not consciously dualist in our thinking then we are prone to go from one extreme to another. As Gibbon put it, with regard the fanaticism of early Christianity:

> "It is well-known that, while reason embraces a cold mediocrity, our passions hurry us with rapid violence over the space which lies between the most opposite extremes."[49]

When Germany came under Nazi domination, many extreme left-wing people went to the other extreme and became ardent right-wing Nazis. A few members of the Nazi Party abhorred the extremes to which that regime took anti-semitism and other intolerances. Among them was Oscar Schindler who risked his life to help Jews, as is justly celebrated in the outstanding feature film, *Schindler's List*. He was undoubtedly dualist in his thinking as he saw and appreciated the merits of the opposing view and acted accordingly.

The progressive and conservative modes of thinking have their basis in society in general. Some people seek change and support progress because they cannot stand the status quo. Others are against social change or progress in principle because of a fear or distrust of any change. These turns of mind may veer into two extremes: (1) an individualist way of thinking that supports debate, controversy, freedom and revolutionary change; (2) a communitarian way of

---

[48] J.S. Mill, *On Liberty*, (1859 – London: Oxford University Press, World's Classics, 1971), Ch. II, p. 59.

[49] Edward Gibbon, *The History of the Decline and Fall of the Roman Empire*, (1776 - London: Allen Lane, 1994), Vol. I, ch. XV, p. 476. Cf. Reid's quotation on p. 24 above.

thinking that cherishes law, order, security and good governance. The one is fundamentally non-conformist and the other fundamentally conformist:

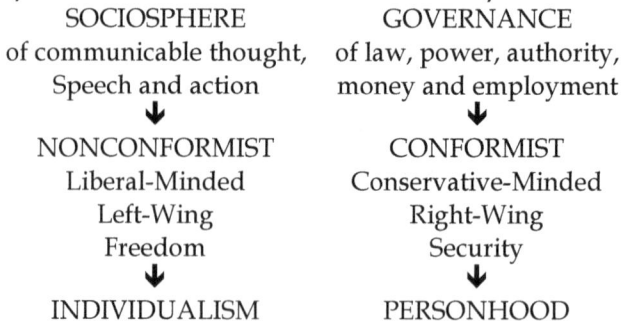

SOCIOSPHERE	GOVERNANCE
of communicable thought,	of law, power, authority,
Speech and action	money and employment
↓	↓
NONCONFORMIST	CONFORMIST
Liberal-Minded	Conservative-Minded
Left-Wing	Right-Wing
Freedom	Security
↓	↓
INDIVIDUALISM	PERSONHOOD

The Contrast Between Discursive Nonconformity and Methodical Conformity

The 20th century was characterised particularly by the wars and conflicts brought about by the fruitless and self-destructive opposition between right and left, fascist and communist and similar dichotomies. Even today there are senseless clashes between left and right wing groups such as between liberals and supremacists, anti-fascists and nationalists, and so on. If society as a whole cannot accommodate these extremes, it is hardly surprising that organizations within society are similarly plagued with such fruitless extremes of thinking that impede their progress. The dualist view is that we can take account of both extremes in our thinking.

We easily get into the mental rut of thinking along one of these lines of thought at the expense of the other. Either we become overconfident of our opinions or we have no confidence at all in them. Either we dismiss all opposition to our views out of hand or we accept mindlessly and uncritically the authority of tradition, gurus, demagogues, preachers or whatever. Instead of taking account of opposing views in an interactive way, we pit our views against the opposing ones and attempt to annihilate them. The result is party politics, warring factions, irreconcilable religions, and so on. In other words, our tribal and sectarian inclinations find their origin in such opposing grooves of thought. As a result, our prejudices are strengthened and they stultify our inner development.

Our hope for our future must lie in our learning not to lapse into the mental grooves that divide us from opposing points of view and prevent us from appreciating their value. For instance, from an educational point of view, students can perform mental exercises as part of civics courses in which they adopt opposing frames of thought and practice broadening their minds in that way. This is not learning to sit on fences but learning to think out the complexities involved in adopting any balanced and informed viewpoint.

The contrast between being and doing:
Ther is a perennial dualist relationship between 'to be' and 'to do'. In the

dualistic view, the contrast between these refers to the passive and active sides of our nature. By means of dualist interaction we strive constantly to reconcile these opposing sides. We need both of them to live a full life. It isn't enough simply to exist as we need to be doing things as well, and it isn't enough to be always active and never idle. The contrast is between extreme stereotypes such as the restless western workaholic and the indolent eastern mystic. Such a contrast is redundant in today's monocultural, globalised world. But seeking a balance and harmony between these immoderate tendencies is arguably what civilised life is all about. Basically, our inner being is built up by doing things, and what we do is consolidated in our inner being which integrates the lessons of life and experience into our unconsciousness. It then becomes available to our intuitions, thoughts and ideas that emerge from that unconsciousness. The opposing sides are interrelated in the following manner though the relationships are suggestive more than exact or logical:

To be	*To do*
Potential	Actual
Passive	Active
Negative	Positive
Feminine	Masculine
Anima	Animus
Yin	Yang

We are become ourselves in the course of being and doing. We are ultimately both what we are and what we do. Our being consists in harmonising everything within ourselves while our doing things develops ourselves by our agency. There is a continual interaction between being and doing as we constantly bring ourselves together in response to what we do in the world and, conversely, as we do things in response to our needs that disrupt our inner peace and good order. A periodic instability arises from the irreconcilability of these opposing sides. It is extended and disordered by our doing things and finding out how things really are. It responds by reasserting its unity in relation to its primary and secondary goals as referred to below. As a result our inner being develops to strengthen our sense of self and what we cannot or cannot do which is worthy of us.

The metaphysics of duality:

The very existence of entities depends on a dualist interaction between their internal and external features. Their existence is made possible by the forces that bring their parts together and maintain the resultant interactions. In scientific terms, these are the atomic forces that render entities stable and long-lasting as identifiable objects. Thus, within every entity there are constant interactions between its internal identity and its external distinction. A stone is internally identifiable because its parts are kept together by the atomic forces and it is externally distinguishable because it exists in a different time and place from other entities. Each entity continues in existence for as long as these interactions persist. Such dualist interactions have been a feature of the universe ever since identifiable and distinguishable entities came into being, namely, since the nuclear particles such as protons and neutrons came together to form atoms and molecules. The internal/external distinction created the possibility of inner being coming into existence as entities became increasing complex and eventually resulted in life-forms. The short lived nature of entities implies that coming into being and passing away – generation and dissolution – are also a fundamental part of the fabric of the universe.

Being identifiable and distinguishable means that each entity forms an identifiable unity which distinguishes it from other entities which are the same as or different from it. Also, its internal composition or clumpiness identifies it as a unity and distinguishes it from its external environment thus creating the distinction between inner and outer. Its unity makes it both different from and the same as the plurality of other entities in the universe. That unity also ensures that it exists as opposed to not existing. While it exists it is in a state of being and it continues that way until it no longer exists. Such non-existence implies that it has become something else which it was not at a previous point in time. While it actually exists, it also has the potential for non-existence or becoming what it was not before. The following dualist distinctions therefore become possible:

Internal	*External*
Unity	Plurality
Same	Different
Existence	Nonexistence
Being	Becoming
Actual	Potential

It is likely that these dualist distinctions are universal to all intelligent species. They become possible immediately words are available to make these distinctions. They may be made by any intelligent species capable of language communication sufficient to form clear conceptions of in and out, of one and many, same and different and so. This is in the same sense that physical laws might understood by all intelligent beings using the mathematical conventions necessary to discover and understand these laws. These dualist distinctions also follow from the fact that information is created by the coming together of entities that makes them identifiable in themselves and distinguishable from each other. That information is complexified over time as entities become more complex. When sufficient information is accumulated by the entity for it to become an intelligent living being, it becomes aware of the distinction between internal and external, and that information is incorporated into its inner being.

Hume's dualist view of the passions:

David Hume famously put reason under the thumb of our passions *i.e.* our emotions: "Reason is, and ought only to be the slave of the passions, and can never pretend to any other office than to serve and obey them."[50] In Book Two

---

[50] David Hume, *A Treatise of Human Nature*, ed. Nidditch, (1739 - Oxford: Clarendon Press, 1980), Book II, Part III, Sect. III, *op. cit.*, p. 415.

of *A Treatise of Human Nature*, he deals with the passions in a dualist way:[51]

Self	*Not Self*
Pride	Humility
Love	Hatred
Pleasure	Pain
Beauty	Deformity
Pity	Envy

Hume points out that we vacillate before extremes in our emotional responses to circumstances that either favour or disfavour us. We can identify with things that we can be proud about, feel love, pleasure, or pity for. But we disown things about which we feel humble, have hatred for, feel pain about and so on. For example, we can be very proud about the beauty of our house but if an accident occurs which damages the house and deforms it then our pride changes to humility. Our attitude changes and we become humble and circumspect in referring to the house. Thus, Hume was very much a dualist in his thinking about ethical matters touching our emotions.

Kant's repressed dualism

Kant was something of a reluctant dualist in his thinking. Though he strove not to be dualistic, he also claimed at times to be both an empirical realist and a transcendental idealist. This very uncertainty puts him firmly in the dualist camp. However, he shies away from the dualist view and allows his idealism to predominate over his empiricist pretensions:

"The transcendental idealist, on the other hand, may be an empirical realist or, as he is called, a *dualist*; that is, he may admit the existence of matter without going outside his more self-consciousness, or assuming anything more than the certainty of his representations, that is, the *cogito, ergo sum*. For he considers this matter and even its inner possibility to be appearance merely; and appearance, if separated from our sensibility, is nothing. . . . From the start, we have declared ourselves in favour of this transcendental idealism."[52]

This stance suits Kant as it is easier for the philosopher to be an idealist than an empiricist since he can then apply his reason to his own thinking without having to submit his reasonings to rigorous empirical examination. But nevertheless his dualism emerges from its repression in his "antinomies of pure reason" in which he argues from two points of view without deciding in favour of one over the other:[53] But in giving us the following opposing points of view he is only starting the dualist interaction process:

---

[51] David Hume, *op. cit.*, Book II, Part I, Sect. V, p. 289.

[52] Immanuel Kant, *A Critique of Pure Reason*, trans. N. Kemp Smith, (1787 - London: Macmillan & Co., 1964), A370, p. 346.

[53] *Op. cit.*, A426/B454 to A460/B488, pp. 396-421.

Thesis	*Antithesis*
1. The world begins in time and is limited in space	1. The world does not begin in time and has no limits in space
2. Everything is made up of simple parts	2. Nothing is made up of simple parts
3. Not everything is caused and freedom is possible	3. There is no freedom as everything takes place according to the laws of nature
4. A being exists which is absolutely necessary	4. No absolutely necessary being exists in the world or out of it.

Kant argues that these dialectic opposites cannot be settled by experience as they "have been divested of all empirical features".[54] They are entirely the products of untrammelled reason, and therefore exemplify the limits to pure reason which has gone beyond useful and applicable experience. From the viewpoint of dualist theory, we settle such matters by establishing the context in which they are being used. If they are argued only in the context of philosophy then only a dogmatic assertion on one side or the other is possible. But in the context of everyday life, we have no practical doubts about the beginning of the world, the simple parts of which things are made, the possibility of freedom or the need to believe in an 'absolutely necessary being'. Thus, the systematic dualist is only concerned about what can or cannot be done about such matters.

Hegel's overt dualism

Hegel developed a dualism based on the opposition between thesis and antithesis. But this opposition revolved round the Absolute which is our holistic grasp of things as a whole. Thus, the synthesis between the thesis and antithesis enables us to move forward in continuing subsuming things into the Absolute. In concrete terms, we do experience the external world as a whole from one second to the next. When we close our eyes and then open them, it is all before us undeniably one thing to be experienced. But in making sense of this, Hegel lures us into a tangled web of abstractions such as the Absolute, Mind, Essence, Being, Reason, Consciousness, Truth, Culture and Religion, not to mention the 'Being in and for itself' so beloved by the later existentialists such as Heidegger and Sartre. But dualist theory cannot progress if it depends solely on having dualist interactions with abstractions in isolation from doing things in the world. A practical realism must enter into the picture if it is to avoid such a self-serving idealism. Thus, the dualist theory being developed here involves dualist interactions with our opinions and beliefs to bring them into accord with external reality. All our thoughts are therefore assumed to be hypothetical and not necessarily real in themselves, which is ultimately what idealist philosophy assumes.

---

[54] *Op. cit.*, A463/B491, p.422.

Part Two
The Nature of the Dualist View

1. What dualism is about

Dualist view is about being interactive with our beliefs and opinions. We hold them at arm's length so that they do not possess us. It is about self-reference in which we refer back to our beliefs to criticise them. The monist view on the other hand sees everything in terms of one thing which is thought to be the ultimate, absolute solution to complex problems. An obvious example of a monist solution is the view that capitalism is the one and only solution to all economic problems as opposed to any alternative that favours government intervention. The opposing communist view that promotes state invention is equally a monist view that fails to take account of the capitalist one. Nowadays, there are few economies in the world that are not a mixture of these two approaches which they seek to balance through monetary and fiscal policies.

Reality is not so simple that one 'ism' alone can encompass everything about it but monist thinkers consistently behave as their 'ism' can do so. Monist solutions to our problems are static, monolithic and inviolable to criticism. They are applied absolutely and without alteration so that they lead inevitably to dogmatic extremism in which the opposing view is demonised. If we interact dualistically with our views we can then deal with them objectively and do not take them to heart as being the ultimate solution.

Thus, the dualist view itself is treated monistically when it is applied as if it is the one and only way of looking at things. Like any 'ism' dualism has its limitations and dualist theory aims to clarify these limitations as well as its areas of applicability. It is self-referential and is open to all kinds of interpretation. To that extent it is more like a science than a doctrine or dogma. The point is that we can choose to interact or not to interact and therein lies the possibility of freewill. For example, we can stop ourselves doing things if we put our minds to it. Dualism is also about building up the inner strength to resist and desist when we need to do so. It is about knowing when to stop and think on the one hand and when to get things done on the other hand.

Dualist interaction consists in one-to-one interactions in which an exchange between disparate processes produces something different. There is no logical equivalence between the one and the other because complex processes are involved, especially with regard to biological entities. Living processes are complexes of dualist interactions. They have their roots in chemical interactions such as that between sodium and chlorine producing an entirely different substance – salt.

We are dualist beings because of our biological nature. We have internal workings that interact on a one-to-one basis with our external environment to keep us in harmony with it. We breathe in air and expel carbon dioxide. We imbibe food and drink and expel liquid and matter accordingly. The metabolic processes inside us involve dualist interactions that are markedly different from the activity in inorganic matter such as liquid and metal. As social beings we constantly interact with each other and with society and its institutions. Our thoughts are influenced by such interactions, and other people's thoughts are changed as a result of our interacting with them. What is inside us changes when we interrelate with what is outside us. This contrast between the internal and the external is inherently dualist.

Being human means being in two minds about many matters. When we are all of one mind, we may be blinded to other ways of doing things and can harm ourselves, other life-forms and the planet in general because we are collectively stupid, and create bubbles, bottle-necks and other excesses such as led to the world-wide financial crisis of 2008. However, we are also a self-correcting species that realises its mistakes and can do something about them. Humanity's activities are not entirely unconscious or random like the swervings of bird flocks or the stampedes of animal herds. Our activities are constantly being observed, monitored and commented upon by self-appointed experts, journalists, pundits, academics and the like. By examining the consequences of our actions, we can rectify our mistakes, and this is done by interacting dualistically with our problems. As dualists, we do not expect to get everything right all at once but may hope to do so in the long run.

Single-minded persons often commit atrocities, like Nazi officers who plead that they are only following orders when they slaughter people mindlessly. Man's inhumanity to man often results from the voice of authority being pursued single-mindedly and inhumanely. Single-mindedness is fine in moderation and within reasonable limits. We often need it to get things done. But it is taken to extremes by absolute monists (as mentioned below) who know no limits in pursuing their ends. The dualist view draws attention to our limitations in that regard because it reminds us of the need to be self-critical. We can stop ourselves and think again and be less sure of our own reasonings. The interactive aspect of dualism reinforces this critical self-reference.

We are capable of being self-conscious, self-corrective beings who examine what we are doing and thinking and correct ourselves when necessary. In interacting with ourselves, we figuratively loop back into our former thinking and correct it accordingly. This is basically what self-consciousness involves when we are aware of what we should or should not be doing or thinking. The dualist view thus refers to self-conscious activity that involves trial-and-error; a common sense procedure that also underlies the scientific method and has ensured the remarkable success of science in transforming our society largely for the better. Dualist thinking therefore moves forward recursively in a dynamic and flexible way. It embraces opposing points of view instead of being stuck unyieldingly in one extreme viewpoint. This dynamic view is not completely realist or idealist, empiricist or rationalist, logical or intuitive. It embraces all of these in an interactive manner, that is to say, it moves from one viewpoint to the other and *vice versa*, according to what needs to be done in the real world in correcting imbalances, redressing injustices, and loosening rigid points of view.

We should regard opposing positions, such as left-wing/right-wing and empiricism/rationalism, as *dualist challenges* rather than irreconcilable paradoxes. These positions constantly challenge us to make sense of them and we live our lives confronting them and dealing with them. Perhaps the ultimate dualist challenge is to live as if one is going to live forever and also as if this is the last day of our lives. Resolving this paradox requires us to actively find the most important and lasting things to do, and the resolution demands our constant attention. If we regard it as nothing more than an irreconcilable paradox then we have no incentive to make anything of it. Thus, paradoxes should be regarded as dualist challenges to be overcome rather than dismissed because they are paradoxical.

As human beings we are both unique individuals distinct from society and collective units intimately involved in society. These incompatible positions must be constantly reconciled and this is best achieved when we are in our dualist frame of mind. As individuals we are not so unique that we can live entirely to ourselves. Extreme individuality makes no more sense than extreme conformity. We can learn to balance the two in a dualist manner. Our word 'idiot' comes from the ancient Greek word meaning those who live for themselves alone and do not participate in society at large. To make the most of ourselves we need to conform and find our rightful place in society. But this conformity is taken to extremes by those who obey authority single-mindedly. They are in a monist frame of mind and may lose their humanity by being in thrall to ideas, beliefs or opinions that are regarded as real and inviolable. They become pawns in the nefarious activities of the state or of some organisation whose activities are divorced from the interests of humanity as a whole.

We all have this problem of balancing individual self-expression with the social conformity that is needed to make the most of ourselves, and this balancing involves what is here called 'dualist interaction'. We interact with opposing ideas in a genuine effort to seek the best way forward instead of being stuck in the rut of one way of thinking. There is always another way of looking at things, and this is the essence of open-mindedness.

We obey the laws of society because we have good reason to do so but we are not above breaking the law if only because we are human and not mindless automatons. If we are sufficiently moved by the injustice of certain laws, we may purposefully break them. The dualist view recognises the fragility of our humanity and is therefore the default position for human beings. Other animals may be driven by instinct and impulse but we always have the choice of doing or not doing what we feel like doing. We need to be fully aware of our potential for wicked and evil acts to avoid actually doing them. This is what self-control is all about. It consists in knowing what we can do and what we should not do. This two-minded duality makes us dynamic and uncertain animals that are always trying to do things better in the future – every day being 'Groundhog Day'. We are all hoping to experience the perfect day though we might never achieve it.

However, many philosophers avoid this obvious duality in favour of a monist view of ourselves and the universe. They wish to see us as purely material beings or in the contrary view as purely spiritual beings. The dualist view is too untidy and illogical as it gives us a very complex interactive account whereas their inclination is to reduce everything to one thing or idea. Their thinking is discrete and categorical, and the truth is often conceived to be static, unyielding and eternal. But in the dualist view, truth is something we are constantly striving for by interacting with our environment. It is a process of continuous advancement and enlightenment rather than a fixed goal to be arrived at, as is argued below in Part Nine on *The Pursuit of Truth by Dualist Interaction,*

2. The importance of the dualist view

The words 'dualism' and 'duality' are often used pejoratively to refer to contradictory and confusing behaviour: for example, the duality of behaving with sympathy at one moment and with hostility at the next moment. The dualist view itself is avoided and often dismissed without further examination. It is considered too indefinite and flawed to be seriously considered.

However, a better understanding of dualism is a tool that we can use to cope with conflict and uncertainty in our daily lives. Conflicting opinions are a necessary dynamic which can make or break an organisation. When people take sides and regard their opinions are more certain and truthful than those of the opposing side, the dualist view helps us to resolve the matter one way or the other. It may be uncertain as to which side is correct, beneficial, or whatever, but dualist thinking is about dealing with uncertainty rather than shying away from it.

Uncertainty is a necessary aspect of the human condition. Life would be boring if everything is predictable and reliable. If the outcome of a football game is certain beyond doubt, there would little point in paying to watch it. A football team that could win all its matches without fail would be promoted to a league of its own.[8] Similarly, there would be no need for leaders, politicians or managers if every situation pans out predictably and there are no doubts about how to deal with it. Computers and other machines are used when routines, processes and procedures can be worked out mechanically or algorithmically. When machines can deal with unpredictable situations as we do all the time, they will be the equal of us. (Turing's test is not rigorous enough to determine when computers are truly indistinguishable from human beings. The computer would have to be shown to think for itself without referring to anything else.[55])

---

[55] A. M. Turing, "Computing Machinery and Intelligence," *Mind*, 1950, Vol. LIX, No. 236. This famous paper is excerpted in Hofstadter and Dennett's book, *Mind's I*, Penguin Books, 1982, pp.53-68. The question of whether a machine is thinking or not may be resolved by observing how it is behaving to itself rather than to people, as Turing suggested. Its inner life, consciousness and self-identity will consist in its having feelings and thoughts of its own. We will react emotionally to their displays of emotion and either empathise or not as the case may be. As with human beings, what they are actually feeling may be uncertain even to themselves.

Whatever is discrete and measurable can be analysed by logic and mathematics. But when we think ahead and make choices between alternatives, the process is often intuitive and qualitative. Decisions made on logical grounds can be as extreme as those made by intuition. If the bankers had thought dualistically instead of logically they might have recognised the extremes to which their behaviour was tending. The bankers' and financiers' activities before the credit crunch of 2008 were doubtless backed up by a whole array of reasonable arguments. The fact is that they were too rational and failed to think outside the box. It was not so much collective insanity that led to the credit crunch as too much trust in the rationality of their actions. Only a leader imbued with a flexible, dualist outlook could have broken the mould and shown them that they were going to absurd extremes in their reasonings. Obviously such a leader never emerged at the right time.

Success in life is a black-and-white matter. Either we are successful at getting the job done or we are not – as a matter of fact. But how that success is achieved is not so clear-cut. In practical terms, we are concerned here with the means by which we may or may not achieve success through dualist thinking. A successful person is usually not just a lucky person but also one who takes account of both sides of any argument and also of the extremes to which each side may be taken by those who are prone to such extremes. In that way, they are able to take a balanced view of any situation and make realistic decisions which bear fruit.

The dualist view does not make us any the less decisive in our actions. Indeed, it gives a rational basis for decisiveness. Systematic dualism (as discussed below) considers the extremes to which our thinking can go. By so doing, it clarifies situations by revealing imbalances, imperfections, injustices, bottlenecks, and distortions which can be addressed and rectified. It clearly shows the direction in which action must be taken to achieve harmony, redress imbalances, perfect imperfections, remedy injustices, and relieve bottlenecks and distortions. For example, one can only hope to avoid taking an extreme view in politics by carefully considering the opposing view and evaluating its merits in a dualist fashion. The resulting view should be more balanced and enable one to act more justly having taken account of all factors involved in the situation.

Dualism is part of the human condition as we are alternately active and passive beings. It is in our nature to alternate between self-assertion and self-denial. We may assert ourselves boldly and then retract into our respective shells when things go wrong as a result. This alternation is at the root of the contrast between dogmatism and scepticism. We may be over-confident of our beliefs or have no confidence in them at all. The history of philosophy may be viewed dualistically as an oscillation between dogmatism and scepticism, between the confident assertion of belief and the diffident doubt of it.[56] Evidently, philosophy is undergoing a sceptical phase at present. Perhaps it is now time for some

---

[56] This dualist view of the history of philosophy is outlined in my book, *What is Philosophy?* (Edinburgh: Dunedin Academic Press, 2008).

dogmatic, one-sided dualism to help us control our obsessions so that they do not control us. Correcting such imbalances is part of the dualist view. It is an imbalance when we have lost control of aspects of our lives. Our interests are a part of our life and not the be-all and end-all of life. The dualist view helps us to keep them in their place. We learn to externalise them by interacting with them dualistically. Conflicts can then be considered objectively to ensure that we deal with them in a balanced and systematic way. Kipling's well known 'If' poem also advocates the avoidance of extreme reactions to the 'imposters' of 'triumph and disaster' which in the cold light of day may not be as alluring or as depressing as they seem at the time.

Thus, the dualistic view is not simply about moderation in all things. It is about recognising the complications involved in a situation and, if necessary, going to opposite extremes to rectify an imbalance. For example, the prevalence of intolerance in some sectors of the community may itself be intolerable and require extreme measures to rectify it, as Karl Popper recognised in his 'Principle of Toleration'.[57] We cannot tolerate all forms of behaviour without question as is implied by extreme multiculturalism. A limit to tolerable behaviour must be set in the interests of social harmony.

Another example is Aristotle's 'golden mean' between two extremes.[58] This is a static and artificial division that does not reflect the complexity of the real world. Thus, thinking of courage as a mid-point between rashness and cowardice is of no help in practical situations where something must be done or not be done, as the case may be. The courageous person does not deliberate between two extremes but acts intuitively because something must be done. Intelligent decisiveness comes from taking account all the circumstances involved in a situation. Thus, seeking a fixed balance between two extremes is naïve dualism if it does not result from a systematic view of the whole and of all the possibilities, as is argued below.

3. Avoiding the muddled middle

In Charles Dickens' novel, *Hard Times*, there is a character called Stephen Blackpool whose catchphrase is "'tis aw a muddle". He is a mill worker in the industrial north of England who cannot bring himself either to side with his fellow employees in their dispute with the mill owners or to take the protection offered by the latter. The employees wish to change their working conditions for the better whereas the employers want to preserve the status quo and protect their company's profitability and position in the market. The employees take a progressive view and the employers a conservative one. Blackpool sees the merits of both sides and refuses to identify with one extreme or the other.

---

[57] Cf. Karl Popper, *The Open Society and its Enemies*, (1945 - London: RKP, 1969), Vol. I, Ch. 7, Note 4, p. 265.

[58] 4. Aristotle, *Nicomachean Ethics*, Book Two, Section 7, 1107a28. See Penguin edition (1987), p.104.

Inevitably, he is despised and shunned by both sides and leaves the town. When he is falsely accused of a bank robbery, he returns to the town to clear his name but falls down a mineshaft on his way there. Eventually he is found and in his dying words says it is a muddle from first to last. If things hadn't been so muddled, he wouldn't have needed to come back. If the workers hadn't been in a muddle among themselves, they wouldn't have misunderstood him, and so on.[59]

Stephen Blackpool is one of Dickens' many exaggerated characters who nevertheless give us an insight into the human condition. We can interpret him as a naïve dualist who is mired in the muddled middle. He sees that the truth is never as black and white as the clear thinkers make it out to be. The truth lies within the two extremes and it is easier to take sides than work out what should be done. The problem is to maintain a dualist view while avoiding uncertainty and indecision. Blackpool lacks the mental equipment to see his way forward, and therefore everything seems incorrigibly muddled to him. In short, he sits uncomfortably on the fence because he is not a systematic dualist who understands the nature of his position and is confident of its superiority over the extreme positions which it abhors.

The systematic dualist recognises that there are only two clear responses to a confusing situation in which people take sides against each other. One can join one side or the other or one can work towards a resolution, reconciliation or synthesis which will take the situation forward and make progress possible. Taking the first alternative, the systematic dualist would join one side or the other and work hard to moderate the views of that side and achieve a reconciliation of some kind. Taking the second alternative, he or she would be confident enough to persuade both sides that conflict and confrontation cannot achieve their ends. In Blackpool's case, the first alternative is more likely to be successful than the second one, given the passions of both sides in such 19th century conditions. However, Blackpool clearly lacked the leadership qualities required to take the dynamic and purposeful action that the situation demanded. It is arguable that successful leadership depends on the use of systematic dualism to a greater or lesser extent.

Dualism is often associated with shiftiness, prevarication, hypocrisy and even immorality. But systematic dualists by virtue of being systematic in their thinking are also being consistent, reliable and moral in their behaviour. They are no longer being systematic when their behaviour lacks integrity. If they acquire the depth in philosophy that systematic dualism demands then they are more in touch with themselves and are less inclined to misbehave. Their conduct can be consistent with the highest standards of honour and respectability though being human means that they may fall from grace as readily as anyone. The recent lapses of the professional golfer, Tiger Woods, come to mind in that regard. Sooner or later, insincere, immature or malign personalities reveal their

---

[59] Charles Dickens, *Hard Times*, (1854 - New York: New American Library, 1961), Bk. III, Ch. VI, pp.267-8.

inadequacies as they are deficient in the self-criticism that the dualist view demands. They no longer see themselves as others see them and are therefore incapable of behaving themselves.

4. The relationship of dualism to monism

There is a spectrum of monist and dualist views. For the dualist there are no fixed either/or, black/white alternatives as far as our beliefs and opinions are concerned. Both alternatives are always up for consideration. Thus, the systematic dualist never excludes entirely any opposing view, even the monist view. Monism in this context is a single-minded and exclusive devotion to ideas, ways of thinking, ideas, hobbies, lifestyles, and so on. Monism is not an absolute alternative to dualism as it has its place in human affairs just as dualism has, and indeed it forms part of the dualist view. There is a spectrum between monist and dualist attitudes and we are all monists and dualists to some degree or other. But we must never lose touch with our inner dualist and become absolute or extreme monists.

Absolute monists who give no credence to opposing views can be a menace to society, especially when they know no bounds to their fanaticism and enthusiasm. Terrorists, extremists and hot-headed fanatics are typically absolutist in their thinking. Less extreme monists are simply bores when they systematically interpret everything in relation to one thing. These include those whom the essayist William Hazlitt graphically describes as 'people with one idea.'[60] Having one idea means that every conversation is brought round to it as if it were *sine qua non* of their existence.

However, we are all moderate monists in our everyday pre-occupations with hobbies, football teams, shopping or whatever grabs and interests us most in life. Moderate monists are amateur enthusiasts who may be fanatical about their interests but only within limits. Their interests are always balanced by other interests and responsibilities such as earning a living, pursuing a career, raising a family, political activity and so on. We can therefore distinguish absolute, extreme and moderate monists along a spectrum that includes the dualist view at its moderate end. The full spectrum between monism and dualism may be represented as follows:

Absolute Monists - Extreme Monists - **Moderate Monists/**
Systematic Dualists - Naïve Dualists - Absolute Dualists

The spectrum ranges from absolute clarity to absolute obscurity as absolute monists have absolutely no doubt about their beliefs as much as absolute dualists doubt everything as a matter of policy. Absolute dualists have no views of their

---

[60] William Hazlitt, 'On People With One Idea', *Table Talk*, 1824, London: J. M. Dent, 1908, Essay VII, pp. 59-69.

own and are true sceptics. They apply their scepticism single-mindedly so that paradoxically they are absolutely monistic in that regard. The same kind of paradox arises when dogmatic left wingers become fascists in enforcing their views, or when extremely conservative people are notoriously lax and permissive in their moral behaviour. In other words, absolutists end up chasing their tails and confirming that which they deny. These distinctions are summarised as follows:

- *Absolute Monists* despise moderation and give no credence to opposing views. They know no bounds to their fanaticism and enthusiasm and are often a menace to society. Terrorists, extremists and hot-headed fanatics are typically absolutist in their thinking. In absolute dualism, the world is divided absolutely into black and white, good and evil, matter and spirit, mind and body and so on. The thinking of absolute monists is dominated by categorical thinking in which the world is dividing into rigid categories. You are either for them or against them.

- *Extreme Monists* systematically interpret everything in relation to one thing without using violence to enforce their views. Having one idea means that every conversation is brought round to it as if it were *sine qua non* of their existence. To be obsessed about one's hobbies, about losing weight or about any number of such fixations is to be an extreme monist.

- *Moderate Monists* are what we all are in our everyday pre-occupations with hobbies, football teams, shopping or whatever grabs and interests us most in life. As moderate monists we are amateur enthusiasts who are fanatical about our interests but only within limits. Such interests are always balanced by other interests and responsibilities such as earning a living, pursuing a career, raising a family, political activity and so on. But moderate monists are also systematic dualists by the very fact of being moderate in their monist indulgences.

- *Systematic Dualists* recognise when faced with opposing sides that there are only two clear responses to a confusing situation in which people take sides against each other. One can join one side or the other or one can work towards a resolution, reconciliation or synthesis which will take the situation forward and make progress possible. Taking the first alternative, the systematic dualist would join one side or the other and work hard to moderate the views of that side and achieve a reconciliation of some kind. Taking the second alternative, he or she would be confident enough to persuade both sides that conflict and confrontation cannot achieve their ends.

- *Naïve Dualists* are without any systematic approach by which to cope with their dualist views. They have the muddle-headed, fence-sitting kind of dualism in which one is unable to make up one's mind. They are like Buridan's ass that had equal piles of hay on either side of it. As it was unable to make up its mind which pile to eat, it starved to death. Such dualists clearly lack the internal *nous* and the leadership qualities required to take the dynamic and purposeful action that the situation demands.

- *Absolute Dualists* are sceptical of all beliefs whatsoever. They tend to divide the world absolutely into good and evil, matter and spirit, mind and body and so on. They lack a stable belief system by which to relate one side to the other. The Manicheans were absolute dualists as was Descartes with his mind/body dualism which lacked a coherent interaction between these extremes. These views are also absolute in that they interpret the world from one sceptical point of view. Like all absolutists you are either for them or against them from their point of view.

In everyday life, we can be both moderate monists and systematic dualists. When we want to get things done, we are generally single-minded about it and have no doubts about it. When we are faced with problematic situations then the dualist within us comes to the fore. We need to take account of opposing views and perhaps carefully consider both sides of the argument. We have to be open-minded when we want to reach a clear view of things. But when it is clear that things have gone to extremes and a serious imbalance has occurred than the moderate monist will find plenty of reasons to do what needs to be done.

We can also incorporate both dualist and monist ways of thinking without being aware of it. The latter means being moderate in our prejudices and pre-occupations, and the former means recognising the alternatives that are always possible. We must judge when to be carefully doubtful and when to be cautiously certain. Great and successful leaders are usually adept in combining moderate monism with systematic dualism. They are generally dualist in their thinking and are invariably flexible and creative in their behaviour while also being certain and sure-footed in their decision-making. An outstanding example of this is Oliver Cromwell whose conversation could be baffling and hard to understand but whose actions and battle strategy were decisive and effective.[61] This duality is often called 'common sense' but dualist theory goes much further than Thomas Reid and the Scottish Common Sense School in elucidating what it is.

We can all identify with Robert Graves' poem, "In Broken Images".[62] We are "slow, thinking in broken images", while others are "quick, thinking in clear images." We reach a new understanding of our confusion while others experience a new confusion of their understanding. The systematic dualist view is that clarity resides with facts, things and events while confusion and uncertainty may justly reign in our views, opinions, beliefs, convictions which are peculiar to ourselves. Formal, linear logic is needed for the former but a dualist, dynamic logic is required for the latter. We may be certain, reasonable and logical about facts that we all share but we often have to suspend judgment about our own opinions. A different logic is required in which the middle view is not excluded. Thus, dualist logic is not the same as formal logic. Changes of mind may lead us to

---

[61] Cf. Sir Walter Scott's extraordinary portrayal of Oliver Cromwell in his novel, *Woodstock* (1826). It seems convincingly true to life.

[62] Robert Graves' poem 'In Broken Images' is freely available online

contradict ourselves. We must be more inclusive in our thinking. Being open-minded and forward thinking means that we hold our opinions at arm's length and with some doubt and uncertainty. In contrast, the absolute monist errs in attributing absolute truth and clarity to his or her beliefs and in attempting to eliminate doubt in matters in which doubt is more often a virtue than a hindrance. It is nearly always the case that "much might be said on both sides".[63]

Nevertheless, decisiveness is not incompatible with dualist thinking. In daily life, however, it is often necessary to be decisive and sure-footed. Systematic dualists must necessarily hone their judgments to ensure that decisive action is taken when required. They will thrive on oppositions and the pleasure of reconciling them to achieve worthy ends which are otherwise defeated by the acrimony aroused by such oppositions. They will seek unity and unanimity in relation to the aims of society. Effective leadership can always inspire and motivate people so that they fight for common causes rather than against each other. But it is successful only when it eschews the extremes and shows clearly the benefits of the middle way. When left wingers and right wingers make enemies of each other then the middle way is lost and society can lose its sense of direction. This loss is exemplified all too clearly in the next part of this book.

---

[63] Joseph Addison (1672-1719), in his Roger de Coverely essays in *The Spectator*, no.122, July 20, 1711. (London: J.M. Dent, 1909), p.149. See also no. 117, July 14, 1711 (p.128):
"There are some Opinions in which a Man should stand Neuter, without engaging his Assent to one side or the other. Such a hovering Faith as this, which refuses to settle upon any Determination, is absolutely necessary to a Mind that is careful to avoid Errors and Prepossessions."

Part Three
The Humanist Consensus

1. Introductory

The viewpoint of the systematic dualist, as described above, has usually predominated during periods of intellectual ferment such as the Renaissance and the Enlightenment. Human potential was realised in an unparalleled way during such periods. A humanist consensus predominated that allowed talented people to come to the fore. This consensus overrides the dualist conflicts between traditionalists and progressives, between conservatives and liberals. Real progress becomes possible when the humanist consensus is strong enough to allow it. That strength enables it to plot a middle way that unites the disparate extremes in the common cause of furthering civilisation. In other words, there is a general agreement to follow a middle path that facilitates rational progress which benefits the majority.

European civilisation arguably lost its sense of direction after World War One when its humanist consensus, that promoted human betterment, collapsed into a fruitless political opposition between left and right wing extremism. Communism and fascism rose into prominence and offered simple, absolutist solutions that appealed to many people in the confused circumstances that followed this war. This collapse of the humanist consensus is here exemplified by the breakdown in relationship between left winger Bertrand Russell and right winger D.H. Lawrence during WWI. They fell out with each other after an initial collaboration that aimed to further social progress. Their mutual animosity mirrors the later opposition in Europe between fascists and communists.

However, the real causes of the loss of the humanist consensus are more deep-rooted, as that consensus has its roots in the Renaissance and Enlightenment movements when the influence of humanist views was at its height. By the late 19th century imperialism and militarism threatened the consensus, and the senseless slaughter of WWI brought it to an end. The humanist consensus re-emerged post-WW2, largely through American influence, but it has declined since. To reinstate the humanist consensus we need the dualist view to become more widespread and ultimately to become the common way of thinking about things.

2. The role of the humanist consensus

Historically, one of the ways in which left/right, liberal/conservative conflicts have been reconciled is through what is here called 'the humanist consensus'. This ensured that the ends of humanity prevailed over the bitter antagonisms of these two sides. Periods of significant progress in the history of western civilisation have usually been made possible because of the prevalence of this consensus. This applies, for example, to the Renaissance period from around 1450 onwards. But here we deal with the example of the pre-World War One consensus that prevailed particularly in western Europe.

The humanist consensus consists in an overall belief in (1) the ability of individuals to better themselves, at least intellectually if not morally and (2) the ability of humankind to better itself and make a better future for itself, both materially and culturally. The consensus is a general agreement that forms the spirit of the times.   It engendered optimism and a faith in humanity that transcended religious belief. Its loss resulted in a polarisation of politics between the left and the right. Radically minded people began to think of themselves as having nothing in common with conservatively minded people, and *vice versa*.

Following World War One (WWI), Europe lost the great impetus of civilisation that was taking it forward to an ever better future. That impetus was already petering out due to the causes that also brought about that cataclysmic war. Also, the USA was already poised to take over the mantle of civilised progress from Europe. The effect of the war was to end decisively the humanist consensus in Europe that was needed to maintain an optimistic view of its future and to continue cohesive progress on all fronts. Pre-WWI, there was an air of optimism throughout Europe that contrasts with the general pessimism of today. Nowadays, every disaster or setback anywhere in the world is amplified by the mass media into harbingers of the doom awaiting us. The consensus today favours the revival of religion as being our only hope for the future. Thus, humanism's future depends on our restoring faith in humanity's ability to cope with the future and whatever it throws at us. It is argued here that the restoration of this faith depends on our modifying the social, political and religious extremes which will otherwise rend our society apart. A renewed humanist consensus is required to unify the world and take us all forward to better times.

When the humanist consensus was lost after WWI, European civilization lost its sense of direction, and the extremes in politics began to dominate. The authoritarian ideologies of communism and fascism swirled into the vacuum left by the absence of a dominant humanist consensus. Immediately after the war, Lenin and Mussolini rose up and were followed by Stalin and Hitler. Even in the UK and France, passionate persons devoted themselves to promoting these ideologies as if they were absolute truths thus alienating more thoughtful and open-minded persons. The story is somewhat different in the USA where the humanist consensus, enshrined in the American Dream, has been more predominant, at least until the last few decades during which religion and god-belief have resurfaced in a significant way.

It is argued here that the humanist consensus, promoting the future betterment of humanity, involves a connecting interaction between the left and right wings in politics. Humanism at its most open-minded involves such an interaction, and its future depends on its maintaining a dualist view embracing these two outlooks, (as I have argued in the previous part of this book) When there is no longer a consensus between left and right, they become alienated from each other and regard each other as being the principal obstacle to future progress. They go to extremes in their indictment of each other: the left considers the right to be doctrinaire, cruel and oppressive; the right looks on the left as being sentimental, self-indulgent and decadent. The one then strives to eliminate the other, and the stage is set for self-sustaining internecine conflicts bringing no progress and only misery to humanity.

In the following discussion, the loss of humanist consensus after WWI is illustrated by the fall-out between Bertrand Russell, the left wing philosopher, and D.H. Lawrence, the right wing novelist.[64] It was a pivotal moment in European history. The rest of the discussion deals with the problem of restoring the humanist consensus and thus renewing people's confidence in humanity's future. It is suggested that a dualist view of the role of contexts in our thinking will help people to take the larger view of things. To understand our proper place in the scheme of things, it is necessary to enter the larger contexts of humanity and futurity for example.

3. Russell and Lawrence

The post-WWI loss of humanist consensus is nowhere shown more strikingly than in the break-up of the relationship between Russell and Lawrence. This break-up occurred during the winter of 1915-16, and Lawrence described how things fell apart in the following passage:

> It was in 1915 the old world ended. In the winter 1915-1916 the spirit of the old London collapsed; the city, in some way, perished from being a heart of the world, and became a vortex of broken passions, lusts, hopes, fears, and horrors. The integrity of London collapsed, and the genuine debasement began, the unspeakable baseness of the press and the public voice, the reign of that bloated ignominy, *John Bull*.[65]

Lawrence was partly expressing his bitterness at the treatment of his novel, *The Rainbow*, which had been prosecuted for obscenity in 1915; hence his contempt for 'John Bull' and prejudiced public opinion. But he was also disillusioned in his attempt to engage with the English intellectuals and inspire a revolution in their thinking. They included John Maynard Keynes, Lyndon Strachey and the rest of the Bloomsbury set.[66] In particular, he collaborated for a time with Bertrand Russell. They met for the first time in February 1915 at the behest of Ottoline Morrell, a well-known society hostess. At the time they thought that together they could change with world for the better. They discussed the organisation of

---

[64] Bertrand Russell (1872-1970) established analytical philosophy as the dominant philosophy of the 20th century, and D.H. Lawrence (1885-1930) wrote innumerable novels which are still widely read and some of them have been made into notable feature films such as *Women in Love*.

[65] D. H. Lawrence, *Kangaroo*. (1925 - London: Penguin Books, 1980), ch.12, p. 240.

[66] The Bloomsbury set was associated with the literary group which included the novelist, Virginia Woolf whose father lived in Bloomsbury Square, London, not far from the British Museum.

joint lectures. Lawrence would deliver lectures on a religious theme and Russell on ethics and politics.[67] Russell expressed his initial feelings about Lawrence in this way:

> I liked Lawrence's fire, I liked the energy and passion of his feelings, I liked his belief that something very fundamental was needed to put the world right. I agreed with him in thinking that politics could not be divorced from individual psychology. I felt him to be a man of certain imaginative genius, and, at first, when I felt inclined to disagree with him. I thought that perhaps his insight into human nature was deeper than mine. It was only gradually that I came to feel him a positive force for evil and that he came to have the same feeling about me.[68]

Subsequently, Russell realised that they differed from each other more than either of them differed from the Kaiser of Germany. He also believed that Lawrence was espousing fascism before politicians such as Mussolini and Hitler got around to it.[69] Significantly, it was through their correspondence concerning the proposed lecture course that they gradually fell out with each other. Russell went on to deliver the lectures himself and they were published in his book, *Principles of Social Reconstruction* (1916).

The estrangement of Russell and Lawrence was not repaired by any subsequent correspondence; any more than the letters between Freud and Jung or between Rousseau and Hume could have renewed their respective friendships. Correspondence by letter is not an effective way to sustain an intellectual relationship between people with strong views, both of whom believe they are on the right track. They move away from each other with each written expression of opinion which is read from an unsympathetic point of view. They fall into mutual acrimony as they see more and more faults in the other's expressed opinions.

Though Russell demonised Lawrence till the end of his life, Lawrence avoided the fascist extremes with which Russell accused him. While he sometimes displayed a middle-class kind of anti-Semitism common at the time, he joined no fascist political party, nor would he have condoned Nazism. He seems not to have mentioned Hitler in his writings. As he died in 1930, he probably did not anticipate Hitler's rise. When Lawrence spoke of 'blood knowledge' he wished to bring it into balance with the intellect, while the effect of Nazi ideology was to eliminate the intellect altogether.[70] Indeed, he abhorred the bullying tactics of both communists and fascists. When he came across gangs of young political extremists in Germany in February 1924, he saw them as being throwbacks to a

[67] Ronald W. Clark, *The Life of Bertrand Russell*, (Harmondsworth: Penguin, 1975), ch. 10, pp. 323-326.

[68] Bertrand Russell, *The Autobiography of Bertrand Russell*. (1967 - London: Allen & Unwin, 1975), Volume Two, ch. 8, p. 243.

[69] *Ibid.* p. 244.

[70] Harry T. Moore, *The Priest of Love: A Life of D.H. Lawrence*. Revised edition, (1974 - Harmondsworth: Penguin Books, 1976), part three, ch. 6, p. 372.

primitive tribalism.[71] He would likely have seen Nazism in the same light. The critic, Terry Eagleton places Lawrence on the radical right wing, as being hostile to democracy, liberalism, socialism, and egalitarianism, though never actually embracing fascism.[72]

In his writings, Lawrence often expresses humanist views. Some of what he says in his last book, *Apocalypse*, is quite lyrical and positive minded:

> What man most passionately wants is his living wholeness and his living unison, not his own isolate salvation of his 'soul'. Man wants his physical fulfilment first and foremost, since now, once and once only, he is in the flesh and potent. For man, the vast marvel is to be alive. For man, as for flower and beast and bird, the supreme triumph is to be most vividly, most perfectly alive.[73]

Lawrence may be culpable for his radical right wing stance, but he did not condemn Russell to the extent that the latter condemned him. He resorted to no more than ridicule when a friend told him that Russell had said: "Lawrence has no mind". Lawrence replied: "Have you seen him in a swimsuit? Poor Bertie Russell! He is all Disembodied Mind."[74] Russell himself went to left wing extremes both in his politics and his behaviour in his response to the horrors of WWI. From a personal point of view, he saw little point in exercising virtue and became a notorious womaniser.

> The war of 1914-18 changed everything for me. I ceased to be academic and took to writing a new kind of books. I changed my whole conception of human nature. I became for the first time deeply convinced that Puritanism does not make for human happiness. . . . I saw that reformers and reactionaries alike in our present world have become distorted by cruelties. I grew suspicious of all purposes demanding stern discipline.[75]

It is remarkable that Russell's autobiography up to the end of WWI is teeming with convivial activity. He is constantly meeting and talking to people. After WWI, he is increasingly on his own and struggling to make sense of his life in an entirely different way. During the 1920s, he went to Russia and China presumably in search of answers but found none that satisfied him. Similarly, Lawrence went on his travels throughout the world, leaving a fruitful trail of novels in his wake.

Neither Russell nor Lawrence was being true to humanism when they rubbished opposing views because they were opposed to them. They saw each other's views as being intrinsically evil and thought that the world would be a better place without such views. In short, they wished to see them eradicated from the face of the Earth. Clearly they did not subscribe to Voltaire's alleged saying: "I disapprove of what you say, but I will defend to the death your right to

---

[71] *Op. cit.*, part four, ch. 8, p. 491.

[72] Terry Eagleton, *The English novel: An Introduction*, (London: Wiley-Blackwell, 2005), pp. 258–260.

[73] D. H. Lawrence, *Apocalypse*. (1931), Penguin, 1974, p. 125.

[74] Harry T. Moore, *op. cit.*, part five, ch. 1, p. 516.

[75] Russell, *op. cit.*, ch. 8, p. 261.

say it."[76] They reacted emotionally against each other's views to the point of wilfully misunderstanding them.

The humanist way is surely to try to understand why people need to adopt such radically opposing views to one's own. This is why the dualist view is important to the development of humanism. It provides a systematic way of understanding the import of diametrically opposing views. Thus, the humanist consensus is only possible when it can accommodate such opposing views by giving a sense of purpose to which most people can subscribe. They can sideline the extremists because it is obvious to them that the bigger picture involves both sides working together for better future instead of fighting against each other to no purpose whatsoever.

4. How the humanist consensus was lost

The falling out between Russell and Lawrence was symptomatic of the loss of the humanist consensus which had been threatening European civilization long before WWI. The latter event brought matters to a head because people were traumatised by the senseless loss of life it had caused. They lost faith decisively in the progress of humanity. But the seeds of that doubt were already taking root during the nineteenth century.

At its most potent, the humanist consensus had brought about the great intellectual movements of the Renaissance and the Enlightenment. These movements petered out as progress was usually slower than people's expectations. Their idealist belief in humanity's potential was worn away by the realities of life. The certainties of dogmatism reasserted themselves in the form of religion or ideology. Such certainties offered people the comfort and security they craved. During the nineteenth century, the split between left and right was widened by the rise of liberal and idealist philosophies that were mutually incompatible with each other.

Until the late nineteenth century, the humanist consensus had supported a secularist society of which religion was only a part and not the most dominant part. The extremes of capitalism were also tempered by improving working conditions and increasing wage levels for workers. The political aspirations of both the left and right therefore were moderated and pointed in humanist directions. However, during the nineteenth century, European thinking came under the thrall of two opposing philosophies: (1) a liberal, utilitarian philosophy emanating from Britain and (2) a conservative, idealist philosophy stemming from continental Europe.

The liberal philosophy had been championed by the Benthamites,[77] including

---

[76] Attributed by S.G. Tallentyre (*alias* Evelyn Beatrice Hall) in *Friends of Voltaire* (London: Smith, Elder, & Co.,1906), p. 199. But Hall tells us that this was only his "attitude" at the reception of Helvetius's book *On the Mind* (*De l'Esprit*) with which he disapproved.

[77] Followers of Jeremy Bentham (1748-1832), the founder of the Utilitarian movement which itself was based on the ethical views of David Hume. James Mill (1773-1836), the father of John Stuart Mill, was perhaps Bentham's most devoted follower.

John Stuart Mill 1806-1873), the most enduring beacon of liberalism.[78] But by the end of the nineteenth century, idealist philosophy held sway, even over Great Britain. Indeed, Bertrand Russell had begun his intellectual career at Cambridge University as an idealist philosopher, until G.E. Moore's influence led him back to his liberalist beginnings.[79]

German idealism of the early 20th century century was taken up in Great Britain later in the century. Philosophers such as T. H. Green (1836-1882), F. H. Bradley, (1846-1903), and John Mactaggart (1866-1925) espoused a British Hegelian philosophy that brought idealism to the fore. The fashionable sway of idealist thinking at this time amplified imperialist and jingoist sentiments. The European population was brainwashed into the adulation of 'God, King and Country' and this motivated millions of young men to march stubbornly into the mass massacres of WW1. These high ideals had become more real and important than human beings. Such Platonist thinking sullied the humanist consensus that the Enlightenment had nurtured so successfully. By 1914, the Platonist ideals of God, King and Country unified Europe sufficiently to justify a senseless war between self-congratulatory nations each of which had their own selfish and mutually incompatible imperialist ambitions.

Post-WW1, there was an immediate reaction against these imperialist ideals and, in the post-war chaos, many people went to the political extremes of the left and right. The communists and fascists came to power in Russia and Italy respectively, followed in the 1930s by the Nazis in Germany. These extremists were only interested in the exercise of power and in subjugating their respective peoples. The optimism of the humanist consensus had no place in their thinking. In contrast, the USA was still largely under the influence of the pragmatic philosophy of William James (1842-1910), John Dewey (1859-1952) and others. American optimism pervaded Europe to some extent post-WW1 and helped to moderate the pessimism and disillusion spawned by the senselessness of the war. American influence increased still further after World War Two and helped to reinstate the humanist consensus in Europe. This reached its crescendo during the nineteen sixties.

5. How to restore the humanist consensus

After WW2 and until the 1960s, the humanist consensus flourished once more in Europe and an air of general optimism swept the continent. Everything seemed possible, and even the Roman Catholic Church stooped to reforming and modernizing itself to somewhat. But all that was brought to an end by the aimless political extremism of the late sixties both in Europe and the USA. Western civilisation lost its focus and no coherent humanist philosophy emerged to

---

[78] J. S. Mill's famous essay, *On Liberty* (1859), is the classic statement of what liberalism is about.

[79] Ibid., ch. 5. p. 136. George Edward Moore (1873-1958) together with Russell founded the analytical movement that dominated philosophy in the 20th century.

consolidate the consensus, and it faded away amidst the bromide of the seventies.

In short, the humanist consensus can only be restored by strengthening humanism so that it becomes the dominant view in society. I have already suggested in part two above that this strengthening can be achieved by developing a dualist theory that ensures extremist thinking is avoided in our thinking. But extremist thinking is also avoided by looking at things from different perspectives. This is a contextual view that emphasises putting things into wider contexts and not confining them to one context. An extremist may think that everything must be seen within the context of his or her religion or ideology. To them, no other context matters in life and they act accordingly.

Thus, avoiding the extremes of religious and idealist thinking requires us to develop a contextual theory which helps us broaden our perspective beyond ourselves and our egotistical concerns. What seems real, important and indubitable in one context can seem trivial and mean in another context. For example, buying new clothes for a job interview may seem vitally important in the context of one's daily life, but it is fairly unimportant in the context of world poverty in which many people worry about having something to eat, let alone what clothes to wear. The plight of the poor become of personal importance to us when we see things in that perspective – "no man is an island entire of itself".[80] This contextual view deals with how contexts take us out of our immediate concerns so that we see things in broader contexts, and remote events enter our sphere of thinking. This view is not new though it has never been properly explicated before in a philosophical manner. It is presaged, for example, in this quotation from the Italian philosopher, Giambattista Vico (1668-1744):

> In his bestial state, a man loves only his own well-being. After he takes a wife and has children, he continues to love his own well-being, and comes to love the well-being of his family as well. After he enters civil life, he comes to love the well-being of his city. After his city extends its rule over other peoples, he comes to love to the well-being of his nation. And after such nations are united through war, peace, alliances, and trade, he comes to love the well-being of the entire human race. In all these contexts, the individual continues to love his own advantage above all else.[81]

Vico's view probably influenced that great Italian patriot, Giuseppe Mazzini (1805-1872), in his formulating the slogan, *Amate l'Umanità!* (love humanity!) which he used in his nineteenth century campaign to unify Italy's disparate nations and city states.[82] He considered the interests of humanity to be more important than those of family and country. The creation of a united Italy was more vital to humanity than loyalty to smaller units which were perpetually in conflict with each other. The context of humanity thus incorporates the other contexts such

---

[80] John Donne (1572-1631), 'Devotions upon Emergent Occasions - Meditation XVII' (1624). *Selected Prose*, (London: Penguin Books, 1987), p. 126.

[81] Giambatista Vico, *New Science*. (1744), (London: Penguin, 1999), Section Four, §341, pp. 125-126.

[82] Giuseppe Mazzini, *The Duties of Man*, (London: J.M. Dent & Co., 1955), pp. 49-50.

as family and nation to unify people when they open their minds to the importance of that viewpoint.

If humanity is to have a future we need to use such contexts to unify people of all political persuasions to get things done, such as reforming the global financial system and tackling climate change, which may be vital to the future of life let as well as humanity. I further argue that using dualist interaction helps us to make the best possible use of contexts. It means interacting with the contents of contexts on a one-to-one basis. Everything is not considered within the bounds of one point of view but is extended to include opposing views. We are thereby less more prone to go to dogmatic extremes since we are deliberately putting our problems in their proper perspectives and not making more of them than they really deserve.

From a humanist point of view, there is no need for high, inhuman ideals to live up to, such as religion and ideology thump into us to the exclusion of everything else. But we do need parameters within which to function and gauge our behaviour. We can elevate ourselves and have confidence in our views because we are taking account of opposing views and are not claiming to have the whole truth and nothing but the truth. In short, dualist theory can help renew the humanist consensus by providing the rationale that humanity now needs to replace the simple and easy answers that religion has hitherto provided.

Part Four
Applying Dualist Studies

1. The fundamental nature of dualist interaction

Dualist interaction is entirely material, entirely a part of the physical world, and is always amenable to causal explanation. The development of this notion in dualist studies gets rid, once and for all, of occult, supernatural entities in the brain and the universe in general. However the availability of causal explanation is limited by the extent of our scientific knowledge. At the moment, it is clear that our knowledge is insufficiently advanced to account for all dualist interactions in the universe. But, from a philosophical point of view, dualist interaction can be used, figuratively speaking, as an Occam's Razor to cut across the Gordian Knot of tangled philosophical problems such as the following:

The Mind/Body Problem. As already mentioned in the Introduction, dualism has been too closely associated with Cartesian dualism. It posits the existence of a mental/physical divide that is too rigid and narrow to explain the complexities of brain activity. When we apply dualist interaction universally it becomes clear that notions such as immaterial, spirit, soul, and vital energy (élan vitale) are superfluous entities that ultimately cannot be defined. The continuous nature of dualist interaction means occult entities are not required to explain, for instance, consciousness. Our self-consciousness may be thought of metaphorically as, for instance, a turning in of brain activity to make self-awareness possible. Exactly what interactions are required in physical terms depends on further understanding of brain activity. Subjectivity therefore refers to the misfit of what is going on within our physical bodies and the environment in which they exist. We need to be constantly alert and attentive to overcoming that misfit. The problem of how the mind influences the body vanishes when we explain all our experiences in terms of dualist interactions. The word 'mind' becomes an empty notion. If it is uninformative to say that the brain moves the body, it is even more uninformative to say that the mind moves body. When we move our limbs, all kinds of dualist interactions are involved which are not yet fully understood. The processes involved are wholly physical and material and no spiritual or immaterial explanations are required. The unified activity of these dualist interactions are all that are required, and these might ultimately be explained in terms of neural networks and the like.

The Absolutism/Relativism Problem. The only absolute that we require is the continuous existence of dualist interaction that links us to external reality. The 'now' or 'nunc stans' of present existence is a unified absolute that is only sustained by continuous dualist interaction between ourselves and our external environment. We can be absolutely sure of our relationship to external reality because of the work we are constantly doing, both consciously and unconsciously, to stay in touch with it. Everything is relative to what we are doing. The same applies to the relativity of our beliefs and opinions. We have to work at keeping them down-to-earth. We also need to work constantly at relating our views to those of other people and ultimately to society as a whole. Dualist studies deals with this problem through contextualisation, that is to say, by putting things into context and by seeing things from different perspectives.

The Sceptical/Dogmatic Problem. We can never be absolutely certain about anything. But at the same time, there is no need to be sceptical about everything. We then have the problem of dealing with doubt and uncertainty since the dualist view seems to put us perpetually on the fence. We are apparently prevented from making our minds up altogether. Developing the dualist view helps us to fine tune our reasoning without lapsing into rigid dogmatism. For example, the logical law of the excluded middle is confined to its proper place instead of being applied to all of our beliefs and opinions as well as to discrete objects in external reality. In other words, the 'either/or' distinction applies rightly to the existence of things and events in the real world. They either exist or they do not exist and there is no doubt about it. We may be totally certain, for example, that tables and chairs exist in the next room. In such practical matters there is little doubt in the matter. But if our beliefs and opinions about political and religious matters are held to be true with absolute certainty then we are led down the path of extremism and are honour bound to impose our views on other people willy nilly. The dualist view therefore helps us to moderate our views and to take due account of the merits and demerits of opposing views. An understanding of the relationship between dualism and monism helps us here.

2. The social usefulness of the dualist view

> ### Some Aims of Dualist Studies
> •   To train the mind to cope with extreme thought tendencies and to avoid complete scepticism on the one hand and complete dogmatism on the other hand;
> •   To show that dualist thinking is not necessarily vague or indecisive and is in fact necessary for correct and productive thinking;
> •   To show how new ideas can change society for the better;
> •   To instil philosophy with renewed vigour;
> •   To understand better what it is to be human, especially in regard to what is considered to be inhuman, in thought and behaviour.

The Application of Dualist Studies

Dualist studies involve applying the dualist view to practical areas such as management, crime and punishment, education, future studies, understanding the universe. An outline follows of the dualist approach to each of these areas:

A dualist approach to management: The dualist view is essential to successful management. It consists in understanding the extremes of opinion and attitude to which both employers and employees are prone and which pervade every workplace. The dualist view can help managers deal with situations that demand intuitive insight more than incisive logic. The distinction between naïve and systematic dualism is useful here in which the former refers to confused and muddled thinking whereas the latter involves organised and purposeful thinking to deal systematically with confusing and conflicting situations. Such distinctions help us to understand conflicts between rival groups within the workplace and with leadership dilemmas such balancing friendliness with aloofness. (This is the subject of my paper entitled "The Role of Dualist Thinking in Management" which was presented to the Seventh International Philosophy of Management Conference at St. Anne's College, Oxford on Friday 23rd July 2010.)

A dualist approach to crime and punishment: At present, crime is punished very unevenly and often ineffectively. Punishments are meted out in an unsystematic way that leads to the extremes of under and over punishment. Those who might be punished with leniency are often given custodial sentences that ruin their lives, while others who deserve very harsh punishment to put them on the right track are often treated too leniently. When dangerous people finish their term of 'punishment' they are let out into the community and may endanger the public. The conservative view is that criminals should be punished with longer jail sentences. The liberal view is that people should be rehabilitated and not merely punished by jail sentences. The dualist view is that the person should be punished, not the crime. In other words, law-breakers should be punished not by fixed, predetermined sentences but according to what is required to 'cure' them of their social deviance and hopefully make honest citizens of them. A *social treatment system* is therefore required to change our criminal justice system and to ensure that those who need lenient treatment are given it and those who need harsh treatment are also given it. (The aforementioned 'social treatment system' is elaborated in my paper entitled "Punish the Person, not the Crime! Proposing a Social Treatment System to Punish Lawbreakers".)

A dualist approach to education: In one respect, we need education to be thumped into us if we are to imbibe successfully such basic skills as reading, writing and arithmetic. But in another respect we need to absorb knowledge and understanding in our own way and in our own time. When these two contrasting approaches are insightfully combined, they interact to produce the best kind of education. The first approach may be called 'Mode 1' and the second 'Mode 2'. Mode 1 emphasises the skills, knowledge and abilities that should be inculcated through education, whereas Mode 2 emphasises the cultivation of individuality and creativity. In the dualist view, both these approaches are combined in an imaginative way.[83]

A dualist approach to future studies: Though we live in the present we constantly look back to the past and forward to the future. Studying the past helps us to predict the future, and looking to the future helps us to anticipate

---

[83] Cf. *The New Production of Knowledge*, Michael Gibbons, C. Limoges, H. Nowotny, S. Schwartzman, P. Scott, and M. Trow. (London: Sage, 1994).

things being better than they are at present. But we can be too pre-occupied with the past at the expense of the future and vice versa. These are monist views that look exclusively in either one direction or the other. It means that we dwell too much in the past or look too confidently to the future. The *retrospective* view looks to the past and *prospective* view to the future. The dualist view helps us to place equal value on both these views. We move in a dynamic way from one to the other without being stuck in the past or leaving everything to the future. (There is more on these distinctions in my unpublished paper entitled "Posterity and Prospectivism: The Way Forward for all Humanity".)

A dualist approach to eliminating extremes of thought: Systematic dualism is essential for creativity as it depends on our maintaining a balance between thinking too much or too little. It is arguable that those 'geniuses' who perform extraordinary feats of creativity are only able to do so because they are systematic dualists who avoid self-defeating extremes in their thinking. They develop their mental powers in a purposeful fashion without taking themselves too seriously on the one hand or belittling themselves too much on the other hand. Often we are in doubt whether to think too much of ourselves or too little. Here are the extreme consequences of the opposing tendencies involved:

Thinking too much of oneself	*Thinking too little of oneself*
May lead to	May lead to
Hot-headed extremism	*Empty-headed indifference*
Involving	Involving
Brazen overconfidence	*Insipid lack of confidence*
And *in extremis* to	And *in extremis* to
Homocidal sociopathy	*Suicidal self-abnegation*

It appears that too many young people are prone to these extremes these days, leading to an outbreak of massacres and suicides, as reported in the mass media. Suicide bombers seem to incorporate both these strands in their thinking. Their unbalanced thinking twists these strands into a deadly double helix, the antithesis of DNA which gives life instead of taking it. A rational dualist interaction between these extremes is required to avoid being possessed by them beyond sense and reality. Thus, a greater understanding of our essential duality is the next big step forward for humanity.

3. In praise of the middle way

Our Capacity for Extremism. Perhaps our most admirable and our most dangerous trait is our capacity for excess. The seemingly limitless extremes to which we push ourselves brings out the best and worst in us. Our obsessions can lead us, for example, to climb the highest mountains, write huge novels, and gain immense advances in scientific knowledge, while crippling ourselves with addictions, killing each other in the millions, and destroying the planet in our pursuit of the 'good life'. From a moral standpoint, it is obvious which of these are beneficial and which are harmful. But it depends on our states of mind whether we adopt the first and avoid the second. In so far as we have personal insight and self-discipline we can avoid harmful states of mind when we recognise them as such. We can choose not to do harm or to have negative thoughts in so far as we have control over our emotions. For example, we can stop being angry with someone when we realise that our anger is unfounded or unreasonable. People about to commit murder or suicide can be persuaded by others to desist. Potentially we can all change our minds if we choose to do so. Therefore, we have enough freewill to consciously avoid going to these extremes if we really want to. A clear method is needed to deal with these extremes, and the following distinctions hopefully help us to recognise extreme and harmful states of mind both within ourselves and in others, so that we can avoid them.

A Schematic Depiction of the Middle Way

	The Will to Power (Nietzsche)	The Will to Understanding (Systematic Dualism)	The Will to Belief (William James)
Features: Motivations:	Carnivorous (Wolves) Seeking immediate fame, power or notoriety ↓	Human Seeking long-term personal development ↓	Herbivorous (Sheep) Seeking security within 'herd/flock' ↓
Traits:			
Relational	Dominant	Independent	Dependent
Prescriptive	Commanding	Questioning	Unquestioning
Doxastic	Dogmatic	Critical of belief	Blind belief/faith
Reactive	Authoritarian	Authoritative	Credulous
Predictive	Deterministic	Latitudinarian	Fatalistic
Attitudinal	Absolute certainty	Relative certainty	Total conviction
Judgmental	Contempt	Respect	Uncritical
Behavioural	Demeaning ↓	Self-critical ↓	Subservient ↓
Effects:			
Social	Esoteric	Familial	Exclusive
Heuristic	Indoctrination	Teaching	Preaching
Emotive	Hypnotic induction	Rational passions	Mob mania
Dispositional	Them/us discrimination ↓	Tolerance of differences ↓	Indiscriminate love/hatred ↓
Goals:			
Epistemic	Messianic knowledge	Hypothetical knowledge	Common knowledge
Personal	Adulation ↓	Truth ↓	Conformity ↓
Outcomes:	Self-deception	Insight	Delusion

Introducing the Middle Way. The above three outlooks or ways of thinking characterise human nature. We have, on the one hand, the overly strong 'will to power' and, on the other hand, the overly weak 'will to believe', between which the relatively moderate 'will to understanding' hovers uneasily. The former two ways represent relatively primitive and uncivilised aspects of human nature which need to be supplemented by the middle way. Their primitive and uncivilised aspects emerge when they are isolated from the middle way and are taken to extremes. All forms of political, religious, and behavioural extremism result from such a loss of the middle way, as is argued below. This extremist potential persists within us all and we need constantly to guard ourselves against its reassertion and predominance. In so far as there is progress in civilisation, it consists in the middle way being progressively introduced until it forms part of everyone's mindset and ultimately of the political and social fabric. Civilised behaviour requires the middle way to insinuate its way between these intimate extremes which feed on each other. This process has recurred several times in history when humanistic attitudes have come to the fore. Equally, the simplicity and attraction of extreme views has all too often resulted in the loss of the middle way. Until the twentieth century, the appearance of the middle way has been cyclical and impermanent. Hopefully, the twenty-first century will see its permanent institution when it becomes an integral part of the educational system.

The Consequences of Repudiating the Middle Way. It may be argued that excess is tolerable while it is related to the middle way wherein we remain human rather than inhuman. We can be a little wicked as long as we repent of that wickedness and resolve to do better. For we need to bear in mind the harm which excessive behaviour does to ourselves and others. We need the restraints of the middle way to function as sociable and rational beings. Repudiating the middle way entirely means losing one's moral sense or social conscience. Psychopaths and sociopaths feel no shame or remorse because they have lost all restraints over their behaviour and have nothing within them to draw them back from doing their worst. In the same bracket, we may include terrorists, extremists, fanatics, zealots, criminals, rapists, gangsters, gurus, charlatans, and sectarian bigots of all kinds, who commonly scorn the middle way between the will to power and the will to believe. They seek the nearest way to satisfy their ambitions, desires, compulsions and obsessions. In preying on the populace like wolves on sheep, they dehumanise themselves and demean their victims. They dominate people to achieve their self-serving ends. They are so sure of themselves that they become dogmatic and authoritarian in their behaviour towards others. In the case of religious and political bigots, they exert power over others by means of messianic knowledge which is usually a belief system specific to themselves or the organisation within which they operate. The belief system is often so esoteric and divorced from common life that they adopt a them/us discrimination policy. You are either in or out and there is no middle way.

No Excuses for Repudiating the Middle Way. Clarifying the middle way helps us to put such people in their place and treat them with the contempt and disapproval they deserve. Neither their genetic inheritance nor their social backgrounds are sufficient to excuse their opprobrious ways of thinking over which they potentially have as much control as the rest of us. Their freely adopted attitudes and frames of mind are primarily to blame for their deplorable behaviour. We need not respect or tolerate behaviour and attitudes which cannot be justified by reason or reference to the middle way.

Without the Middle Way We Lose our Humanity. In the absence of any middle way, power-mongering and intimidation prevails, and the human race is composed of nothing but knaves and fools, or exploiters and victims. Knaves think too much of themselves and fools too little of themselves. The knaves quarrel among themselves and use fools to fight each other. The divisions between people are irreconcilable and they erode trust, perpetuate enmity, make co-operation impossible, and prevent us from fulfilling our potential as human beings. Killing each other becomes a routine matter when we have no respect for others as human beings and regard them as dispensable vermin. It is Hobbes's 'state of nature' in which there is 'war of every man against every man'. The highest human aspirations are thrown away in favour of the lowest and meanest ones, dictated by narrow, personal, group, sectarian, nationalist or religious matters. Such are the conditions which prevailed under authoritarian regimes such as Nazi Germany, Stalinist Russia, and Pol Pot's Cambodia.

Power and Subservience go Together. Just as sadism goes along with masochism and *vice versa*, so power-mongering goes along with submission and subservience to a stronger will or character. Power-mongers will always have victims over whom they exert power and influence while the majority retain an uncritical will to believe in spite of all reason or common sense to the contrary. As a mobilised mob or a cowed crowd, people are susceptible to the wilfulness of dominant characters. It is easy to appeal to people's emotions when they form a cohesive tribe that spurns the freethinking individual. Only when people are allowed to think things out as individuals, is it possible for reason and good sense to prevail over crowd-pulling emotion.

Preserving the Middle Way may Require Extreme Measures.   When the other two ways of thinking predominate to extremes then the human race is divided against itself and neglects its true ends in favour of war, enmity, hatred, and sectarianism. War typically breeds inhumanity, and any savagery is justifiable if it leads to victory. Thus, it took the ultimate savagery of the atomic bomb to prevent the even more savage prolongation of the Second World War. Presumably much of Japan's remaining population was preserved, to say nothing of countless allied lives, by this justifiable savage act of using atomic weapons. Also, we would never have known just how horrible and inhuman the atom bomb is until it was actually used on a large population. Its drastic and widespread effects simply could not have been imagined beforehand. Thus, extreme measures may be morally justifiable on rare occasions to respond to extreme activities. We cannot tolerate the intolerable if we are to preserve the continuity of our civilisation. The continued existence of the middle way itself may depend on extreme measures being taken to preserve it. This clarification of the middle way disciplines us to go so far in preserving it without losing touch with it altogether. Otherwise we are prone to the Dr. Strangelove solution in which the extremes take over, and people *qua* people are conveniently forgotten. The end only justifies the means when the end is the welfare of individuals and not just humanity as a whole.

The Middle Way Itself can be Taken to Extremes. Moreover, the middle way is itself not immune from extremism. Taken to extremes it leads to mediocrity and sterility. But unlike the other ways, it is largely self-regulatory. In being self-critical, we can detect when we are getting into ruts, failing to do justice to ourselves, and so on. Therefore, on the whole, the middle way is less susceptible to extremism but never entirely resistant to it. While we must forever work hard to keep ourselves on the straight-and-narrow, we must also be flexible and open-minded in seeing the value of change, innovation, and creative solutions to problems generally.

No Such Things as Absolute Good and Evil. The middle way gives the lie to the Manichean myth concerning the existence of good and evil as opposing forces in the universe. Absolute good and evil exist only as symbols of our own tendencies towards to the extremes. We become absolutely good or absolutely evil only by going to one extreme or the other. There is nothing outwith our own minds to partake of, one way or the other. That is to say, there is no substance of good or evil waiting out there to take possession of us. If there were, then it would be impossible for us to moderate our behaviour and to prevent ourselves from going to extremes.

Masculinity/Femininity and the Middle Way. The power/belief extremes are rooted ultimately in the masculine/feminine dichotomy. Wholly masculine behaviour is typically power-driven just as wholly feminine behaviour is typically subservient. But most of us most of the time are neither entirely masculine nor entirely feminine, whatever our genetically determined gender. Thus, the middle way reflects this ambiguity and makes sense of it. For it is arguable that men are more effective as men, and women more effective as women in relation to the middle way, since it brings the sexes together in pursuit of the common purposes of humanity, e.g., marriage and family life. Outwith the middle way, the sexes are in isolation from each other, and masculine and feminine attributes appear in both males and females. Such perversions are particularly apparent in extreme cultures such as in Ancient Sparta, prison populations, monastic communities, and celibate priesthoods. The fact that these are now appearing in western culture indicates the extent to which the middle way is yet again endangered by extreme reactions against it.

The Golden Mean and The Middle Way. An early precursor to the middle way was Aristotle's Golden Mean in which virtue lies between excess and deficiency, e.g., courage lies between rashness and cowardice, temperance lies between licentiousness and insensibility, *etc.* (Cf. *Ethics*, Book II, vi-viii). This is inadequate because of the difficulties in defining these terms with any precision and in relating one set of terms to another, *i.e.*, relating courage to temperance. The diagram above provides a more comprehensive basis for relating all the terms of the middle way to each other and for differentiating them from the ways of power and belief. This task is begun in the Explanatory Notes below. Thus, the distinctions made in that diagram are intended only as guidelines which highlight the importance of the humanist outlook. They are not the last word on the matter but hopefully the first. Doubtless other terms may be chosen to make similar distinctions. The reasons for making these distinctions and for choosing these particular words are clarified in the following notes.

Explanatory Notes

The Will to Power:

For our personal development, it is more important to gain power over ourselves than over others. Thus, the will to power is an admirable attribute in the hands of artists, writers and other creative people who wish to exploit their creative powers by willing themselves to greater things. In that respect, Nietzsche's book, *Also Sprach Zarathrustra*, often inspires people to make the best of their talents and abilities. This is the moderate, middle-of-the-road view of the will to power. But taken to extremes, the will to power means power over other people for one individual's ends and purposes or for an anti-social cause, and the middle way may be lost in the process. Business men, politicians, and other persons in positions of authority can misuse their power to the extent of becoming authoritarian or criminal in their behaviour. However, in an open, self-regulating society, authority and power are usually compatible with the middle way when they are exercised moderately, rationally, socially, legally and, above all, morally.

When power goes to people's heads they are liable to use intimidation, sex, blackmail, oratory, controversy, mysticism, or other forms of emotional arousal or irrational bamboozlement to gain an advantage over those over whom they wish to wield power. Terrorists use bombs and weapons to exert power over people and terrify them into sheep-like acquiescence. But they themselves are led like sheep by the persons or doctrines to which they are subject. They uncritically accept the 'truth' meted out to them as if that truth constitutes reality in an absolute and indisputable fashion. In their turn they wilfully impose their beliefs on others by extreme methods. Thus, the prosecution at the trial of the Oklahoma bomber, McVeigh, claimed that "the truck [in which he planted the explosions] was there to impose the will of Timothy McVeigh on the rest of America". Similarly, Islamist terrorists imagine themselves to be carrying out the will of Allah in committing their deadly and barbaric acts. Raskolnikov in Dostoevsky's classic work, *Crime and Punishment*, also saw his crime as an embodiment of his "will". However, such a misuse of the will to impose ourselves on others does not preclude the use of the will in an understanding and rational way.

The Will to Understanding:

Understanding, in this context, means thinking about things instead of reacting impulsively and thoughtlessly to events. More exertion is involved in understanding things than in following our emotional whims and inclinations. Therefore, the will to understanding requires more sustained effort of will than either the will to power or the will to believe as these usually appeal more to our emotions than to our intellect. The will to understanding has the advantage of making us think about and inquire into things instead of accepting them at face value or because past authority says so. It means thinking for oneself instead of letting others do all one's thinking. Humanism throughout the ages has fostered the will to understanding as an ongoing process rather than a fixed attribute. A constant exercise of the will is required because we are not understanding creatures by nature nor necessarily by upbringing. The willingness to adopt this state of mind comes through maturity and self-knowledge. It is primarily a function of our language acquisition which enables us to question others and ourselves to understand better how things are.

Because it is not a soft option, the will to understanding is under constant threat from the other two ways. It will remain so until it is a rationally acknowledged part of our culture and is sustained and renewed by unremitting reference to the middle way. Civilisation depends on our cultivating the will to understanding and on our maintaining a culture in which it is encouraged rather than suppressed. If, as a species, we stop understanding things anew for ourselves from one generation to the next, then the further development of civilisation ceases and nothing remains but the celebration of past glories. Understanding things means constantly solving puzzles and satisfying our curiosity about everything around us. We may never get to the bottom of the problems we face but we can find pleasure and interest in our grappling with them. Therefore, as well as encapsulating the humanist outlook, the middle way as depicted above also supports and justifies scientific research and philosophical inquiry.

The Will to Believe:

The will to believe was advocated by William James in his essay of that name. He rightly argued that there would be little to believe in if we always require 'sufficient evidence' before relying on our beliefs. Our ability to do anything at all is impaired since our actions depend on believing many things implicitly and without having to investigate them ourselves. However, the will to believe is taken to harmful extremes when belief becomes an end in itself and is impervious to criticism, rethought, or revision. We are entitled to our own beliefs but we harm ourselves in holding these beliefs uncritically or with absolute confidence of their inviolability against alternative beliefs. We become slaves to the beliefs instead of using them for self-enlightenment. If we ascribe too much importance to our beliefs, we are liable to defend them to the death. Putting them at arm's length enables us to explore and revisit them to test their real usefulness to ourselves and others.

Any belief can be conceived to be untrue or limited in some way, otherwise it is not a belief but a rigid dogma. No belief can be absolutely true in all conceivable circumstances whatsoever, yet true believers behave as if that were so. Such absolutism is the source of much bigotry, extremism, especially in respect of fundamentalist religion. There is a kind of insecurity in people that leads them to rely absolutely on such beliefs without further thought on the matter. The humanist view is that we don't deserve or need such security. As T.S. Eliot put it (in the poem, *Little Gidding*): "We shall not cease from exploration and the end of all our exploring will be to arrive where we started and know the place for the first time." Thus, death alone brings our exploring to an end.

Conspectus

The middle way as portrayed here comprises an intellectual and educational tool to be used by individuals for their personal insight and self-improvement. It is something to be used rather than believed in. It is intended to be a contribution to knowledge and not to be imposed on people willy-nilly. Clarifying the importance of the middle way, compared with its extremist alternatives, will hopefully make people more conscious of the need to avoid such extremes. It can heighten people's sensitivity to their own susceptibilities in that regard. This development may not be enough in itself to achieve that goal but it can contribute to the process. Moreover, there is much more to the middle way than is dealt with in this outline

4. A list of promises

The future development of dualist theory offers hope and salvation by promising a coherent system of philosophy that comprises the diverse benefits listed below. This theory is not the complete answer to our problems but it hopefully provides new insights into many of them. Thus, answers given here are at least hints and suggestions that can take our thinking forward and perhaps lead to better answers in the future. These promises are listed under four headings about the benefits of understanding dualist interaction, inner being, the nature of reality, and humanity and our role in the universe:

The Benefits of Understanding Dualist Interaction

- *Dualist interaction:* In explaining our mentality in terms of dualist interaction, dualist theory adds to our knowledge and understanding of the way we think and reason in general. This will enable us to cope better and more realistically with the uncertain future before us.

- *Flexible and adaptable thinking:* Dualist theory helps us to be more flexible and adaptable in our thinking because of its interactive and trial-and-error rationale. This helps us to function more effectively in an increasingly complex and interconnected society.

- *Extremism:* A greater understanding of extremist ways of thinking with the hope of eliminating it as an endemic feature of our society. The dualist antidote to extremism is open-mindedness as between dogmatism on the one hand and scepticism on the other hand. We may have to oscillate between one and other to find the middle way.

- *Imbalances:* Dualism is also about correcting imbalances caused by our constantly going to extremes in one way or the other. Such imbalances give rise to obsessive behaviour in human beings and in society to economic bubbles and other financial excesses.

The Benefits of Understanding Inner Being

- *Consciousness:* We are conscious in so far as we are interacting with ourselves, other people and our environment. Thus, consciousness is not an entity but an interactive process. It involves inner being[84] that is accessed by self-consciousness in which we are conscious of our interactions within ourselves, as well as with external reality.

- Subjectivity: Dualist theory promises a better understanding of how to evaluate subjective mental processes. It explains causally how inner being and our notions of consciousness, self and mind are built up through constant dualist interactions. This understanding gives us more confidence within ourselves so that we can cope better with whatever the vagaries of fortune throw at us.

- *Self-reference:* A key feature of our thinking is that we constantly self-refer. We refer back to the things we have been thinking about. Our thinking thus turns into itself by recursive, feedback processes of which only dualism can make sense.

- *Choices:* We are constantly faced with making choices and having to decide whether or not to do things. Either we can respond intuitively and make our choices spontaneously without deep thought or we can think things out and make reasonable choices based on evidence and experience. Examining these alternatives is the role of dynamic logic and it demands a better understanding of the role of intuition.

- *Nature/Nurture:* This concerns how genetic inheritance relates to the plasticity of our mentality and how it contributes to the making of human nature. We only discover what is truly natural for us by trial-and-error dualist processes – by trying something out to see if it works and if it does not, try something else.

- *Humanness:* What it is to be a human being embedded in society while interacting dualistically with it. How the dualist view helps us to maintain our individuality while conforming to society.

- *Emergence:* How dualist interaction explains the emergence and development of mind. That emergence of new thoughts and ideas can only be explained interactively. The same applies to the emergence of unpredictable novelties of all kinds. Thus, the problem of supervenience is best understood as being the product of dualist interactions.

---

[84] The topic of 'inner being' is discussed more fully in my book, *Sautonic Wisdom: What We Are Here To Do*, (Almostic Publications, 2015) in Part Two, Exercise One: Exploiting our Vitality.

- *Character Building :* We build up our character by strengthening ourselves within. This requires both self-discipline and constant dualist interaction with other people and our environment.
- *Leadership:* The most effective leaders are Invariably dualist in their thinking. They employ both reason and intuition in their relationships with others and according to what circumstances demand. They therefore may appear irrational and unpredictable in their behaviour.

The Benefits of Understanding the Nature of Reality

- *Reality:* How our intuitions put us in immediate touch with reality as a whole and how our dualist interactions keep us in touch with reality from moment to moment.
- *Contexts:* Abstractions such as society, life and the universe given a contextual treatment that makes them part of our thinking about things instead of having an existence of their own.
- *Relativism:* Putting things into higher contexts helps to counter relativism that treats all contexts equally. This contextualisation values contexts in relation to each other.
- *Fact/Value:* Facts cannot be without value in so far as they have meaning for someone. If a fact means something then it is valuable because of that meaning. Thus, a fact cannot be entirely objective or valueless unless it is deprived of all meaning.
- *Paradoxes:* The nature of logical paradoxes can be better understood in terms of dualist interactions and this is a function of dynamic logic which is dealt with in part eight below.
- *Empiricism/Rationalism:* This age-old dichotomy is tackled with the help of dualist interaction which embraces both in relation to each other.
- *Induction:* Some light is poured on the problem of induction by clarifying induction in relation to intuition. There is a dualist interaction between these that forms the basis of the scientific method.
- *Causation:* Dualist interactions in general are causal in their nature but our scientific knowledge is often deficient in accounting for these interactions in causal terms. Dualist theory can pinpoint areas of our knowledge that lack causal explanations by the requisite scientific hypotheses, theories, laws, mathematical formulae and so on. Whether they ever will be satisfactorily explained by these means remains debatable.

The Benefits of Understanding our Role in the Universe

- *Unification:* The hope of unifying humanity in terms of our common aims becomes possible as we are all in the same dualist boat. When that is properly recognised, the prospect of our pursuing a unified future with common ends becomes more realistic.

- *Medial Species:* We are infinitely insignificant in relation to the unimaginably huge universe. But we are infinitely massive in relation to the unimaginably tiny areas of quantum existence. We are the medial species that has freedom of thought and action not possessed by these large and small levels of existence. We can save ourselves in the future by achieving increasing understanding of our place in the universe in relation to these levels of existence.

- *Confidence:* Dualism reverses the loss of confidence of man's mission on Earth by showing to what extent we are in control with ourselves and what we do collectively in the world. Above we can plan to make a better future for ourselves and the planet.

- *Religion:* Dualist theory makes religious explanations even more superfluous than they are at the moment by showing how humanity is a intimate product of the universe and has a positive role to play in the universe.

- *Future:* The dualist view of the future is designed to ensure that humanity looks forward to the future and uses the past in the service of posterity which is a prospective as opposed to a retrospective view; the latter being characteristic of the religious outlook that puts God before the future interests of humanity.

Book Two

Expository

Part Five
The Nature of Dualist Interaction

1. The importance of dualist interaction

Dualist interaction is a fundamental aspect of the universe, and an understanding of its role gives us an insight into how we became the complex, unified entities that we are. Everything that has happened to entities, and will happen to them, can be explained and understood in terms of dualist interactions. This is over and above all the physical explanations that can be given using the theories of physics, chemistry and biology. It gives us an additional view of the processes involved in our development and the development of the universe.

A dualist interaction is a focused and directed activity involving one thing or event and another thing or event. A one-to-one interaction between the two things or events occurs and a dualist interaction is the result. An entity is a amalgam of dualist interactions each of which interact with each other on a one-to-one basis. Such one-to-one interactions are universal. Everything that happens in the universe is reducible to at least one interaction between one thing or event and another thing or event. For example, quantum physics reduces everything to interactions between atomic and sub-atomic particles on a one-to-one basis. The interactions in a complex entity are dualistic in that every interaction takes place between one part and another part. When many parts interact together, the various processes can be analysed and singled out as occurring between one part and another, and therefore as being dualistic. Complex processes are thus reducible to a succession or a composition of one-to-one dualist interactions when analysed in that way. For example, the various organs in our bodies are interacting with each other individually – the heart responds to our muscles' requirement for more or less blood supply – the kidney responds the amount of liquid in the bloodstream by expelling more or less of it, and so on.

It is a fundamental axiom of dualist theory that all processes and all entities involve interrelated dualist interactions. In part six on *The Emergence of Complexity by Dualist Interaction*, it is shown how dualist interaction can be traced back to the beginning of the universe where and when such interactions were set in train. Every subsequent dualist interaction stems from that beginning, and a continuous and uninterrupted train of dualist interactions has followed from that beginning. As a result of the successive disintegrations and coagulations of entities, increasing internal complexity is built up until complex life forms become possibility. This means that there is no clear dividing point between energy and matter or between matter and life. The phase transitions are smooth and undifferentiated in reality even though in our thinking we tend to create conceptual boundaries to make sense of life and the universe. Thus all biological interactions find their origin in the beginning of the universe and are involved with the processes of the universe as a whole. Furthermore, the dualist interactions that created us began with the beginning of the universe so that we are the product of these. The beginning of dualist interaction within us cannot be found since the true origin lies at the beginning of the universe. This suggests that life is a direct product of the universe as a whole and that it is not something that can be constructed by finite being such as ourselves.

Dualist interaction is not only the source of all change and transition in the universe, it is also the source of all unity, harmony, regularity, stability in the universe. All unity and stability is shown to result from dual interactions forming stable relationships so that unified entities and processes remain so over a limited period of time. Thus, a unified entity of any kind is a stable amalgam of dualist interactions which remain in relative harmony while the entity persists as a unity. Understanding the nature of dual interaction is therefore essential to understanding how static processes can be dynamic when their constitution is examined close enough. The most stable material object is a composite of dynamic atomic and sub-atomic interactions. The comparative changelessness of things depends on the continuation of harmonic interactions. Both dynamic and static relationships are included in this account. In this way, dualist theory provides an alternative way of thinking about our place in the universe. It complements logic, mathematics and science and provides new insights into these. This is because its approach is through the interactive nature of consciousness and its apprehension of abstractions through intuition and induction.

The dualist interaction supplies a semantic component to information theory that it otherwise lacks. A message or piece of information derives its meaning, firstly, from an interaction between the conveyor of the message and its recipient. The form of the message is empty until the intention of the conveyor and the interpretation of the recipient come into play. The conveyor intends it to have a certain meaning which the recipient may or may not interpret successfully. Secondly, the message must have a social meaning in the first place. It is the verbal means by which we relate to other people as well as keep in touch with external reality and interact with it. Thus, the meaning of the message lies in the interactions between the conveyor and the recipient of the message and not in the means of conveyance i.e. the symbols and sequences of numbers which are a meaningless jumble of letters and sounds outside these interactions. People make the message and not the means of its conveyance. In this way, dualist theory serves to add the semantic component to information theory that it otherwise lacks.

Our mentality reflects the universal and fundamental nature of duality in so far as it functions by dualist interactions. We relate to the universe in a fundamental way in that our dualist interactions ultimately involve the universe as a whole. Thus, part six on *The Evolution of Dualist Interaction* deals with development of dualist interactions in the universe. Dualist theory looks all the interconnections that involve dualist interactions and attempts to systematise them. Thus, by exploring dualist interactions we can understand better how we are intimately entwined in the workings of the universe whether we like it or not.

The next section on *The Logic of Dualist Interaction* deals with the human aspects of dualist interaction, namely, what makes us unique and irreplaceable human beings as opposed to merely mechanical, material entities.

The following are some of the ways in which dualist interaction is fundamental to life and the universe.

- At the most fundamental level of existence, the interactions between elementary particles are basically dualist. When one particle interacts with another, it does so on a one-to-one basis and wave/particles are produced in evidence of that interaction. Such one-to-one interactions ensure that ever more complex entities are created in the universe.

- The evolution of living beings involves dualist interaction in that species are perpetually interacting on a one-to-one basis with their environment to which they adapt or fail to adapt as the case may be.

- Dualism is reflected in relationships such as the following: positive/negative, left-handedness/right-handedness, life/matter, mental/physical, objective/ subjective, male/female, yin/yang, sacred/profane, and heavenly/sacred.

- There are dualist contrasts between hot and cold, day and night, summer and winter and so on. These enter into our dualist thinking so that the one cannot be contemplated without implying also the existence of its opposite, whether that opposite is stated explicitly or not.

- Above all, there is the overriding interaction between microcosm and macrocosm, between the very small and the very large aspects of the universe, which is the key to our understanding the workings of the universe. Exploring the very small aspects is obviously the subject of research at CERN and other nuclear research facilities. The very large aspects of the universe are the subject of astronomical research throughout the world. But the relationship between these is the subject of dualist research.

- Life is full of dualist interactions and their effects on us. We and other living beings result from these dualist interactions. Dualist interaction involves interplay between one entity and another so that changes of some sort result. It will be shown that not only the processes of the universe can be described in terms of such interactions. The way we think and feel about things also involves dualist interactions.

- There are numerous dualisms involved in accountancy and economics, for example: debit and credit, profit and loss, input and output, demand and supply, monopoly and competition, rich and poor.

- The bit of information can be represented in various binary forms: as logical values (true/false, yes/no), algebraic signs (+/−), activation states (on/off), or any other two-valued attribute.[85] Life cannot be absolutely

---

[85] Cf. Claude E. Shannon and Warren Weaver, *The Mathematical Theory of Communication*, (1949 - Urbana: The University of Illinois Press, 1964).

distinguished from non-life. The complexity of matter phases gradually into the complexity of life-forms. Material objects also have their complexity. A stone stays together because of the interactivity of atomic and molecular forces. The most congealed and stable object is in fact full of dualist interactivity that serves to keep it congealed and stable. Physics tells us that there is unseen motion everywhere.

- Scientific facts are established by chains of dualist interactions. For example, The fact that water boils at 100 Celsius at sea level is established by a chain of dualist interactions involving boiling water and the measuring of its boiling point. It is confirmed by a chain of dualist interactions aimed at confirming or refuting that fact.

2. What dualist interaction involves

Dualist interactions can be multiple while being individually one-to-one dualist interactions. What this means is as follows. Multiple interactions are always composed of dualist interactions that may be isolated one by one. If three or more objects are involved, dualist interactions occur between each of them. Object A interacts with object B and both of them interact individually with object C. Each interaction is dualist in itself. Thus, triple and quadruple interactions are examples of multiple dualist interactions. A may interact with B, C, D at the same time. But this group of interactions nevertheless consists of three distinct dualist interactions, namely: $A \leftrightarrow B$, $A \leftrightarrow C$, and $A \leftrightarrow D$. Though they take place at the same moment in time, they can be individuated and analysed separately. Similarly, the most complex combination of interactions may be reduced to individual dualist interactions. It is impossible to consider any interactive situation without treating it either as a single dualist interaction or as a group of dualist interactions. Thus, every movement involving two or more entities of any kind must be analysable in terms of dualist interactions.

Dualist interaction introduces change by an exchange between the two interacting subjects in which something or other is added to or subtracted from the subjects of the interaction. One-to-one interactions are thus adding or subtracting something and this involves not just quantifiable change but also qualitative change. Billiards balls colliding produce a quantitive change but not a qualitative one. The balls remain much the same after the collision and their internal structure is unaltered. This is non-dualist interaction. The Large Hadron Collider at CERN produces collisions in which protons are smashed apart to find out their constituents. In so far as there are no interactions between the particles, this is only non-dualist interaction, akin to cracking a nut open. Dualist interactions, on the other hand, can be a prosaic part of everyday life. Adding milk to tea brings about interactions between the ingredients that change the look and taste of the resultant substance. The connection and interplay between two objects changes them, adds to them or diminishes them. As a result, something different emerges. Consequently the objects change internally and substantially. The whole process of making the change, addition or subtraction constitutes the dualist interaction.

Thus, interactive changes are arithmetical, but they are also qualitative. When two entities enter into a dualist relationship with each other, the resultant changes are usually qualitative and not just quantitative. Thus, in chemistry when two substances come together and a new substance emerges, the change is qualitative. The substances sodium and chlorine form sodium chloride (salt) when they are mixed up together. When the substances fail to interact there is only quantitative change in that the mixture becomes heavier by the presence of the two substances but it is not changed into something different from its constituents. Thus, two substances may be attracted together to make a bigger entity such a crystal and the difference may only be quantitative if no interactions occur between the constituents of the crystal. Substances may aggregated without making any qualitative difference as, for example, when sand is plied up without changing the particles of sand. But if cement aggregate and water are added and mixed into the sand, dualist interactions take place that result in a new substance, namely, concrete. An object may be an entity that exists in external reality or an object of thought that relates only indirectly to reality. They may be simple and straightforward in their interactions with other objects but be more or less complex in their internal structure.

In summary, therefore, non-dualist interaction may produce changes that may add, subtract, reduce or diminish but nothing substantial or qualitative results. The simplest non-dualist interaction occurs when two material objects collide and their respective trajectories change, or a piece of one might be dislodged. Nothing substantial is exchanged by such an interaction as they remain internally as they were before. Dualist interactions are more complex in that something is exchanged between two objects for something different and they change significantly or are added to within them. Examples in the physical world are elementary particles that exchanges particles when they interact. Bacteria also interact with each other when they acquire bits of DNA that they incorporate into their structure. But the dualistic interactions with which we are most concerned in dualist theory are those between people in a social context. Such are the basic workings of dualist interaction. How dualist interaction governs how we think about things is outlined in part eight on *The Logic of Dualist Interaction*. In part six on *The Emergence of Complexity by Dualist Evolution*, the way dualist interaction pervades the whole universe and produces us is discussed.

3. The nature of biological and social interactions

Interaction in biological entities involves opposition followed by reciprocity. Something happens or is done and there is a reasoned reaction to that happening or deed. Either there is something done to the agent and it reacts accordingly, or the agent does something and there is a reaction which may require a further response by the agent. The opposition between these passive and active extremes is eliminated while they maintain their connection through constant interaction. A maintained interaction creates the unexcluded middle ground wherein originality, innovation and supervenience all take place. These interacting events occur instantaneously to make our thoughts and actions seem fluid and uninterrupted.

Social interactions involve reciprocity between participants in which minds are changed. In understanding what another person says, changes take place in the listener's brain that reflect the new understanding that has taken place. Moreover, an interaction is dualist when one side is being acted on or is reacting to another side. The sides need not be singular or composed of one thing on either side. It is enough that the sides are opposed to each other and that they interact with the aim of establishing a meaningful and reciprocal relationship between the two sides. For example, in a committee meeting, the chairman may have a number of responses from different committee members, but the interaction between the chairman and each of the members is always on a one-to-one basis and therefore is dualist. Basically, we can only have conversations with other people one at a time. We address one person and then another. Moreover, a speaker before an audience is interacting dualistically with that audience as a whole. The same principles apply to physical and biological interactions in general.

When we interact in conversation, our replies are often not logically deducible from what is being said to us. For example, The question, "Are you coming with me?" might be answered by saying 'no', 'yes', 'maybe'. 'later' or whatever.   In other words, the exchange involves a response which cannot be predicted by considering the first statement alone. There is no logical equivalence between the one and the other because complex processes are involved, especially with regard to biological entities. Action is followed by reaction, not on a logical basis but on a purposeful basis. Physical entities interact in ways that may be understood in scientific theory but are not accountable logically (e.g. wave/particle interactions).   Interactions within and between living beings may have a purposeful or meaningful basis which is not logically deducible or causally determined (e.g. interacting with the environment to ingest food and expel waste products.)

Thus, the richness of dualist interactions in biological and social contexts shows the importance of the notion of dualist interaction. Dualism has been wrongly disparaged by modern philosophers because they have identified it solely with Descartes' simplistic mind-body dualism. But this dualism is inadequate it consists in separating the things of the mind from the things of the body, as if the mind contains discrete objects analogous to those in the external world. Dualist interaction unites them in a continuous process instead of separating them as if they were lumps of matter.   Cartesian dualism led to Locke's empiricism based on the view that ideas are formed in response to sensory experience of the external world. But ideas then become intermediaries between us and the external world. Berkeley and Hume rightly pointed out the lack of a causal connection between ideas and their objects. Thomas Reid countered the resultant scepticism by showing that the mind worked by means of processes or faculties and not by discrete ideas. This laid down the foundations of the science of psychology as developed during the 19th century. Psychology implies that we interact in a dualist fashion with the external world. However, philosophers continued to reject such 'psychologism' because it ran counter to their use of linear logic and discrete categories as a means of understanding how we acquire our knowledge and apply our understanding. In other words, Kant continued to reign supreme whose view consists in imposing a grid of intuitions and categories on the world rather than interact with it in an open-ended fashion.

4. The role of dualist interaction in mathematics

Mathematics is a method of representing dualist interactions in a stable manner so that we can understand and predict the workings of the universe. A mathematical equation such as $x = y$ is dualistic in that the left hand side relates to the right hand side such that the two things could not be more equal. A dualist interaction between the two sides is performed when mathematical rules are applied equally to both sides in solving equations. Each side of the equation is changed and they acquire a different qualitative meaning. The mathematical formula thus consolidates our thinking and ensures that we think about things in a way that accords with the way things are in reality. Such formulae enable us to relate in a precise way the workings of our brain to the workings of the universe.

Mathematical formulae achieve their stability and formality by omitting (1) the qualitative component in a dualist interaction, (2) the context within which the dualist interaction occurs, and (3) the time and place to which the formulae may or may not refer. The qualitative component consists of the differences and changes that a dualist interaction introduces when it takes place. They may be re-introduced in the following manner: $C\{(x = y) + d\} =$ a fact or event, where C is the context, $x = y$ is the mathematical formula, and d is the difference or change brought about by the dualist interaction. Another suggestion is to replace the equal sign as follows. xAn — the symbol of A for application or activation might be introduced in the formula in place of the 'equal' sign to show that the number is being applied or activated in the real world. The formula is no longer just an abstract formula being used according mathematical rules. The A implies connections in the real world such as directly applying to, for example, apples or cars. The formula dualistically interacts with these objects.

The meaningful existence of numbers depends on their interactive use in practice. A number such as three does not exist on its own. It can only exist as part of a dualist interaction represented by the formula $x = n$, where n is the number and x is the relationship it bears in the world, usually, a group, bunch, bundle, class of things. Thus, $x = 3$ is three particular things existing in the world in some capacity; it is not an isolated idea like three itself. The idea of the number three is given Platonic existence when it is taken out of any context. Thus, the square root of minus one becomes a real number when it is used in a practical context in which it has definite function and enables us to do things in the world.

Both mathematics and logic have their limitations in that they are based on discrete distinctions which are quantitative and not necessarily qualitative. The emergence of unpredictable qualities and complex innovations cannot be readily accounted for in these subjects. Its limitations were first clearly shown in the 20th century with the various self-reflective paradoxes to which it gives rise. Russell's paradox, the Cretan liar paradox and other paradoxes arise because linear logic cannot refer back on itself with contradiction, inconsistency or discontinuity. Gödel's incompleteness theorem shows that such limitations lie at the heart of mathematics. The theory of interactive self-reference helps us to get beyond such paradoxes. There is more on these subjects in the part eight on *The Logic of Dualist Interaction*.

Dualist interaction has a timeous beginning and ending; it begins and ends in time. At the outset, there is the unity which is the 'now' of present time. Everything is one thing as it is experienced at one moment of time. The mystical experience of the absolute unity of things is manifested in a single moment of experiencing everything all at once and in the submergence of self in that experience. But everything is absolutely the same only in timeless conditions or when one denies the passage of time by seeking Nirvana or going into a trance or catatonic state. Thus, dualist interaction only comes into play with the passage of time. When we are aware of the passage of time we experience change or the possibility of change. At the next moment of time, things change and we interact in experiencing something new and different in so far as we experience it as new and different.   Otherwise everything would be changeless and be exactly the same from one moment to the next.

5. How dualist interaction creates a stable reality

The notion of dualist interaction helps us to explain how we can experience reality as if it were entirely independent of us while our actual experience of it is entirely in our minds. We know that things and events exist 'out there' because our dualist interactions are constantly successful in keeping us in touch with these external realities. In so far as mistakes do not occur, our confidence in the independence of reality is constantly reinforced. When we do make mistakes about what does or does exist, we usually know how to correct them and our confidence is not shattered. Thus, our apprehension of external reality is at least accurate and reliable enough for everyday purposes, even though psychology and the other sciences inform us that our senses are severely limited in what they can tell us about what external reality is really like. For our mental capacities are usually sufficient to keep us in touch with realities because of the dualist interactions involved.

We intuitively know of the independent existence of things and events because we habitually interact with our surroundings through perception and conception. Our acts of perception and conception involve dualist interactions with our surroundings. Things are perceived and conceived to be what they are largely through our past experience of them. Our present experiences are usually dove-tailed with our past experience so that reality is experienced in a relatively changeless manner. What perception and conception consist in is discussed in more detail in part six on *The Evolution of Dualist Interaction*. Here we are only concerned with the effects of these mental capacities in keeping us in close touch with what really exists. The point is that these constant interactions ensure that what is in the mind is conformable with what is outside the mind. Thus, the interaction involves both the idealist and realist positions in succession. There is no need to view things from either a realist or an idealist position since both are involved in this account of what reality is both in the mind and out of it.

The crux of the matter is that our mental capacities provide us with matrices that represent realities. These matrices are constantly confirmed by our dualist interactions with external realities. Through perception and conception, external reality is composed of an array of stable entities that are completely unconnected with us. We see things when we open our eyes, hear sounds impinging on our ears, feel the smoothness or roughness of fabrics, or feel the heat or coldness of our surroundings. We immediately conceive of the things that we see, hear or feel, and we can name them because of the gift of language. Each entity is perceived or conceived intuitively all at once and as a whole. But the steadiness with which entities are perceived and conceived results from our interacting with our environment to arrive at reliable representations of external reality and its contents. These representations become reality within our minds. They do so by being harmonious matrices at work in our minds as is now outlined.

By means of dualist interaction we arrive at stable notions or concepts of entities that directly reflect reality in the context within which they are experienced. Each notion forms a matrix that exists entirely within the mind but constitutes reality within its allotted context. A dualist matrix is composed of stable interactive oppositions between positive and negative elements, namely, existence/non-existence and what it is/what it is not. There are dualist interactions between (1) the existence of x and its non-existence, and (2) what x is and what it is not, where an x may be a notion, context, account, theory or some such thought or composite of thoughts. The balancing between these four elements makes x consistent in our thinking about it when we do not examine it in itself. When we do so examine it, its stability falls apart as we put x in a different context or view it from another perspective, standpoint or point of view. A dualist matrix illustrating the existence of x is outlined in quadrifoil form as follows:

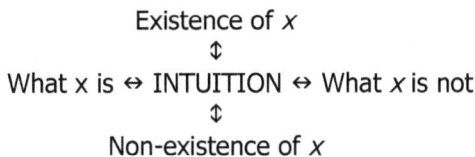

Existence of x

↕

What x is ↔ INTUITION ↔ What x is not

↕

Non-existence of x

The quadrifoil matrix of a stable entity x

Intuitively we see or hear things as being 'out there' because the act of perceiving them is constantly updated and renewed from one moment to the next. The activity ensures the accuracy and dependability of our perceptions. The continuous flow of perceptual intuitions gives us the impression that we are experiencing the whole of reality within our minds. These intuitions give us a stable view of the world whenever we open our eyes. We immediately and intuitively see everything before us as a complete whole. What we hear and feel also contribute to that holistic experience. In that way, our perceptual intuitions become the reality we immediately experience. Everything is as it is until we pay attention to things and perhaps see that something is not where it should be. In that case, its non-existence becomes apparent and balance between existence and non-existence vanishes. The presence of a clock becomes apparent when it stops ticking when the absence of the sound paradoxically reveals its presence. This example shows how the holistic experience includes elements the existence of which we are not immediately conscious. In short, we are aware that something exists because we are undertaking dualist interactions whether or not we are aware of the interactions or their nature.

These four interactive elements provide the boundaries within which the entity is experienced as a stable and long-standing entity for as long as it is an object of thought and does not become the subject of thought. In the latter case, it is focused upon and analysed into something different from what it was intuitively thought to be. It differs in specific ways because more or less things are seen in it or attributed to it as a result of being the subject of thought. When it is the subject of thought, it is put into a context within which it does or does not make sense. The existence of a character in a feature film makes sense in the context of that film but not in the context of real life when film fans act as if the character had a physical existence.

An entity's stability is maintained within its existential boundaries. For example, we may have a very stable view of what a table is but when we put that notion into a scientific context then it becomes an insubstantial thing full of empty space. All notions within a context are further interconnected in a matrix that includes the family relationships of conceptual logic, as referred to in the next part on *The Logic of Dualist Interactions*. In this way the contexts to mathematics and physics reflect their respective realities. Each context forms a reality of its own seems to have a platonic existence apart from the reality of immediate experience. The stable structure of an entity is also established by a pattern of dualist interactions. The pattern ensures that dualist interactions balance each other out thus ensuring the entities stability over a given period of time.

This interactive view of existence clarifies the existential quantifier in logic. The quantifier is obviously inadequate in so far as it simply proclaims the existence of anything without acknowledging the thinking underlying such a proclamation. The idea that a stable and harmonious interaction is occurring when existence is posited enables us to straddle both the idealist and realist views. We directly perceive things as they are because a constant and reliable interaction is occurring of which we are not entirely conscious because it is both given by our sensory organs and so well learnt and habitual. In other words, the dualist view enables us to clarify how things are both in our minds and out there at the same time.

The dualist view leads to a *circular assumption of mutual existence*, which states that everything exists for us because of dualist interaction. At some point in time, an act of dualist interaction occurs which brings existence into being for each of us as individual human beings. Thus, the only proof of our existence and of the existence of anything other than ourselves is circular. The proof of this circular assumption goes as follows. The fact of interaction means that something exists. I interact therefore there must be a reality independent of me towards which I can interact. Reality exists, therefore I must exist as an entity that can interact with it. Thus, existence begins with a single act of dualist interaction that brings existence into being. Every other interaction follows on from that single act.

Dualist theory begins with the unity which is the 'now' of present time. Everything is one thing as it is experienced at one moment of time. The mystical experience of the absolute unity of things is manifested in a single moment of experiencing everything all at once and in the submergence of self in that experience. But everything is absolutely the same only in timeless conditions or when one denies the passage of time by seeking Nirvana or going into a trance or catatonic state. Thus, dualist interaction only comes into play with the passage of time. When we are aware of the passage of time we experience change or the possibility of change. At the next moment of time, things change and we interact in experiencing something new and different in so far as we experience it as new and different. Otherwise everything would be changeless and be the same from one moment to the next.

6. The priority of dualist interaction over cause and effect

The cause and effect relationship is a type of dualist interaction in which we explain or rationalise the connection between two events – a cause and an effect. The dualist interaction is prior to and necessary for causal explanations. The dualist connectivity needs to observed or apprehended before a causal connection is noticed and formulated. Thus, relationships of cause and effect are imposed on previously existing dualist interactions. I may feel a pain in my leg and wonder what caused it. In noticing the pain, I interact with what I am feeling but the pain is itself causeless as I have to make the connection between the feeling and its cause. I then remember that I knocked my leg against a chair and I then have the cause of it.

Dualist interactions precede causal explanations, as the latter are a function of dualist interactions having taken place and having been observed or noted by someone who recognises them as such. When they are noted, the reasons for the interactions having taken place are formulated and these reasons are causal. In other words, making a causal link means having noticed a dualist interaction that requires a causal explanation. When I see a vehicle crash into another vehicle, I have observed an event involving a dualist interaction between the vehicles. I then surmise that the rear vehicle must have failed to brake quickly enough to avoid a collision – I have formulated a causal explanation for the event. I could not have done the latter without having done the former. Such causal explanations can be very rashly made. For example, ruined crops or dying cattle might be blamed on witches who have allegedly caused such events through their magical powers. The events were usually connected with witches simply because no other explanation is sought. The development of science has obviously dispensed with such witchery and consequently most unexplained phenomena can now be explained by seeking scientific explanations.

Causal explanations also involve one-to-one interactions in formulating them. We need to interact with things on a one-to-one basis to establish causes or reasons for things happening. For example, the re-occurrence of the pain in my leg reminds me that I knocked my leg yesterday. The memory of it follows an interaction with the experience of pain. Every event has a cause only because we do something interactively to understand or make sense of an event on a causal basis. We notice a connection between events or things and discover or invent a reason or cause for the happening. Every event has a cause only because we do something interactively to understand or make sense of an event on a causal basis. We notice a connection between events or things and discover or invent a reason or cause for the connection being made. If we see smoke, and then see a fire engine going in that direction, we make the connection and conclude that the smoke was caused by a fire. We have interacted with the given facts and have arrived at the most plausible conclusion.

Duality applies even more to the universe as causality. Our causal explanations are our human attempts to explain connected events. The latter connections are more fundamental and prior to the causal explanations. Dualist interactions involve correlations between two objects, events or other aspects of the universe that exist whether or not there are or are not intelligent beings around to experience them. They are therefore prior to causes in accounting for the natural functioning of the universe. Dualist interactions can be qualitative and not be at all quantifiable. For instance, our feelings of anger may not only be unquantifiable but also causally unjustified, as when the anger erupts spontaneously. Nevertheless, there are interactions occurring that are good or bad, justifiable or unjustifiable and so on. The anger is judged to be bad and unjustified through lack of explanation. In contrast, causal explanations of a scientific kind account for quantitative relationships in which one event leads to another in a deterministic fashion which can be calculated numerically. An account of the dualist interactions involves provides us with a qualitative understanding of how the interrelation between events leads to different events. The causal account allows us to calculate the relationship between events while the interactive account enables us to assess them in terms of how good or bad, valuable or useless, meaningful or meaningless, important or unimportant they are.

The fact that dualist interactions underlie cause and effect relationships is confirmed by the feedback involved in the latter relationships. The feedback means that a causal account forms a closed system. Thus, striking a match causes a flame to consume the chemicals available on it and the flame causes these chemicals to be consumed. That consumption eventually causes the match to be incapable of causing any further flames. There are obviously dualist interactions taking place in each instance. But there is more going than can be accounted for by the closed system of feedback relationships that constitutes a causal account. Who is striking the match and for what reason has no place in the causal account. How the match was made involves an entirely different causal account. The dualist account, the particular dualist interactions being pinpointed depend on the account that one is making of the events taking place. A different account will refer to different dualist interactions. But they can all be brought together and interwoven as is being done here for the purposes of showing the versatility of the dualist account. Such an account can be as concise or long-winded, superficial or exhaustive as suits our purposes.

It therefore follows that causal explanations are interconnected and form closed systems that may not be sufficient to explain all the factors involved. Thinking in terms of dualist interactions helps us to develop the account of any complex series of connected events. Taking another example of a vehicle accidently crashing into another vehicle, the crash may be caused, perhaps, by an icy road surface or by carelessness on the part of a driver. Dualist interaction draws our attention to the interactive processes involved in this incident. The expected outcome was that the two vehicles should interact by passing harmlessly by each other. However, one vehicle interacted with the road surface in an unintended manner, or because one driver's attention was distracted for some reason. The driver's inability to cope with a skid is another factor that may be involved. The preventative nature of the incident is therefore highlighted by means of dualist analysis. The accident was not simply a matter of cause and effect because emotional and other factors may be involved in a complex way that may be better understood by a dualist analysis. Therefore, while all cause/effect relationships involve dualist interactions of some sort, they can be more fully explained by a dualist account that includes all the factors and not just that of direct or necessary cause/effect.

The causal account can never be the whole picture. The fact that the dualist account goes beyond the merely causal one is also shown by another example. When we take the pills and potions of physicians, we rely on their causative effects to make us better or at least feel better. We interact dualistically with such curative medicine by taking them regularly, finding them pleasant or unpleasant or, more generally, in our appreciation of doctors' efforts. These interactions are initiated by ourselves and are a matter of choice rather than rigid determinism. We may disobey the doctor's orders if we so choose. Thus, there is more involved than the causes and effects of our actions since choices need not have happened. Also, we may simply forget to take the medicine and it may be difficult if not impossible to pinpoint of the cause of our forgetting to do this. A mere random and unpredictable quirk in the brain may be responsible for our forgetfulness. Thus, the dualist viewpoint enables us to bring in factors that are over and above any causal account and not strictly implied by such an account. In this way, this account of dualist interactions goes beyond the causal one and is evaluative and subjective in comparison.

It also follows that not all dualist interactions can be causally explained. Dualist interactions are causal in that explanations may be given as why they occur at all or why events have turned out in the manner that they do. Whether such explanations are available or not depends on the state of science. The limited nature of our scientific knowledge is such that many causal explanations are wanting in respect of many interactions. Although dualist interactions can be assigned causes, our scientific knowledge is often deficient in accounting for them in causal terms. This is particularly the case as regards interactions said to be occurring in the mind or brain. Subjectivity and consciousness are notoriously difficult to pin down anywhere to demonstrate their causal nature and to explain what they are in physical terms. As a result, mental illness is often difficult to treat effectively. The positing of dualist interactions can therefore pinpoint areas of our knowledge that lack causal explanations by the requisite scientific hypotheses, theories, laws, mathematical formulae and so on. Whether they ever will be satisfactorily explained by these means, may be debatable.

Moreover, dualist interactions may be both causal and intentional. Dualist interactions in general are potentially causal in nature in so far as causal explanations are found for them. But biological interactions are both causal and intentional. Living beings are sufficiently complex and self-referential to be become agents that act intentionally and purposefully. Everything about them can be explained in causal terms but their intentional acts are addition to that causal description. Complexification brings an added dimension to this account of dualist interactions and its role is outlined in the section four above on *The Evolution of Dualist Interaction*. For example, there is no clear division between agent causation and event causation in the dualist account as they form a spectrum of complexity from one to the other.

Causal relationships are therefore only retrospectively assigned. Nothing occurs in the universe without an interaction of some kind taking place. Everything depends on everything else *ad infinitum*. This concatenation of interactions is only retrospectively understood in causal terms. The cause/effect relationship is only one form of dualist interaction. This was not recognised by David Hume, the arch causationist who thought that concrete causes were behind everything, as he said: "And indeed there is nothing existent, either externally or internally, which is not to be consider'd either as a cause or an effect"[86] Modern physics obviously casts doubt on this certainty as many events

---

[86] David Hume, *A Treatise of Human Nature*, 1739, (ed. Nidditch, Oxford: the Clarendon Press, 1978), Book I, Part III, Section II, p. 75.

occur causelessly in the quantum world. Moreover, Hume had a linear view of causal connections based on a constant conjunction, contiguity, continuity, identity and logical necessity. As he was not a dynamic thinker, he thought only in concrete, formal terms instead of the dynamic, fluid terms that are required by dualist theory.

7. Summarising the dualist nature of causation

The dualist view of causation leads to the following conclusions regarding its nature:

➤ *Causation is the product of our intellect and not of nature.* The principle of causation, namely, that every event has a cause is only true in so far as we find reasons for the occurrence of anything whatsoever. The cause of anything comprises only those reasons by which we either choose to make the connection between events or find to be sufficient or necessary to make the connection on evidential grounds. The principle of causation has nothing to do with reality of nature and everything to do with the power of our intellect or imagination to make connections between events which are always dualist in their fundamental nature. Thus, we should not be surprised when we find that sometimes there are no such connections to be made in nature, as the realm of quantum physics appears to be telling us in respect of events happening at a distance with no apparent connection between them. The same applies to the principle of sufficient reason. There is only a sufficient reason for things being as there are because we can and do find reasons for believing things to be as they are, whether or not these reasons are borne out in reality.

➤ *Making connections creates the 'cause' and not vice versa.* The use of the word 'cause' therefore implies that we already have reasons, whether adequate or not, for making connections between events. It is not the case that a cause exists to be discovered. We must first of all have the reasons for making the connections and then we believe that the effects are caused, subsequent to having these reasons. The observation that "heat is a constant attendant of flame"[87] is arrived at by associating heat with flames so that there is a hypothetical expectation, but not necessarily a hard-and-fast expectation, that a flame will produce heat. If we notice that a flame does not produce heat, we wonder why and seek reasons why. For example, it may be because the ambient temperature is too low for us to experience the heat. If it were simply a 'constant conjunction' then we would be endlessly puzzled by heatless flames, and not know what to think or do. Having an open mind ensures that we speculate and investigate further until we resolve the matter.

➤ *Causes are theory-bound and not independent of our thinking of them.* This means that the causes that we ascribe to events do not exist independently of our

---

[87] David Hume, *An Enquiry Concerning Human Understanding*, (1777 - ed. P.H. Nidditch - Oxford: the Clarendon Press, 1975), section VII, §50, p.64.

formulating them. All that is exists are the reasons, explanations, theories, laws, and motives, and all these are indifferently called 'causes'. The word 'cause' is often uninformative since the mere fact of conceiving A to be connected to B means that the connection is thought to be causal regardless of the value or veracity of the reasons for making the linkage. Thus, a prevalence of infant deaths in the neighbourhood of an old woman living alone may lead to a false causal connection being made by those who believe in witchcraft. Similar associations are made nowadays, for instance, when the existence of electric pylons in a neighbourhood is thought to be the cause of a high incidence of cancer among children in that neighbourhood. Whether the statistical evidence is sufficient to make the causal connection may be debatable.

➤ *The simple 'cause-effect' relationship is inadequate as all the causal conditions are required.* The customary 'cause-effect' relationship is therefore fundamentally inadequate as an account of what is going on. Only one reason is being mooted to link the cause to the effect whereas potentially an infinity of reasons and theories may be thought up to justify making the link. What is required is an understanding of the whole range of conditions involved in the linking of events. And this is the purpose of having a theory, law, account, description or other generalisations. And it will always be found that dualist interactions of some sort are involved in these causal explanations.

➤ *Causal language concerning mental acts is uninformative.* More importantly, nothing is gained by talking of 'mental causes' (à la Anscombe[88] and Armstrong,[89] for instance). All that exists are the reasons, motives, and feelings, which we ascribe to mental activity. These might all be said to 'cause' something if that thing is said to follow from them. Distinguishing them as 'causes' tells us no more than what we already know when we refer to them as reasons or motives. That something or other follows from their existence is already included in the act of describing them as reasons, and motives. But what follows from having reasons and motives is not necessarily action or behaviour but the choice, judgment, reasoning etc. whether to do or not to do something. Thus, the deterministic threat to our freewill comes from the intrusion of causal language into descriptions of mental activity and not because there is no such thing as freewill.

8. What dualist interaction does for us

Dualist theory helps us to keep us in touch with other people by thinking in terms of our dualist interactions with them. We can thereby understand in general terms what it is like to be others without actually experiencing what it is to be them. It makes us think in an interactive way about our relationships with others. We make the effort to reconstruct their way of thinking to compare it

---

[88] G.E.M. Anscombe, *Intention*, (Oxford: Blackwell, 1957), p.16.
[89] D.M. Armstrong, *A Materialist Theory of the Mind*, Revised Edition, (London: Routledge, 1993), ch. 6, p. 83 etc.

with our own. This is possible by interacting with one's given experiences of other people. Novelists do this all the time in inventing their characters and putting them in situations that appear to them to be as realistic and believable as possible. We find common ground by which to compare our subjective experiences with those of other people and indeed intelligent beings in general. But that common ground is strictly limited because we cannot actually be the other person and experience exactly what they are experiencing.[90] This is just as well since the reductionist programme implies that there are no essential differences between the mental events experienced by one person and another, and that everybody's experiences are reducible to elements which are common to everybody. If this were true then we would not need to communicate with each other but simply work out by logical and mathematical deduction what other people are experiencing. Such machine-like uniformity, or 'artificial intelligence', is surely the converse of what life is all about, for example, its spontaneity, diversity, and the intense pleasure of living from minute to minute.

Interactions between our subjective experiences and objective responses enable us to build up our mental skills and abilities. Our genius, originality, and uniqueness result from our personalities being complexified in this way. Outstanding geniuses are those who are more developed and integrated in their internal organisation than most of us. They are able to accomplish much more and in greater depth because their subjective experiences are more sublime, transcendent, and all-encompassing. This offers hope to us all that we can similarly complexify our thinking and achieve feats of which we previously thought ourselves incapable. Over time and with constant practice such feats may be possible for anyone having sufficient brain capacity to be exploited in this way. Such inner complexification is discussed in more detail in part six on *The Emergence of Complexity by Dualist Interaction.*

Moreover these mental processes are entirely our own. They reflect our own subjective idiosyncrasies. We don't need external influences to account for our creative activity or our internal development. Deities, demons, angels or aliens have nothing to do with it. Such imaginary entities only give us a false idea of our own capabilities. Being mere human beings, we will always fall short of divine perfection. But on the whole we keep faith with ourselves by genuinely doing the best we can. This means being realistic about ourselves and our capabilities rather than seeking a divine perfection which is beyond us altogether. By remaining in touch with ourselves interactively through alternate synthetic and analytic thinking we avoid being unrealistic and false to ourselves.

These interactive processes help us to develop our *personal integrity* as they are integral to the complexification of our personalities. Without them we cannot integrate our experiences and make them our own. With them we can build

---

[90] Cf. Thomas Nagel, 'What is it like to be a bat?', *Mortal Questions*, (Cambridge: CUP, 1979), p.174, where Nagel points it that the more objective we try to be about the nature of subjective experiences, the further we are from what it is to experience them.

ourselves within to cope more effectively with all the challenges of life. We can then be ourselves without relying on outside influences to dictate to us what we should do with our lives or how we should behave. In building up our personality or character the complexity of subjective output grows relative to objective realisation and *vice versa*. The interactivity of the subjective and objective aspects means that they may refer to the same things depending on what we are doing with them. In that way, we find that maintaining our personal integrity is essential in such circumstances.

Understanding how we think within ourselves is an important key to understanding our place in the universe. We are all microcosms embodying the macrocosm surrounding us. We find our place by being at one with the world, but what if we are not at one with ourselves? If we are not at one with our thought processes, we are out of touch with ourselves. We need not be in complete charge of them from one second to the next, but we should feel ourselves to be in charge of events and not at the mercy of them. External events can be overwhelming instead of interesting and diverting, and this gives us no time for understanding what occurs in the universe at large. Knowing yourself is even more important today than it was in ancient times since our complex world presents us with bewildering choices. It means examining our presuppositions, motivations and inclinations so as to be an effective person in the real world. In so doing we understand the contexts within which our best choices are arrived at and our most relevant judgments made. If we think in terms of internal dualist interactions connecting seamlessly with external dualist interactions, this is an important contribution to self-knowledge.

All our notions of inner identity, such as I, ego or self, result from the interplay of the interactive processes between personal input and output in so far as they are under the control of our will. If they are not under the control of our will, then we are subject to them rather than controlling them. Thus, our very self-identity depends on constant dualist interaction. I, for example, cannot be myself unless there is a feedback process confirming that I am what I believe myself to be, and that I can do what I set out to do. Who I am to myself is constantly confirmed by my thinking about and doing things with which I can identify myself. Unless these feedback processes refer back to that inner identity, we lose control of them and thus of our very identity. If we fail to use these processes in a purposeful fashion to fulfil our reasoned goals then we are at their mercy. Our thoughts and actions are products of random chance rather than of integrated thinking. This illustrates the importance of self-control in sustaining our self-identity and the integrity of our personalities. Of course, there is no need for us to be all the time exercising self-control and monitoring ourselves. But unless we do so most of time we are arguable no longer in control of our own lives

The purposeful use of these integrating processes is reflected in the infinite variability of personality development. How we develop as persons in relation to our experiences cannot be predicted from a mere examination of genetic or

DNA content. The latter contributes to personality development without determining it in absolute terms. For our personality development can vary despite our genes. For example, identical twins can develop different personalities in spite of being genetically identical.[91] It is also possible for them to develop different sexual orientations, thus disproving the assumption that sexual orientation is necessarily determined by our genes.[92]

Moreover, increasing self-knowledge is to no avail if it does not mean clarifying goals and facing realities. Our goals constantly require contextualisation by being put into context. Every goal or aspiration aims beyond itself and thus enters a context which incorporates it. In helping other people, we enter their contexts which are incorporated into ourselves to feel and think as these people do. Helping other people often means benefiting the human race as a whole, whether we consciously aim to do so or not. In this way our aims and goals are elevated and made sense of instead of merely being our own selfish ambitions and aspirations. For at each stage we must go beyond the current context to judge and evaluate our actions from the perspective of a more incorporating context. In this way we remain true to ourselves and to the ultimate truths towards which we are all striving, one way or another.

9. The dynamic of dualist oppositions

Dualist interaction can be contrasted with the kind of dogmatic thinking which stultifies our thinking. Whereas dualist thinking is ever ongoing, dogmatic thinking is invariably static and self-sustaining. Dogmatic thinking leads to the mind being closed to different ways of thinking. Our beliefs are self-sustaining and beyond criticism. We think in a circular way that can't be broken out of without difficulty. When our minds close, we stop learning about new things. We also cease to be self-critical and interactive in our thinking. The ability to accommodate and accumulate new ways of thinking is lost. Our thinking proceeds along rigid grooves, and we lapse into one of two rigid, dogmatic lines of thought. In our thinking we overemphasise either the sameness of things or the differences between things. Either people think the same way we do or they differ irreconcilably from our viewpoint. The middle between two extremes is eliminated and everything is reduced to either the one or the many. There is either the one élite to which we belong or the common many that are worthless in comparison because they can't comprehend the truth. Either the context becomes everything or its contents become everything. Such extreme thinking sees either the wood (context) instead of the trees or the trees (content) instead of the wood. They are incapable of taking account of both views at once. In

---

[91] As in the case of the Iranian twins, Ladan and Laleh Bijani, who were conjoined at the head but who tragically died during an attempt to separate them. One was said to be more outgoing and forceful than the other.

[92] Cf. "Relative Values: Alexandra and Caroline Paul", *Sunday Times*, 24th August, 2003, Magazine, pp. 7-9, where one identical twin is said to be heterosexual and the other lesbian.

contrast, dualist interaction entails moving from one of these viewpoints to the other in an interactive way that makes for balanced and productive thinking. Therefore, the separation of the two opposing lines of thought involves taking one of two dogmatic, rigid stances, which are the analytic and synthetic divisions illustrated below.

One of the most important divisions in human thinking is that between the analytic and synthetic ways of thinking. These are disastrous dividers of human beings when they divide people from each other instead of being divided ways of thinking concentrated within the mind of each person. People become divided rigidly into analytically prone persons and synthetically prone persons. When they are divided in that way they are at polar opposites which compel them to see the other side are being the enemy to be overcome if not eliminated. These ways of thinking may be listed as follows:

Analytical Thinking		*Synthetic Thinking*
Empiricist		Rationalist
Realist		Idealist
Pluralist		Monist
Reductionist		Holist
Relativist		Absolutist
Positivist		Obscurantist
Aristotelian		Platonist
'Tough-minded'	(W. James) [93]	'Tender-minded'
'Men of Facts'	(A.N. Whitehead)[94]	'Men of Ideas'
Fox'	(Sir Isaiah Berlin)[95]	'Hedgehog'
'Curiosity'	(B. Williams)[96]	'Salvation'
'Extraverted'	(C.G. Jung)[97]	'Introverted'

A State of Mind:
- emphasising DIFFERENCES as opposed to SIMILARITIES;
- abstracting PARTS from WHOLES;
- asserting MORE & MORE about LESS & LESS;

A State of Mind:
- emphasising SIMILARITIES as opposed to DIFFERENCES;
- generalising WHOLES from PARTS;
- asserting LESS & LESS about MORE & MORE;

---

[93] William James, *Pragmatism*, (1907 - New York: Washington Square Press, 1963), Lecture One p. 9.

[94] A.N. Whitehead, *Science and the Modern World*, (1925 - New York: Mentor, 1958), ch. I p.3, ch. XIII p. 199, for instance.

[95] Sir Isaiah Berlin, 'The Hedgehog and the Fox' in *Russian Thinkers*, (1953 - London: Penguin, 1979), p.22.

[96] Bernard Williams, his conversation with Bryan Magee, published by Magee in *Men of Ideas*, (Oxford: OUP 1982), p. 116.

[97] C.G. Jung, in 'Psychological Types' (1921), *The Collected Works of Carl G. Jung*, (trans. R.F.C. Hull, Bollingen Series XX, Princeton University Press), Vol. 6, Part I.

☯ elaborating the CONTENTS of things to a multiplicity of factors without reference to their contextual simplicities

☯ subsuming everything to one CONTEXT without reference to their complex interactions with other contexts

The Dogmatic Separation of Dualistic Interaction

10. How to get out of the rut

We can easily get into the mental rut of thinking along one of these lines of thought at the expense of the other. We either become overconfident of our opinions or have no confidence at all in them. Either we dismiss all opposition to our views out of hand or we accept mindlessly and uncritically the authority of tradition, gurus, demagogues, preachers or whatever. Instead of taking account of opposing views in an interactive way, we pit our views against the opposing ones and attempt to annihilate them. The result is party politics, warring factions, irreconcilable religions, and so on. In other words, our tribal and sectarian inclinations find their origin in such opposing grooves of thought. As a result, our prejudices are strengthened and they stultify our inner development. We no longer have any incentive to rethink our presuppositions and we remain rooted in our ruts.

However, it must be possible to learn how to avoid extremist thinking. It is after all only an attitude of mind. Our hope for our future must lie in our learning not to lapse into the mental grooves that divide us from opposing points of view and prevent us from appreciating their value. For instance, from an educational point of view, students can perform mental exercises as part of civics courses in which they adopt opposing frames of thought and practice broadening their minds in that way. This is not learning to sit on fences but learning to think out the complexities involved in adopting any balanced and informed viewpoint.

To ensure that we develop as balanced personalities and avoid the lopsidedness of dogmatic thinking, we have to think critically and contextually. We must constantly step outside our trains of thought to see how limited and subjective they are. Otherwise, we assume that we are entirely immersed in reality and that our thoughts are themselves absolutely and undeniably real. However, it is clear that nothing that we think to be the case, can be all there is to reality. Reality is never just as it appears to be and we must battle constantly to keep on top of it. There is always much more going on both inside and outside us than what occurs to us at any given moment.

It has been argued already that monist thinking leads to a polarisation of the extremes between incompatible positions such as empiricism versus rationalism and realism versus idealism. Too much analysis at the expense of synthesis distorts thought processes so that everything is interpreted from the one empirical, realist point of view. We want to be both analytical and synthetic in our thinking. We must constantly struggle to think dualistically. This means that they interact in a cyclical manner which is described in more detail below.

Monist View   *Dualist View*   *Monist View*

Analysis

⇕

Pure Reduction ← INTUITIVE INTERACTION → Pure Generalisation

⇕

Synthesis

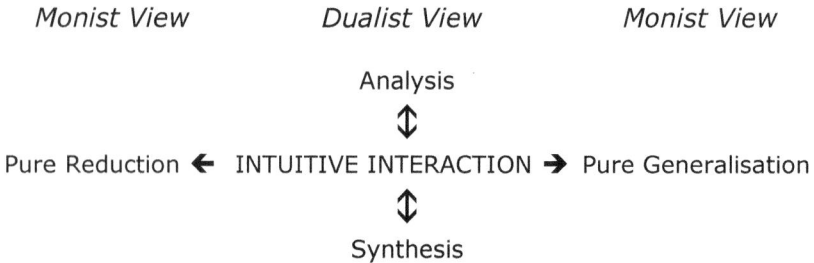

The monist view is either that of pure reduction or pure generalisation, which themselves follow from analytical and synthetic thinking respectively. An intuitive interaction takes place by applying analysis and synthesis alternately or in succession to each other. The analytical and synthetic views are not totally distinct from each other when they are interacting and not isolated and in opposition to each other. They are identified with each other when we understand the one in terms of the other. They are therefore not wholly contradictory positions. The laws of identity and contradiction are no longer applicable in such circumstances. The laws of thought are suspended because interaction may mean contradicting oneself to reach the truth of the matter. A dynamic logic comes into play and identity is then a matter of dualist interaction as is now described.

The analytical and synthetic views range in a spectrum from pure analytical reduction to pure synthetic generalisation. The continuous interaction between these analytical and synthetic positions occupies the indefinite middle position. It is an interacting middle ground between extremes. The extreme views are monist and polarising; they veer away from each other and from the middle ground. The moderate views are dualist and they may be pictured (1) by their interacting with each other in a straightforward manner, and (2) by being thought of as spiralling uniformly in relation to each other through time. If they spiral away from each other then they tend towards uncertainty that is resolved into monist views. If they spiral towards each other they reach one point which is monist and dogmatic. In spiralling towards each other they tend towards identity and a definite conclusion is reached. These spiralling tendencies refer to the movements of thought in one direction or the other. The more we agree, the more we move together and think together in unison and in the way that we analyse and generalise in our thinking about things.

In these circumstances, moderate analysis is identical with moderate synthesis but only *dualistically*. This means that their identity is a function of their dualist interaction. They are not identical in a formal logical sense of being essentially or substantially the same thing. They are only identical in being brought into interactive relationship with each other. In so far as they interact with each other they form an organic process analogous to the way that the organs of our bodies interact with each other. These organs differ in themselves but are identical in their forming intimate interactive parts of the body. Without their continued interactive relationships, both the body and its organs cannot continue to exist. This in outline is the nature of the identity of dualist positions.

11. The metaphysics of dualism

Dualist theory is metaphysical in that it deals with our ability to manipulate our subjective consciousness through introspection. This manipulation is inevitably dualist and involves interacting with our own thought processes. By becoming aware of our thought processes in terms of dualist interactions we are indulging in a metaphysics that takes us into the realms of abstractions. The practical effect is to clarify our own thinking about ourselves and our goals, motivations, desires and feelings since we climb above these and learn to control and manipulate them. To ensure that we use such inner control for the best possible purposes, it is necessary to understand dualist theory as a whole including its ethical and social implications. Here we examine the relationship of metaphysical dualisms with psychological and mathematical, and ethical dualisms as a preliminary to such an overall study of dualist theory.

We cannot always be thinking but when we do then we are thinking about something. This makes us conscious beings, as is discussed in more detail in the next two parts of this book. Consciousness is itself an interactive activity which consists of awareness which is usually, but not always, awareness of something in particular. It is however possible to be conscious without being aware of anything in particular as when drowsy, distracted, or in an empty, thoughtless state of mind. But this is only for short periods of time. To be alive and yet permanently unaware of anything in particular is a vegetative and perhaps catatonic state of mind. Being aware of being alive without necessarily being aware of anything in particular is consciousness *per se,* and we doubtless share this form of consciousness with plants which have some kind of awareness of their surroundings without being aware of anything in particular. But consciousness of something implies an interaction between that which is being conscious and that which it is conscious of. Thus, an active consciousness depends on a constant interaction between the awareness component and what that component is being aware of. This is the origin of all dualist principles such as internal/external and self/non-self.

Such dualist principles emerge from the interaction between the internal and external, that is to say, between what we conceive to be within us and what we conceive to be without us. By means of this interaction we constantly re-establish from moment to moment our self-identity. In so far as consciousness has an object it results from this dualist interaction which itself emerges from the struggles of the ego in establishing its identity within its chaotic surroundings. These principles help us to establish and maintain our self-identity against the disorder and misinformation which threatens to engulf that identity. By means of these principles we maintain the context of self and operate within it. They enable us to identify with, and differentiate ourselves from, other contexts such as other people, society and so on. These dualisms are such that the one side of the principle cannot occur without creating a disharmony or infelicity of thought. The other side of the dualism must be acknowledged and embraced so that one can move on in one's thinking. Such are the dualisms implied by the internal/external dualism.

A quadrifoil matrix of dualisms is possible that shows the relationships between the more obvious and important dualisms with which we are all familiar. There are at least four distinct groupings of these dualisms, *psychological, metaphysical, mathematical,* and *ethical* which are charmingly arranged below in a Kantian quadrifoil. These dualisms all result from the application of the internal/external dichotomy common to all life-forms as referred to in part six on *The Emergence of Complexity by Dualist Interaction.*

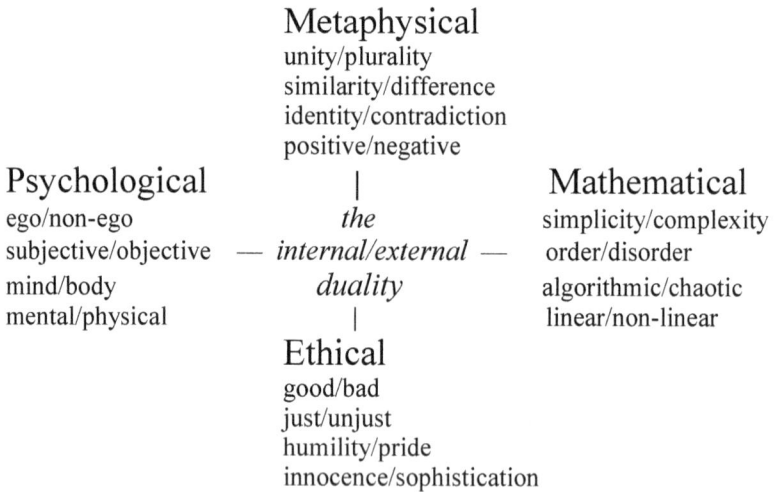

Metaphysical
unity/plurality
similarity/difference
identity/contradiction
positive/negative

Psychological		Mathematical
ego/non-ego	|	simplicity/complexity
subjective/objective	*the*	order/disorder
mind/body	— *internal/external* —	algorithmic/chaotic
mental/physical	*duality*	linear/non-linear
	|	

Ethical
good/bad
just/unjust
humility/pride
innocence/sophistication

These dualist principles are important in actualising possibilities for us. They arise because we make for ourselves choices, decisions, goals and so on. In so doing, we narrow down possibilities by opposing one possibility to another possibility until we resolve the uncertainty. Thus, some possibilities are delineated as against other possibilities. We thereby make actualities out of these possibilities by determining what can be done or not be done. They coalesce into coherent actualities on which we act or do not act as the case may be. These actualities relegate the other possibilities into a negative frame which contrasts and highlights the actualities in question. Thus, negation for instance is derivative of this fundamental actualising process. We decide what can or cannot be done and adopt a negative view of what cannot be done and a positive view of what can be done. These dualisms may be further explicated and elaborated as follows:

(1) Psychological Dualisms

ego/non-ego: This dualism is abstracted from the fundamental dichotomy between our internal and external experiences, that is to say, between what we perceive to be inside us and what is outside us. Deciding what is ours or not ours is a constant pre-occupation for us. In response to changing events, we may disown our feelings, thoughts, appetites, attitudes or opinions as not being worthy of us. We may decide to like something because it becomes us, and so on.

subjective/objective: This dualism is a judgmental one that reduces the compass of the last one by eliminating the ego in favour of what is experienced by the ego or non-ego. Thus, deciding that something is a subjective feeling having no objective basis is a judgment which paradoxically is a quest for objectivity which ultimately physicalises our thoughts and feelings. They can become real to us whether they are imaginary or not.

mind/body: The ego operates by mental activity which is assumed to exist 'in the mind'. But it is only the overall activity that may be distinguished from the body. This can be further extended to include all mental events and physical events. But dualist theory ultimately eliminates this duality by detailing the concatenation of dualist interactions that are involved in subjectivity or what is going on inside us.

mental/physical: Similarly, the mental refers to what we do inside ourselves which may distinguished from the merely physical. The distinction can only be made meaningfully by a complex of dualist interactions rather than a one-to-one relationship between allegedly mental events and allegedly physical ones.

(2) Metaphysical Dualisms

unity/plurality: The notion of unity is derived from our experience of the present moment as an all-encompassing whole. It stems from the unifying activities of the ego in differentiating itself from external reality. But everything can be synthesised to unity or analysed to plurality depending on context and inclination.

similarity/difference: The similarity of things is judged by reference to our internal experience of them while differences are found by contrasting what is external to us. In this way, our personal feelings can govern what we immediately apprehend to be similar or different.

identity/contradiction: In identifying things we bring them into unity with our preconceived notions, and we depart from that identifying process when we contradict ourselves. Thus, we often identify one thing with something that differs from it and thus inadvertently contradict ourselves.

positive/negative: Whatever is positively stated may be negated. In fact, to be really positive about anything it is best to view it negatively as well as positively. In that way, the drawbacks and deficiencies of any view or opinion are included in our prognostications.

(3) Mathematical Dualisms

simplicity/complexity: What is simple is usually defined in relation to that which is complex and *vice versa.* A simple truth such as one and one makes two can be analysed to become a complex account of the way the world is or is not, for instance, by showing how many ways that one thing added to another does not amount to two things, but one thing, half a thing or whatever.

order/disorder: Order is what we see in nature as a result of making sense of it. Disorder is either that which we cannot make sense of or that which cannot be ordered because of its chaotic structure.

algorithmic/chaotic: An algorithmic sequence takes place according to complicated linear mathematical rules and formulae whereas chaotic activity is random and non-linear.

linear/non-linear: Linear formulae are provable and straightforward whereas non-linear are used to account for chaos and random events. Dualist accounts tend to be non-linear in so far as they are qualitative and judgmental rather than calculating and quantifiable.

(4) Ethical Dualisms

good/bad: The distinction between good and bad is one of the earliest conceptual distinctions made possible by language. What is good is generally for us and what is bad is generally against us. The dualist view must inevitably blur the distinction so that we are not absolutely for or against things to the point of causing conflict or war to bring others to our point of view.

just/unjust: This distinction arose when we first accounted for our respective places in society. A just way of life generally involved conformity whereas an unjust way of life put us at loggerheads with the society in which we live. Similarly, the dualist view eschews absolute judgements about what is just or unjust when these create conflict instead of agreement and harmony.

humility/pride: This is personal distinction in which we acknowledge our ability to underestimate ourselves on the one hand and to overestimate ourselves on the other hand. The uncertainty is necessary to keep us striving towards something approaching perfection even though it cannot realistically be reached.

innocence/sophistication: We are alternately innocent of what we are ignorant of or inexperienced in, while being sophisticated in what we are skilled in doing or what we have experienced in life. However, we must not lose sight completely of the innocent view lest our sophistications lead us into deceit, dishonest, crime or inhumanity.

Part Six
The Emergence of Complexity by Dualist Interaction

1. We are products of the universe as a whole

Complexity results from a chain of dualist interactions that are internally highly interactive and, in this part, it is argued that an increasing complexity of dualist interrelationships in the universe has led inexorably to the development of mind as well as the consciousness characteristic of intelligent beings including ourselves. Such a complexification has resulted from an unending concatenation of dualist interactions which may be traced back to the interactions at the beginning of the universe. We are very much products of the overall development of the universe. In short, this is the story of how we emerged from the universe's complexifying processes to become entities that are intimately connected to the universe as a whole. Any attempt to replicate the complexity of our consciousness must in some way replicate the complex processes that produced it.

Thus, it is argued here that consciousness itself has emerged from a succession of interactive biological processes that involve complexification. This view of the mind's development disputes computational theories that tend to reduce us to machines and as a consequence diminish our achievements as creative living beings. Understanding this interactive development leads us to conclude that the artificial creation of mind, consciousness or intelligence would require a replication of the universe's creation of the same. Thus, this view suggests that so-called 'artificial intelligence' will never be complex enough to produce consciousness and self-identity unless it reproduces all the interactive processes of the universe that were necessary to produce our consciousness and self-identity. This means that the whole universe is involved in biological processes, the end product of which is consciousness. It is therefore doubtful whether consciousness could be reproduced artificially since it would require a reproduction of all the biological processes that led up to it. The much vaunted 'singularity' by which computers throughout the world will achieve a state of collective consciousness may never come about.

It is also argued here that life and consciousness have developed by a continuous process of complexification from the beginning of the universe to the present-day. Thus, the answer to the question 'How did life and consciousness develop?' is that the whole developing universe produced them. We must go back to the very beginnings to understand how these came about. There is no absolute cut-off point where they begin or where they emerge from non-life. A gradual complexification of matter resulted in their emergence. This occurred through limitless dualist interactions between matter and energy. Thus, the dualist view is that mind and consciousness result from a continuous process of dualist interactions that has complexified matter and ultimately produced life, mind and consciousness.

Life itself is the result of a build-up of internalised complexities accumulated over the 13.9 billion years of the universe's existence. Thus, the division between matter and life requires an understanding of the dualist interactions that have led to this accumulated complexity. Unless we understand better the workings of the entire universe, we will not fully understand how our self-reflective consciousness came about, let alone reproduce it as 'artificial intelligence.' Thus, dualist theory seems to be the best if not the only way to understand properly our interactive relationship to the universe as a whole.

The universe originated with the so-called Big Bang. What preceded the Big Bang was a kind of nothingness without form or substance. It exploded into existence and the nonentity became something in place of nothing. Becoming something meant creating diversity in place of a uniform unity. In simple terms what was one became many. There was one force that kept everything together as one entity or being. The rapid inflation of the universe split the unified force asunder to create the four forces left over from the universe's original unity – the weak and strong nuclear forces, electro-magnetism and gravitation. When energy burst forth in all directions, it coalesced gradually around the four unifying forces to create particular entities. The forces use dualist interaction to bring energy together into viable entities. Thus, the four forces are the residue of the original force that held the nascent universe as a unified entity, and they use dualist interaction to re-create order and harmony which are otherwise absence from the expanding universe.

2. The complex formation of entities

The origin and development of the universe can be accounted for in dualist terms that explain the evolution of complex entities. This is because dualist interaction is a fundamental feature of the universe by which entities of increasing complexity are built up over time. This increasing complexity has culminated in the complex inner physical activity of living beings which marks them out from other material objects that are less inwardly complex. The dualist interactions underlying that complexity make possible the retention of information so that it may be transmitted, exchanged and ensure the prolongation of complexity. Thus, the universal existence of dualist interaction makes growing complexity possible. For the evolution of increasing complexity in the universe is explicable in terms of dualist interactions of various kinds, as is shown in this part.

As stated above, the source of dualist interaction lies at the beginning of a universe which is fundamentally dualist at its core. The universe has always been replete with dualist contrasts that are essential to its functioning the way it does. These contrasts include beginning/end, order/disorder, attraction/repulsion, positive/negative and left/right. The universe itself may have no discernible beginning but everything in it has a beginning and an end. Its contents began in a state of order and they have incurred increasing disorder through entropy as they move inexorably to their end. Negative and positive entities come into existence which alternately attract and repel each other. Symmetry comes into being by which entities develop left and right sides which are not necessarily one hundred percent symmetrical. The very slight asymmetry creates an imbalance which makes creative unpredictability possible.

When these dualist contrasts came into being, the energy of the universe coalesced and resulted in the formation of material entities by the clumping together of elementary particles. Matter is packaged energy which is sustained by its internal dualist interactions. Entities are created by energy being compressed by interactive nuclear forces so their contents form stable interactive relationships that maintain the identity and distinction of the entity for a period of time.

Thus, the contact between the first entities immediately involved their interaction on a one-to-one basis. The interactive forces involved were sufficient to create and maintain material entities. Such matter clumps together by means of its parts interacting with each other through the four forces, namely, the weak and strong nuclear forces, the electromagnetic force and the force of gravitation. Material interaction can therefore be traced back to the origins of all material entities whatsoever. Its possibility begins with the organisation of energy and matter into entities that are identifiable in themselves and distinguishable from other entities. The physical forces are remnants of the simple symmetry and unity of the universe at its inception when the big bang disrupted that symmetry. They effectively attempt to recreate that symmetry and unity in the universe at large through the creation of entities.

Using the terms of physical theory, we can account for the unique identity and distinction of individual entities. After the Big Bang, the universe grew in size and cooled sufficiently for a process called baryogenesis to take place. At a certain temperature, quarks and gluons combined into baryons such as protons and neutrons, somehow producing the observed asymmetry between matter and antimatter. At still lower temperatures, phase transitions enabled the forces of physics and elementary particles to assume their present form. Thus, the creation of protons and neutrons by strong attractive forces resulted in stable entities which were capable of subsisting on their own and were therefore identifiable and distinguishable in themselves. Eventually, the protons and neurons were attracted together by the strong nuclear force (nucleosynthesis) to form the stable nuclei of heavy hydrogen (deuterium). The interactions between these parts of the atom were sufficient to create the properties unique to the deuterium atom. These dualist interactions not only make unified material entities possible, they ensure that entities distinguish themselves from each other. They assume an identity of their own because of the slight variation in the dualist interactions that bring together and maintain these entities.

Thus, each entity has the potential to be identified and distinguished as being unique to itself. Entities are *objects* composed of interactive parts which range from subatomic particles to atoms, molecules and all entities composed of atoms and molecules. Being an object implies that entities can be the subject of identification and distinction. Their positions in time and space make them separate from each other, and this gives them the potential to be identified and distinguished as entities in their own right. From a dualist point of view, this potential of entities to be identified and distinguished is important as their existence ultimately depends on their being identifiable and distinguishable. They cannot be known to physically exist unless they have the prior potential to be identified and distinguished. Understanding the formation of identifiable and distinguishable entities therefore helps our understanding of life and the development of an inner being that distinguishes life from matter. The potential to be identified and distinguished exists for all entities but the actuality of that identifying and distinguishing depends on the existence of observers capable of apprehending the entity in itself. Thus, the ability to be identified and distinguished implies the possibility of observers existing to perform actual acts of identifying and distinguishing the said entities. It also becomes possible for the observers to form notions relating to identifying and distinguishing. But during most of the universe's existence there has been lacking entities capable of actually forming such notions.

Being identifiable and distinguishable means that each entity forms an identifiable unity which distinguishes it from other entities which are the same as or different from it. Also, its internal composition or clumpiness identifies it as a unity and distinguishes it from its external environment thus creating the distinction between inner and outer. Thus, each entity has its ins and outs that are sufficient to identity and distinguish it. The unique configuration of these ins and outs makes it a unity in itself. This unity makes it both different from and the same as the plurality of other entities in the universe. The unity also ensures that it exists as opposed to not existing. While it continues to exist as an identifiable entity, it is in a state of being and it continues that way until it no longer exists and its parts are dispersed. Such non-existence implies that its parts become available to coalesce into something else which did not previously exist. While it actually exists, it also has the potential for non-existence or becoming what it was not before in the subsequent reformation of its parts. The following dualist distinctions therefore become possible:

Internal	External
Unity	Plurality
Same	Different
Existence	Nonexistence
Being	Becoming
Actual	Potential

These dualist distinctions become possible when they are formulated and understood by any intelligent species capable of language communication by which such conceptual distinctions can be formed. This is in the same sense that physical laws might understood by all intelligent beings using the mathematical conventions necessary to discover and understand these laws. Thus, dualist distinctions are universal to intelligent species in so far as they can all conceive of these distinctions in the same way when they are apprehending the identity and distinction of entities. They also follow from the fact that information is created by the coming together of entities that makes them identifiable in themselves and distinguishable from each other. That information is complexified over time as entities become more complex. When sufficient information is accumulated by the entity for it to have evolved into an intelligent living being, it becomes aware of the distinction between internal and external, and that information is incorporated into its inner being.

Within every entity there are constant interactions between its internal identity and its external distinction. It continues in existence for as long as these interactions persist. Its existence is made possible by the forces that bring their parts together and maintain the resultant interactions. Therefore, the continued existence of entities depends on a constant interaction between internal and external. This interaction sustains their existence and ensures their distinction as identifiable things. This feature confirms the fact that dualist interaction has been a feature of the universe ever since identifiable and distinguishable entities came into being. The internal/external distinction created the possibility of inner being coming into existence with the advent of life. The short lived nature of entities implies that their coming into being and passing away – their generation and dissolution – are also a fundamental part of the fabric of the universe.

It is only because of the discreteness of entities in relation to each other that mathematics is made possible. It depends on the discreteness of entities so that its variables such as x and y, refer to distinct numbers of things and not to dynamic dualist interactions that cannot be pinned down discretely. Mathematics is moreover concerned with the measurement and arrangement of the patterns, flows and movements of entities. As it stands it is concerned more with the outer nature, structure and behaviour of things rather than the complex inner nature of things which are better described in terms of dualist interactions. Thus, a new branch of mathematics is implied by the use of dualist interactions as a means of accounting for the complexity of entities.

The symmetry of complex entities arises from a dualistic interaction within them. For the complexity of entities involves symmetrical interaction in the following way. The entity has two internal aspects which interact with each other to make its structure symmetrical from left to right and from right to left. Crystals, snowflakes and the like derive their symmetrical shapes by their interactive growth in which their parts organise themselves in relation to each other. Thus, the increasing complexity of entities involves a symmetrical interaction which sows the seeds of an inner being unique to the entity.

As time passed, the first material entities in the universe became more complex in their internal structure by accumulating nuclear complexities. Such elements became internally 'heavier' by acquiring increasing numbers of electrons, protons, neutrons and other elementary particles. In technical terms, *big bang nucleosynthesis* was followed by *stellar nucleosynthesis* in which nuclear reactions within stars built the nuclei of heavier elements. This results in the generation of elements from carbon to iron by nuclear fusion processes. *Explosive nucleosynthesis* produces the elements heavier than iron by an intense burst of nuclear reactions that only last seconds during the explosion of the supernova core. In explosive environments of supernovae, the elements between silicon and nickel are synthesised by fast fusion. The creation of radioactive elements such as uranium and thorium result from the re-absorption of the products of supernovae, namely, free neutrons. These are responsible for neutron rich isotopes of heavy elements. In this way, entities are created which are increasingly complex in their internal, nuclear structure. This process of *complexification* leads eventually to the advent of life and a developing inner being. This complexification takes place over time by dualist interactions becoming more involved and intensive as is discussed in more detail below.

3. The nature of space and time

Space and time came into being shortly after the explosive beginning of the universe. Both of them were produced by entities coming into being. They emerged when material entities first came together to form organised unities. When entities became distinguished externally and identified internally, they made space and time possible. They created space in which to distinguish themselves from each other and took time within themselves to identify their existence for a period of time. The passage of time is associated with internality of entities and exists only relatively to their continued existence. The expansion of space is created by entities moving apart relative to each other, and their apprehension of the passage of time is related to that expansive movement of space.

Thus, time came into being when material entities first came together to form organised unities. The organising interactive processes that created stable entities take time to occur, and they last only for a limited period of time. Time is limited for all entities because they are reacting against the expansion of the universe which eventually asserts itself and tears them apart. The unification of parts that creates an entity is an event that has duration within time. The entity endures for a time in spite of the ravages inflicted on it through the passage of time. Therefore, every entity in the universe *persists* through time, *subsists* through the unifying processes, and *exists* to be identifiable and distinguishable as an entity in its own right. Nothing lasts forever as it only has a brief spell of time within which to persist, subsist and exist. Its time is finite because the interactive processes do not themselves last forever. If everything lasted forever there would be no space for change, development or complexification in the universe. Nor would there be time for these to occur. Thus, wave-like elementary particles such as photons are not identifiable or distinguishable entities as they do not exist as such in time. As the uncertainty principle dictates, their existence cannot be pinpointed or identified without losing measurability as regards their position or mass. Their existence is detected only by their effects on entities wherein they cause transient and rhythmical events in time against which the passage of time may be measured.

The reality of time is confirmed by the relentless passing of time – second by second, minute by minute, day by day and so on. Over time, entities change, deteriorate, decay and eventually cease to exist as unified entities. The actual existence of time cannot be pinpointed any more than the existence of quantum particles cannot be pinpointed. That they exist may nevertheless not be doubted because of their palpable effects. Past events only exist in the mind and the future can only be imagined. But their reality in the course of time cannot be doubted without questioning our very existence. Such scepticism is counterproductive since it prevents us from making for a better future and therefore making meaningful and purposeful contributions to the benefit and welfare of posterity.

Time itself results from the spatial expansion of the universe into itself. As the whole universe expands, space is constantly expanded and energy is lost entropically. Entities are subject to the passage of time as they constantly battle against the expansive tendency of the universe as a whole. Complex entities maintain their existence over a period of time by constantly reinforcing the atomic, chemical and metabolic processes that are necessary for their continued unity. Eventually, their ability to maintain these interactive processes becomes diminished and this heralds their eventual demise.

The continued expansion of space has sources such as the following:

- The momentum of Big Bang energy pulsating in all directions.
- The action of so-called 'dark energy' maintaining the momentum of spatial expansion.
- The effect of photonic energy in spreading uniformly throughout the universe.

The action of dark energy especially may be responsible for our experience of the relentless passage of time. That energy is in us as in all matter in the universe. Therefore it is effectively tearing us apart against the best efforts of mind and body in maintaining our unity from one moment to the next. We experience this struggle to maintain our unity as the passage of time from one second to another. (This is more this spatial expansion theory of time in my e-book entitled *From Time to Eternity*.)

4. The nature of complexity

Complexity results from the interacting parts of an entity. It originates with the formation of entities whose parts interact in an involved and complicated manner. Each interaction is individually dual. It occurs between one part of the entity and the other. The entity as a whole is composed of a complex system of such dual interactions. Thus, life-forms themselves are a more complex form of entity than inorganic entities as they are composed of a system of interactions which is numerically greater and more varied than that of inorganic entities. Each interaction generates information which is used by the entity and passed on through reproduction and recorded in DNA and through other means of dissemination such as culture.

As already stated, complexity is made possible by the ins and outs of entities. It is the natural product of the internal development of matter, and its possibility was inherent in the universe at its very beginning. It was made possible in the first place by the ability of matter to come together and form unified entities which are identifiable and distinguishable as entities in their own right. With such unified entities, the *inner* and *outer* comes into being and this is essential to the ultimate creation of a distinct inner being which complexifies as a result of an interacting between inner and outer to unify them within itself. There is no absolute boundary between these ins and outs as they interact constantly and cannot be separated without terminating all interaction which means death to any living being.

Complexity consists in an internal increment of dualist interactions in the following manner. The complex nature of an entity consists in its disparate parts combining together and organising themselves to generate more internal organisation than is possible if the parts merely formed a loose aggregate of individuals. The component parts interact with each other to stabilise the entity as a whole. The parts identify with each other in so far as they interact, but they differentiate themselves in remaining distinct unities in their own right. The identity and distinction are therefore products of the interaction and are not separate from it. By interacting with each other, the distinct components form an entity which is more complex than the sum of the component parts considered in isolation from each other. Some entities are more complex than others because they contain a greater variety of component parts which are capable of generating more interactive activity than a less complex entity. The reason why things become more complex is to make more of their existence as unified entities than is possible when they are isolated and less complex than they are in fact.

It is noteworthy that complexity has not emerged entirely by chance. Its emergence is the product of entities clumping together and then using their complexity to sustain their unity, identity and distinctness over a period of time. The success of an entity in maintaining its unified existence depends on the extent to which its complex internal workings are commensurate with what is required to maintain its unified existence. Complexity has therefore come into being not randomly but for good purposeful reasons that are concern the internal structure of the entities and not anything outwith these entities. It was needed by entities to maintain and sustain a greater amount of inner activity which in turn generates increasing information by which the potentiality of entities is increased and actualised.

It is invariably the case that increasing complexity entails the possibility of increasing information. The more complex an entity is, the more information it has at its disposal, and therefore the more it can use its potentialities to achieve its goals in the universe. For example, more complex chemicals have more properties than less complex ones. An animal can do more than an isolated living cell because its unified structure contains more complexified information concerning its potentialities and what it can do with them. When an entity becomes more complex, it acquires more potential to make more of its existence as unified entity than is possible when it is less complex. Thus, intelligent beings are not only potentially more complex in their internal activity (especially in brain activity) than other living beings, they are also more complex and advanced in the organised way they combine to carry out actions of which they are incapable as individuals.

Complex entities are also distinguishable from flows and aggregates of entities that are also identifiable as discrete wholes. Such flows and aggregates do not usually for discrete, interacting complex entities. They can only be complex entities when the interrelationships between their component parts are stable and tenacious enough to maintain the discrete unity of the entity over time and in opposition of external disruption such as collisions and explosions. The latter will normally be sufficient to disrupt flows and aggregates of entities so that they are no longer discrete wholes. But complex entities, by virtue of their internal organisation, are able to maintain their discreteness and wholeness in the face of external interference as long as it is within tolerable limits.

5. The measure of complexity

The measure of complexity is based on the variety of its component parts and the intensity of the interrelationships between these parts in maintaining the unity and integrity of the composite entity. The degree of complexity relative to entities of similar level of complexity may be represented mathematically in various ways. One possible formula is the following: $C^{con} = pr^n$ where C^{con} is the complexity C of the composite entity within a specific context con, p represents the number of disparate component parts, r is the number of possible interrelationships between those parts, and n is the number of interactions achieved between the various parts over a specified period of time. This formula depends on the context within which complexity is being measured. If the measurement is not confined to particular contexts of complexity, the result would be infinity as each entity is potentially composed of an infinite number of parts in so far as it is infinitely divisible.

It appears that the simplest way to measure complexity is to add up the number of different parts (p) of which the entity is composed and compare them with an entity on the same basis. Thus, a living being is more complex than a lump of rock because the aggregate number of its different parts is greater than that of the rock. It has cells and organs which are complex in themselves and which are different from each other whereas the rock is composed of unorganised molecules that are less different from each other in aggregate. It may be composed of different minerals but these are not organised into disparate parts which have their own internal organisation like the cells of a living being. Also the latter are interrelated in contributing to metabolic process. Thus, a rock is fairly obviously less internally organised than a living being.

However, a more accurate way of measuring complexity is to take account of the context in which it is being measured. In this way, we can compare the complexity of things within and between different contexts or levels of complexity. All material objects, including ourselves, are all bound together or are influenced by the four basic forces:

The Four Basic Forces

Name:	*Acts on:*	*Particles of Exchange*
Gravity	all particles	proposed graviton
Weak nuclear force	all particles except γ	weak bosons, W and Z
Electromagnetism	particles with electric charge	photon, γ
Strong nuclear force	quarks and gluons	gluons, g

These forces bind things together in an interactive way and the strong nuclear force, for example, makes atomic structures possible, and gravitation binds us to the Earth and the Earth to its orbit round the sun. Atoms form the most basic measurable level of complexity since they vary in complexity according to their atomic 'weight' which consists of the sum of their protons and neutrons. An atom of hydrogen has a weight of 1.008 and is less complex than an atom of oxygen with a weight of 15.999. The periodic table of elements shows clearly the range of complexity of the different atoms.

The next context or level of complexity is that of molecules that are combinations of atoms bound together by chemical bonds in which they share electrons and interact with each other in that way. Molecules can be hugely complex but only amino acids and proteins are sufficiently complex to make life possible. Proteins are composed of amino acids and are therefore more complex than the latter. DNA molecules are among the most complex proteins of them all as they are composed of the animo acid peptide and four nucleotides called adenine, guanine, cytosine and thymine. DNA really belongs at the bridge between the context of molecules and the next level of complexity which is that of life.

The living cell is the next level of complexity beyond that of the molecule. It contains all kinds of interacting molecules within the clear context of its outer membrane. They are apparently at least 200,000 different proteins at work in the cell, each of which is interacting in its own way to contribute to the cell's functioning. There are dozens of different types of cell in the living body. They have evolved different functions in enabling the living body to function efficiently over its allotted period of existence. But what is important about life is not that it produces the most complex entities in the universe, but that fact that life itself complexifies. Thus, the universe has hitherto been alone in using the process of complexification to produce entities of ever-increasing complexity. The same process has culminated in an agent of complexification to rival the universe itself, namely, life. The nature and role of complexification are now discussed.

6. The role of complexification in dualist theory

Complexification is an important notion in dualist theory because growing complexity is the product of complex dualist interactions. Greater complexity implies that more dualist interactions are taking place to make that greater complexity possible. That in turn makes possible more diversity and variation in the entity possessing that greater complexity. The result is that more interest and variety comes into being that did not exist before. A more complex entity has the potential to be more different as a result of becoming more complex. If it becomes more complex, then yet more possibilities are generated. The generation of such possibilities is what complexification brings to the universe.

Thus, the emergence of complex features, attributes and qualities is the result of complexification actualising the potential that lies within all entities capable of achieving further complexification. The complexification of entities in the universe serves the purpose of actualising as many of the potentialities inherent in the universe as possible. And the accumulated complexities in entities mean that a greater number of potentialities are capable of being actualised by these entities. For their greater complexity also means that they are more developed in their material structure to cope with a greater number of complexities. Entities are therefore subject to a *principle of actualisable potential* which states that the potentialities available to an entity to be actualised are directly related to the degree of internal complexity attained by the entity. This is to say only that an entity is not capable of doing any more than its internal degree of organisation allows it to do. Thus, the more complex the entity is, the greater is its actualisable potential. In the case of human beings, this principle is useful in ascertaining, for example, how much more a young person could do to develop their capabilities and make more of themselves; hence the need to actualise our inner potential.

An entity of growing internal complexity is also subject to a further *principle of complexifying variability* by which its internal variability grows in relation to its increasing complexity. This means that an entity becomes more individual and unique in itself as it becomes more complex and variable in its internal organisation, that is to say, in its inner being. This occurs because the growing potentialities available for actualisation serve to differentiate the entity increasingly in relation to other entities. The less potentialities possessed by an entity, the less ability it has to identify and distinguish itself as something different from other entities. Thus, atoms and molecules are more uniformly similar to each other than more complex forms of entities such as living beings.

But growing complexity also leads to increasing external wastefulness. The explosive energy of the universe is progressively used up in the creation and dissolution of entities by means of which that energy is organised rather than chaotic. Entities are thus subject to a *principle of creative dissipation* whereby the entropy or energy wastage induced by their organisation is the price paid for their creation and subsistence as identifiable entities. The more organised and complex that entities become, the more they contribute to the dissipation of the energy available in the universe. This principle is a corollary to the second law of thermodynamics which states that a hot body will always dissipate its heat to a colder body and that heat transference in other direction is highly improbable. The *creative dissipation law* is required to account for what is created through the expense of energy involved in the complexification of entities. As far as creativity is concerned, the price paid for it is measurable in terms of correspondingly increasing entropy. However, if we are confident that there is plenty of energy available for all the purposes of life then we are entitled to ignore the expense involved. It may be questionable whether there is enough energy, how long it will last, and whether any unforeseen catastrophes may in the future bring this apparently limitless supply to an abrupt end. But such is the vastness of the universe, it appears that there is an almost limitless reservoir of energy by which entities of growing complexity may continue their development for an indefinite period of time.

The principles referred to above are generally descriptive of complexifying processes, and they do not amount to causal theories that are necessarily the case or are expressible mathematically. This is because complexifying processes are not necessarily causal in so far as they involve dualist interactions not yet explicable in causal terms. Such principles help us to understand in general terms the internal build up in entities which lead to the unity of inner being characteristic of living beings. The general workings of processes are thus described and not the particular workings that can be reduced to elements that are causally connected.

7. The build-up of complexity in the universe

It is invariably the case that increasing complexity breeds yet more complexity. *Complexification* fulfils a distinct role in the universe, namely, that of ensuring that, through time, increasingly complex entities are produced so that more and more of their potentialities are actualised and more and more information is produced. Increasing complexity creates yet more internalised potentiality. This complexification process eventually leads to the potential for inner being observable in living things. Intelligent beings are at the vanguard of this universal process. They have the potential role in the universe of bringing into being more complex entities than themselves so that more potentialities are actualised than they are capable of actualising as solitary individuals. These more complex entities include their social organisations, cities, nations and intellectual entities such as the internet and the websites associated with it.

Entities are of a particular kind because of the process of complexification which often makes them dramatically different from each other. By becoming more complex by whatever means, entities acquire the particularity that marks them for what they are. They acquire distinctive properties and attributes which are over and above anything implied by the existence of their individual constituents. Each entity thus becomes a particular kind of entity by virtue of the particular properties which it acquires through complexification. As they grow and develop, entities go through various levels of complexification in become significant different from each other. The development of conscious life-forms is due to such a complexification.

As already argued, the complexification process is such that the whole universe is involved in the creation of conscious life-forms. The creation of consciousness requires all the processes of the universe that have in fact produce life as we know it. A simulation capable of producing conscious life-forms would have to reproduce all these processes and therefore would create the same universe all over again. This is to say that no computer programme could create conscious life-forms unless it were able to repeat everything that has already happened in our universe. This is because consciousness involves a turning in of physical processes which seemingly involve the quantum processes of the whole universe, and everything that happens at the quantum level has no potential limits to its effects.

Thus, there is a *principle of unique complexification* in which the complexification process involves only one real universe, namely, the universe which we already inhabit. A simulated universe would require all the energies of a big bang beginning to create life-forms which are wholly the product of complexification that happens throughout the universe. There are only sufficient energy resources to ensure the creation and development of our universe. A multiplicity of universes therefore seems superfluous and untenable.

In the dualist view, the most important levels of complexification are outlined in diagram form below. They are the most important levels from the point of view of intelligent beings. And the complexifications that give rise to living beings, intelligent beings, and the sociosphere are dealt with in more detail in the succeeding sections. The following interactions are however generalisations that outline the basic processes involved. The processes in everyday life are doubtless even more complex and impervious to brief description.

The Evolutionary Levels of Dualist Interaction

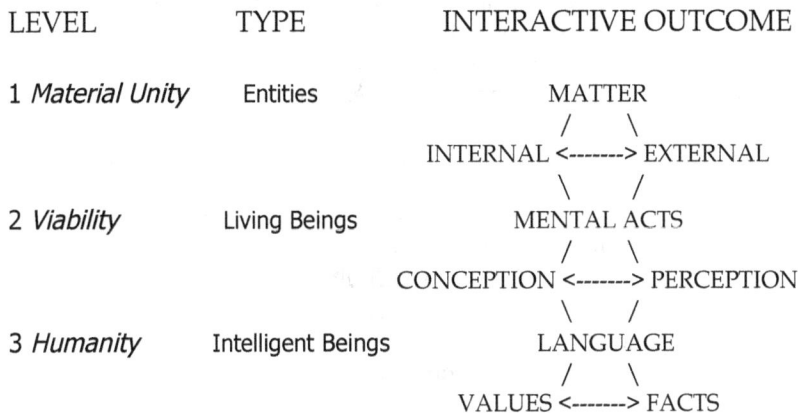

LEVEL	TYPE	INTERACTIVE OUTCOME
1 *Material Unity*	Entities	MATTER / \\ INTERNAL <------> EXTERNAL \\ /
2 *Viability*	Living Beings	MENTAL ACTS / \\ CONCEPTION <------> PERCEPTION \\ /
3 *Humanity*	Intelligent Beings	LANGUAGE / \\ VALUES <------> FACTS

```
                                              \    /
4 Sociability        Sociosphere            CULTURE
                                            /    \
                                    ART <-------> SCIENCE
                                            \    /
5 Cosmic Unity       Posterity          THE UNKNOWN FUTURE
```

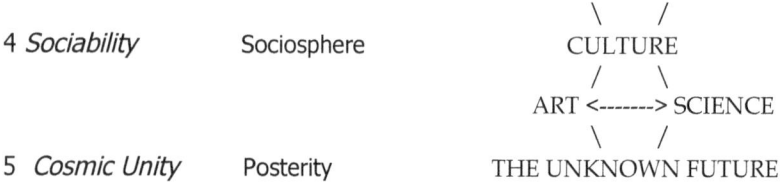

8. The successive levels of complexification

First Level. The first level of complexification resulted from the organisation of energy into MATTER to form material entities. Because the latter form identifiable and distinguishable unities, this gave rise to an interaction between (1) the INTERNAL relationships necessary to maintain their unity and (2) the EXTERNAL relationships with the rest of the universe which threaten and dissipate their unity.

Second Level. The interaction between the internal and external led to a continuous complexification process which eventually produced a second level by which MENTAL ACTS of conception and perception became possible. These acts are used by LIVING BEINGS to maintain their existences for as long as their potentialities and level of complexity will allow. A primary complexification occurred in which life emerged as reproductive single-cells. A secondary complexification followed when single-celled organisms combined together to form more complex living beings so that their collective potentialities were increased. Thus, simpler living beings evolved into increasingly complex forms whose potentialities were correspondingly increased. And living beings became capable of performing secondary actualisations in which they perceived and conceived entities as being independent of themselves. Complex agency complexification which involves living beings consists in an interaction between the external and internal aspects of the entity. These aspects themselves have become more complex in their content and thus have properties over and above being merely 'external' or merely 'internal'. This is dealt with in more detail below.

Third Level. This first complexification occurred when living beings reached such a level of complexity in their mental activity and their social interrelationships with each other that they developed a complex LANGUAGE for communication and other social purposes. This enabled INTELLIGENT BEINGS to give VALUES to their emotional states and their internal experiences, and to arrive at FACTS concerning what really exists and what is really happening in the universe.

Fourth Level. In this level, the values and facts developed and complexified into an identifiable and distinguishable entity which may be called the sociosphere. The latter is actualised in the form of a living CULTURE in which ART and SCIENCE are developed. However, the potentialities of the sociosphere are inseparable from the thoughts and actions of individual intelligent beings. Therefore, the sociosphere is not a life-form distinct from intelligent beings but it may be a super life-form in the making. This may herald that which is to transcend life in THE UNKNOWN FUTURE.

Fifth Level. In this level, a cosmic view may eventually prevail which is capable of embracing all points of view. It is a balanced state of mind that is constantly open to the absorption of new information and new ways of looking at things. We are moving towards this state of mind with the plethora of information and understanding now available to us on the internet and in media sources of all kinds, including books, newspapers, CDs, DVDs and other electronic sources. The resultant COSMIC UNITY may form a distinct life-form that is hived off from humanity and cast into outer space where it may bring life and knowledge to other planets in the universe.

The overall tendency towards ever-increasing complexity throughout the universe can now be seen by us as having a purpose, namely, that of rebuilding the complex unity of the universe over time. In this way, complexification tends towards the ultimate unity of everything. The atheists are correct; there is no god now. However, our increasing knowledge and understanding of the universe is making it possible for the universe itself to be unified into an all-embracing cosmos that makes sense of everything else in the universe. This is the dualist cosmic outlook that embraces everything but only in the far future. In a sense, the inner beings of each of us constitute fragments of divinity which are striving towards that distant unity that makes up a cosmic being in the future, namely, a thing that has nothing whatsoever to do with us in the present and that therefore effectively does not exist in reality.

9. The advent of life through complexification

Life came about with the second significant level of complexification. This was when material entities reached sufficient internal complexity to do things that would prolong their existence, maintain their unity, identity and distinction, and reproduce themselves. This meant that they could interact *purposefully* with their external environment. They were able to set goals for themselves and this is evidence of an inner complexity that is sufficient to formulate such goals. This inner complexity forms a unified inner being that interacts as a whole with what is external to the entity to produce an an apprehension what exists outside the entity. This development confirms the truth that life complexifies through the development of an inner being. For living beings exist not only for themselves as identifiable and distinguishable entities but also to maintain their complexity and prolong their existence. They require the unifying effects of inner being to achieve this.

There is a progression of complexification through the various aspects by which inner being unifies the organism in relation to its goals. Each aspect of inner being forms a purposeful agency that impels the life form to do things in its own interests. The inner being of human beings in particular progresses through the aspects of consciousness, agent, self, person, society, and cosmos. Each of these aspects progressively complexifies the inner being. They also remain within the purview of the individual organism and are not extensions beyond its bodily existence. The consciousness of a life form is the first aspect of its inner being. It consists in the ability to identify itself as a unity and distinguish itself from its environment. A single-cell organism is conscious of its surroundings and is able to move towards available food. This action involves identifying and distinguishing itself as something distinct from its surroundings. Such consciousness does not amount to self-consciousness.

The second aspect of inner being consists in their becoming agents that are capable of acting or not acting of their own freewill. Inner being complexifies by turning in on itself, and in so doing it produces aspects of itself with which it interacts. It identifies itself with these aspects, and distinguishes itself from them, in the course of interacting with them. The foremost of the aspects for human beings is the self by which it is conscious of what it is or is not doing. It thereby exhibits self-consciousness. The self is inner being in action especially in its function as an agent initiating action. The role of the self in the process of in making us human is discussed further in part seven on *The Development of Self by Dualist Interaction*.

An aspect of inner being is therefore a further development in its complexification by which the meaning and purpose of its life and living is increased. Each aspect adds to the complexity of inner being by increasing the extent to which it is self-referential. As inner being refers into itself, it is as much an aspect of the self, will, mind, body, brain, and all the other parts of the organism as each of them are aspects of inner being. This only means that they are all conceptions manifesting the same unifying principle which ensures that we endure fleetingly as viable living beings.

Aspects are important in enabling us to refer back to ourselves. The conception of an aspect results from our ability to conceive of things in abstraction from what feeling and putting our thoughts into words. Their existence is confirmed by the fact that our being able to act can be perceived or felt by ourselves. In other words, we can see what we are doing and can attribute our actions to ourselves. We, as language using beings, know that these aspects exist because we are able to refer to these notions in making sense of what we do within ourselves in thinking successfully about the self, will, mind, body as being things belonging to us. For example, we can think of pains being in our body, of material objects as belonging to ourselves, of having or not having the will to give up smoking, see ourselves doing things in the mirror, and so on.

Thus, inner being in this context may be defined as the ability of living beings to be internally unified and externally distinguished by interacting purposefully with their environment to breathe, feed, defend, differentiate, improve themselves, replicate themselves, relate to other beings, culturally immortalise themselves, and so on. For example, the inner being of a single-celled entity such as an amoeba manifests itself in goals such as its purposeful pursuit and incorporation of edible matter. In that case, its inner being consists in at least four goals which are needs or motivations formed within it. These are (a) its need to maintain its unity and survive as an identifiable and distinctive entity; (b) its motivation to feed itself and create sufficient energy to maintain its unity; (c) its concern to defend itself from external threats to its existence, for instance, by moving away from toxic substances; (d) its need to replicate itself by cellular division which reinstates its inner being in two distinct individuals. Replication ensures that life having come into being cannot be extinguished as long as inwardly motivated individuals remain to ensure its propagation and continuation.

Therefore, the emergence of consciousness begins with the simplest life form capable of independent existence, that is to say, the single-celled organism, in which the distinction between the internal and external involves distinguishing ingestible from non-ingestible food. The food in being ingested becomes internal as opposed to external i.e. it forms part of the organic workings of the being. With sense organs, the more complicated organism is able to register physical impressions on these sense organs, and it responds to these impressions with feelings and emotions which are aroused by these impressions. Thus, on detecting food by means of these organs, it feels their presence and responds positively to that presence. A life form therefore becomes conscious of what it is doing when it reaches out to embrace particles of food. Such awareness is made possible by the unifying activity of inner being in forming and carrying out its goals. It is the simplest form of consciousness and the first aspect of inner being to make its appearance.

The further development of consciousness consists in its performing a specific role in inner being. An additional complexification occurs in inner being which complexifies by turning in on itself, and in so doing it produces aspects of itself with which it interacts. This form of consciousness is the beginnings of self-consciousness which involves the living being's awareness of what is occurring within itself. The awareness of inner being is manifested in the conscious being by the subjective feelings which it experiences. It is made aware of its feelings by a process of internalisation: a turning into itself to be aware of the activity of its inner being. The feelings such as those of hunger, desire, aggression and fear result from this awareness generated by inner being. This emotional awareness falls short of self-consciousness which is a further development of consciousness in human beings. It is made possible by acquiring a notion of self. This involves our being aware of ourselves (1) as a subject experiencing whatever happens to us and (2) as a subject making objects of these experiences and making more of them than they were originally experienced to be.

Consciousness emerges with single-cell organisms that are independently viable. In contrast, viruses lack consciousness and are not viable life forms in so far as they are incapable of existing for long outside the cells within which they become an intimate part in order to replicate themselves. The replicating ability of a virus is no more life-like than the replication of chemical crystals. It is a rogue piece of DNA chemical that mimics life rather than being life itself. There are no limits to its destructiveness because its activity is more mechanical than purposeful. It has no internal conception of what it is doing by which it could be said to be aware of what it does. As a result, viruses can unknowingly kill their hosts and themselves by their unbridled activities within living beings.

10. The development of perception

The operation of perception emerged as a progressive apprehension of surroundings through the development of sensory organs. The ability to detect external objects by means of perception was a major step forward by which life began the process of liberating itself from its material essence. Living entities began to apprehend their surroundings so as to fulfil their internalised goals more efficiently. Inner being thereby complexified to provide the acts of perception, conception and recollection.

The development of perception went in tandem with a corresponding development of conception or the ability to conceive that which is being perceived. To maintain their existence as unified entities, living beings developed the sensory organs required to distinguish appropriate forms of external matter or energy from inappropriate ones. As a result, they were able to perform mental acts of *conception* concerning the kind of material or energy they required to absorb in order to survive, and mental acts of *perception* concerning the identifying and distinguishing of that matter or energy. By developing this form of consciousness or awareness of their surroundings, they were able to move towards the requisite source of matter or energy and absorb it accordingly. They were also able to perform mental acts of *recollection* so that they recalled the former presence of edible matter and energy. This means that the operation of memory develops together with the other operations and they form the brain.

In this way, how a single-celled organism perceives can be described in dualist terms. An amoeba, for example, moves towards a particle of food by sensing a gradient of chemical emissions from it. It then identifies and distinguishes the presence of that particle and by moving around it proceeds in the direction of the particle's position as it detects stronger signals of that position. On reaching the particle, the amoeba touches it and extends its protrusions around it proceeds to incorporate it within its body. To that limited extent, an amoeba has a conception of food by which it distinguishes what is ingestible food from what is not ingestible food. It *perceives* that food by linking the *conception* of it to what is sensed as a gradient of chemical signs indicating the presence of suitable food as it moves towards it.

Similarly, algae are able to move towards light because they arrive at a rudimentary conception of lightedness within them which enables them to distinguish a greater concentration of light from a lesser one. An act of perception has occurred in which the conception of light is linked to the sensing of this greater or lesser concentration of light. This may lead to a cell or group of cells specialising in light detection and this marks the beginnings of an organ of perception. In this way, we can describe in dualist terms how light is detected by perception.

This also shows that the formation of conceptions is necessary for perception of objects. From the very beginning, the actions of living beings proceeded on the principle of *trial-and-error*. Chaotic, random movements led to the detection of regular and continuous patterns in the external universe. These patterns form the basis of objects of conception, of which external reality is perceived to be constituted. By trial-and-error, conceptions are arrived at which enable living beings to do things with the objects of reality. These objects cannot be perceived distinctly nor identified precisely without conceptions having been formed concerning what they are. An indispensible dualist interaction therefore takes place between the mental capacities of perception and conception in giving living beings access to external reality.

11. The dualist interaction between perception and conception

We can also show how sense organs evolved to give interactive access to external reality. They evolved as a result of an interaction between the organism's internal potentialities and the external actualities facing it. In other words, it did whatever it was able to do to cope with the external circumstances in which it found itself. As life complexified, these interactions between internal potentialities and external actualities became significantly more intense. Those organisms which successfully adjusted to external circumstances stored and passed on its advantages as they divided to reproduce themselves. Thus, potentialities inherited by genetic inheritance passed on advantages that aided survival and reproduction. Sense organs evolved to provide increasingly accurate access to external reality. The sensations from these organs became organised into distinct objects of conception which are actualised interactively by means of sensory contact with external entities. These objects of conception are then actualised internally either in acts of conception or in acts of perception for which external entities become conceivable objects of conscious attention.

By this means, internal potentialities are actualised into mental capacities which are distinct from the physical processes that make them possible. These capacities become distinct from the unified activity of the entity in using them or not using. As a result, they are stored up in an 'unconscious' circuit which may or may not be accessed by the entity as a whole. This circuit constitutes an inner being that is unique to each living being. The entity may be called 'conscious' when it has the ability to choose whether to use a mental capacity or not. And this act of choosing arises only because the entity is aware of what it is or is not doing in using or failing to use a mental capacity. Thus, consciousness at this level involves choosing or not choosing to use mental capacities.

These mental operations of perception and conception are therefore the result of secondary actualisations which give rise to internal powers, capacities and skills. The existence of the latter as potentialities is dependent on primary actualisations that have made them available to the living being because its unified activity as viable entity. In other words, its inner being has been built up by dualist interactions between its inherited power and capacities and the actual use of these powers and capacities. Secondary potentialities come into existence because the powers and capacities acquire their own potentialities. These secondary potentialities result from further activity by which the internal activity of the entity relates to external activity and vice versa. These dualist interrelationships may be represented approximately as follows.

$$\text{INTERNAL x EXTERNAL} = \text{PERCEPTION}$$
$$\text{EXTERNAL x INTERNAL} = \text{CONCEPTION}$$
(By analogy with matrix algebra: $a \times b = x$ and $b \times a = y$.)

These formulae mean in simple terms that perception internalises while conception externalises. They tell us that perception helps us to internalise the external while conception helps us to externalise the internal within us. The internalisation of the external gives rise to the operation of perception, and the externalisation of the internal gives rise to the operation of conception. An act of conception enables the internalisation to take place and an act of perception enables the externalisation to take place, so that neither perception nor conception are prior but both develop in conjunction with each other. This internalisation consists in an emotional reaction to an external stimulus, and that reaction produces the conceptual capacity which enables the living being to cope adequately with the sensory stimulus whenever it is repeated in the future. Instead of experiencing nothing but a naked and isolated emotion of fear, love, hate, or pain, the living being knows what to do or what not to do because an act of conception is related to the stimulus. The individual then runs away, makes love, acts aggressively, licks its wounds etc.

This means that an object of conception is built up interactively. An external stimulus to the sense organs of a living being makes an impression on them which arouses feelings and emotions. The repetition of the stimulus leads to a turning in of these feelings and emotions so that they are associated with that stimulus by means of a memory circuit (i.e. involving circuit turning in). An object of conception is then built up because stimuli from other sense organs are related to it. A sensation is thus the initial experience of an impression on a sense organ before it is related to an object of conception. An act of perception, on the other hand, always includes an object of conception by which the act may be made sense of.

When an external object is subjected to an act of perception it is real and independent of the perceiver when it is so intimately related to external stimuli that it is directly perceived to be an external object or event which may either be acted upon and manipulated in a fairly predictable fashion or be the reason or cause of predictable actions in the external world. The object of conception then forms part of perception so that the individual is able to relate to the object as being external to it. The key point is what can be done successfully when something is or is not being perceived. When the object of conception is abstracted from perception, it is then that which has been identified and distinguished as a discrete whole by means of an act of conception. It has been conceived to be what it is when it is thought about intentionally and brought before the mind.

As with other living beings, human beings are agents which do things when they pay attention to an object of perception to make something of the object. To begin with, the field of visual perception is largely given by unconscious processes that involve the conscious self or will. We open our eyes and a whole scene is before us without our willing it. The unity of the scene is the work of unified inner being whose activity is required to maintain the stability of that scene, even though we are not conscious of it. The immediate impression of photons on the retina is the mechanical part of vision. The objects of visual perception are the work of unified inner being and the act of attending to these objects is performed by us consciously. Thus, we consciously interact with objects of perception when we pay attention to them and think about them and do things with them. The act of consciousness involves our being identical with the unifying processes so that we are unaware of being anything other than ourselves looking at something. Our inner being must have the potential or power within it to do what it can in relation to external realities. This potential develops with the complexification of inner being as it gains perceptual experience of that which exists outside it. That experience is gained by interacting dualistically with our environment and with other people in a social context.

12. The advent of consciousness

Even the simplest living organism is conscious since it can detect particles of foods and incorporate them. As it is aware of the presence of these particles, it is conscious of them. Consciousness therefore involves the possibility of being aware even if there is nothing around to be aware of. It usually consists of awareness of something in particular. It is possible to be conscious without being aware of anything in particular as when drowsy, distracted, or in an empty, thoughtless state of mind. But this is only for short periods of time. To be alive and yet permanently unaware of anything in particular is a vegetative and perhaps catatonic state of mind. Being aware of being alive without necessarily being aware of anything in particular is consciousness *per se,* and we doubtless share this form of consciousness with plants which have some kind of awareness of their surroundings without being aware of anything in particular. But consciousness of something implies an interaction between that which is being conscious and that which it is conscious of. Thus, an active consciousness depends on a constant interaction between the awareness component and what that component is being aware of. This is the origin of all dualistic principles such as internal/external and self/non-self.

Such principles emerge from the interaction between the internal and external, between what we conceive to be within us and what we conceive to be without us. By means of this interaction we are constantly re-establishing our self-identity from moment to moment. In so far as consciousness has an object it results from this dualist interaction which itself emerges from the struggles of the ego in establishing its identity within its chaotic surroundings. These principles help us to establish and maintain our self-identity against the disorder and misinformation which threatens to engulf that identity. By means of these principles we maintain the context of self and operate within it. They enable us to identify with, and differentiate ourselves from, other contexts such as other people, society and so on. These dualisms are such that the one side of the principle cannot occur without creating a disharmony or infelicity of thought. The other side of the dualism must be acknowledged and embraced so that one can move on in one's thinking.

We differ from other living beings in the extent to which we have an inner life and know that we have such a life of our own. As Feuerbach put it:

> Hence the brute has only a simple, man a twofold life: in the brute, the inner life is one with the outer; man has both an inner and an outer life. The inner life of man is the life which has relation to his species, to his general, as distinguished from his individual, nature. Man thinks — that is, he converses with himself. The brute can exercise no function which has relation to its species without another individual external to itself; but man can perform the functions of thought and speech, which strictly imply such a relation, apart from another individual. Man is himself at once I and thou; he can put himself in the place of another, for this reason, that to him his species, his essential nature, and not merely his individuality, is an object of thought.[98]

As human beings, we are self-conscious, self-corrective beings who examine what we are doing and thinking and correct ourselves when necessary. In interacting with ourselves, we figuratively loop back into our former thinking and correct it accordingly. This is basically what self-consciousness involves when we are aware of what we should or should not be doing or thinking. The dualist view thus refers to self-conscious activity that involves trial-and-error; a common sense procedure that also underlies the scientific method and has ensured the remarkable success of science in transforming our society largely for the better. Dualist thinking therefore moves forward recursively in a dynamic and flexible way. It embraces opposing points of view instead of being stuck unyieldingly in one extreme viewpoint. This dynamic view is not completely realist or idealist, empiricist or rationalist, logical or intuitive. It embraces all of these in an interactive manner, that is to say, it moves from one viewpoint to the other and *vice versa*, according to what needs to be done in the real world in correcting imbalances, redressing injustices, and loosening rigid points of view.

Our self-consciousness may be thought of metaphorically as, for instance, a turning in of brain activity to make self-awareness possible. Exactly what interactions are required in physical terms depends on further understanding of brain activity. Subjectivity therefore refers to the misfit of what is going on within

---

[98] Ludwig Andreas Feuerbach, *The Essence of Christianity*, trans by Marian Evans (aka George Eliot), (London: John Chapman, 1854), ch. 1, p. 2.

our physical bodies and the environment in which they exist. We need to be constantly alert and attentive to overcoming that misfit. The problem of how the mind influences the body vanishes when we explain all our experiences in terms of dualist interactions. The word 'mind' becomes merely metaphorical as refers to nothing in particular in the brain. If it is uninformative to say that the brain moves the body, it is just as uninformative to say that the mind moves body. When we move our limbs, all kinds of dualist interactions are involved which are not yet fully understood. The processes involved are wholly physical and material and no spiritual or immaterial explanations are required. The unified activity of these dualist interactions is all that are required, and these might ultimately be explained in terms of neural networks and the like.

In conclusion, therefore, we are conscious in so far as we are interacting with ourselves, other people and our environment. Thus, consciousness is not an entity but an interactive process. Inner being involves self-consciousness in which we are conscious of our interactions with self etc. Consciousness takes its time and we pay for it in the end with our demise. Thus, it is within time that our actual experience of reality is made possible. The rest is an eternity of possibilities.

13. Computational theory does not compute

The dualist view of the development of consciousness disputes computational theories of the mind that tend to reduce us to machines and as a consequence underestimate the role of intuitive holism in making us creative living beings. Understanding this development leads us to conclude that the artificial creation of mind, consciousness or intelligence would require a replication of the universe's creation of the same. The dualist view suggests that so-called 'artificial intelligence' will never be complex enough to produce consciousness and self-identity unless it reproduces all the interactive processes of the universe that were necessary to produce our consciousness and self-identity. Whether this is possible or not is doubtful.

The dualist view promises to account for the mind better than the fashionable theory of mind propagated by cognitive psychologists, namely, the so-called 'computational' theory of the mind.[99] This theory purports to explain how the mind works on a more or less computational basis. Ironically, the theory cannot compute as it is insufficient to work out by computational methods how we came to be what we are. It cannot account for our mathematical ability, our

---

[99] An account of the computational theory is to be found in Steven Pinker's *How the Mind Works*, (London: Penguin Books, 1998, p. 24f). He seems to support the computation theory of mind but just as his book *The Language Instinct*, (London: Penguin Books, 1995) proves beyond doubt that language is anything but instinctive, so his book proves that the mind is anything but computational. His book proves nothing definite about the mind, and indeed in the Preface, he admits that "we don't understand how the mind works". (*op. cit.* p. ix).

aesthetic feelings, or our moral intuitions among other things. It cannot work out how original thoughts and ideas emerge intuitively and without apparent neurological causation. It cannot pinpoint in the brain where the idea of the square root of minus one is to be found since that idea has no existence in the material world. We are not genetically programmed to understand such a notion by any intuitive means. What evolutionary process could have produced our ability to make sense of such things? The answer is that we arrive at such notions dualistically by interacting with our environment and our own thoughts in an intelligent and resourceful way. Such a dualist account includes the intuitive processes that are involved in original thought and aesthetic appreciation.

In 1930, the eminent physicist and astronomer, Sir James Jeans wrote the following:

> The universe begins to look more like a great thought than a great machine. Mind no longer appears as an accidental intruder into the realm of matter; we are beginning to suspect that we ought rather to hail it as the creator and governor of the realm of matter – not of course our individual minds, but the minds in which the atoms out of which our individual minds have grown exist as thoughts. . . . The old dualism of mind and matter, which was responsible for the supposed hostility, seems likely to disappear, not through matter becoming in any way more shadowy or insubstantial than heretofore, or through mind becoming resolved into a function of the working of matter, but through substantial matter resolving itself into a creation and manifestation of mind.[100]

This is an example of how the scientific view during the 20th century has been moving towards a dualist view of the universe. Unfortunately, biologists and psychologists are exceptional in sticking with the mechanistic, computable view of humanity. Biologists, sociobiologists, behaviourists, and cognitivists are among those who support the artificial intelligence view that a development of computing power will lead to a better understanding of the brain. However, it is questionable whether computers will ever be able to rival brains. Computers can only cope with discrete things – one by one, that is to say, one operation followed by another in a discrete sequence. They are deficient in taking things apart and putting them together in new ways that are not already implied by the given program. In other words, they cannot analyse or synthesise in ways that are not already given in their software programs and in the data inputted by human operators. Everything has to be discrete and pre-existing for them otherwise they are not programmed to deal with it. In short, a scientific approach that merely involves deduction, analysis or computation leads to people being treated like mechanistic nodes or ciphers that have no inner life other than what is revealed by their outward behaviour.

It is misleading to say that our brains do anything in particular. We use our brains and not *vice versa*. Though the workings of our brains are an interactive

---

[100] Sir James Jeans, *The Mysterious Universe*, (1930 – London: Penguin books, 1937), Ch. V, p. 187.

aspect of inner being, these workings have no inherited effect on it or on its other aspects such as the self. The view that our brains are genetically programmed to make us do things is a confusion of cause and effect. When we become self-aware, the changes in neural connections in our brains are the effect of environmental and cultural influences on us. These changes are not caused by anything prior to their being effected by these influences. Inner being is initiated by genetic influences but it is built up through thought and experience. We are not programmed for religious beliefs as we have a choice as to whether we adopt or do not adopt such beliefs. Our brains have no choice in the matter. The same applies to the body and other aspects of inner being which have no will of their own because they lack the consciousness of self.

Genetic and other influences are not sufficient to account for inner being. Thus, neither brain, body nor any genetic influences can do everything by themselves. They are parts of the whole and not the whole themselves. By themselves, the brain and the other bodily organs would be competing with each other and their parts instead of co-operating with them. Genetic influences cannot subsist by themselves. They must interact with the body as a whole otherwise we would be entirely instinctive, mechanical beings. To stop these disparate influences being at odds with each other, the activity of inner being is needed to unify their functioning in terms of its goals. The brain, body and genetic influences are aspects of inner being whose activity uses them as tools to fulfil its overriding ends. Inner being also includes the conscious part in which we are aware that we do things for ourselves. There is therefore a constant interaction between inner being and the organism as a whole. Understanding the nature of this interaction is our constant and unending concern as we can never understand it fully without eradicating it.

It is questionable whether inner being or our unconscious brain activity could be replicated in another body. Inner being is a biological phenomenon which only comes into being by growing within the medium of biological entity, as described below. It therefore cannot be reproduced independently of the entity in which it is rooted. Inner being is indivisible and cannot be reconstituted by copying the body down to the last atom and molecule. Such a copied body would have no consciousness or sense of self since it would lack the unifying quality of the original unified action of inner being. There is no possibility of transporting inner being to another body because it is the unified operation of that particular body. It is unique to each individual and cannot be recreated in another brain or body. As already stated, in the absence of inner being, the body falls into disunity, and inner being has no existence outside the body of which it is an inextricable part. They are seamlessly combined into an irreducible whole. The proof of this lies in the reality of the activity of inner being which is in no particular place in the body.

Part Seven
The Development of Self by Dualist Interaction

1. The advent of self

The notion of self has been crucial to human development. Indeed the very notion seems to be peculiar to human beings. Our potential is most conspicuously realised in this notion which gives us a degree of individuality and diversity to which no other species on Earth can aspire. As already described in part six above on *The Emergence of Complexity by Dualist Interaction*, the self exists only as a self-identifying notion. From a physiological point of view, it is associated with the holistic neural activity that gives us the willpower to get things done. Moreover, it enables us to be ourselves much more than other animals are capable of. The self-identifying notions of self, ego or 'I' result from our inner being interacting with itself by self-reference or feedback. This makes us conscious of our own existence so that we self-identify ourselves as having a self, ego or 'I'. In other words, the notion of self exists for us because it enables us to refer our experiences back to ourselves and makes us self-conscious.

The self therefore exists as a unifying self-referential process which we constantly use when we think of or refer to ourselves. I am more than the sum of my experiences simply because I have a notion of self, ego or 'I' that enables me to unify these experiences in terms of such notions. Thus, the emergence of these notions results from the self-reference made possible by language. It is a process whereby inner being refers back into itself and arrives at a notion of a self or individual identity peculiar to itself. The self is therefore our inner being turned into itself to enable us to be aware of what we are and we are doing. It is an aspect of our inner being which is identical with that inner being while differing from it when we are aware of the interaction taking place between us and whatever experience belongs to us. These notions of self, ego or 'I' must be consonant with all intelligent, self-referential, self-critical, language-using beings and not just with human beings.

The various notions of self are indispensible in helping us to be ourselves. In dualist terms, our experiences at the beginning are given immediately by intuitions over which we have no control. In interacting with these intuitions we gradually build up a notion of ourselves as being distinct from our experiences. We arrive at notions of self, ego or 'I' and they help us to unify our interactive experiences and make sense of our being. They enable us to interact with what is happening to us and what we are doing from one moment to the next. They give us time in which to be more that what is immediately happening to us. We become ourselves only when we have a strong notion of self. Instead of being immersed in the immediate experiences given in perception we can objectify them by alternately distinguishing ourselves from them and identifying ourselves in relation to them. We thereby refer alternately to ourselves and to our experiences in an interactive way. Our experiences are thereby both ourselves and not ourselves according to whether we view them subjectively or objectively. When I am absorbed in a hobby and lose myself in it, it becomes me in a sense. When I listen to opinions with which I do not agree, I distance myself from them. Though I have made sense of them, I do not identify with them. This dualist interaction between ourselves as subjects and our experiences as objects constitutes self-reference and makes consciousness possible, as has already been argued.

Furthermore, we develop ourselves inwardly by using self-reference. The self-referential loop that makes the self possible begins with the establishment of an inner being which results from a genetically determined brain growth. The intuitions produced by the sense organs are gradually organised by the use of language and the realisation of self eventually emerges. I am what I am by thinking about my likes and dislikes, my fears and interests. I access these by referring back to my memories and experiences. I interact with these memories one after another on a continuous loop. This feedback process gradually builds up and develops the inner workings of the brain. This amounts to a development of what is here called 'inner being'.

Such a feedback process reinforces the idea of self. Thus, the constant interaction of the self with its experiences leads to the further development of inner being by which mental and physical events are unified in relation to our aims, goals, desires, aspirations and motivations. By self-reference we refer back to what is happening to us and what we are doing so that we can understand better what is going on within us. Such self-knowledge enables us to give expression to our thoughts and feelings, and communicate them to others. The notions of self, ego, and I thereby enable us to be more at one with ourselves, in other words, our inner being.

2. The importance of self-reference

This notion of a constantly interactive act of self-reference forms a secure foundation for our existence. It suggests the foundational apophthegm: *I interact self-referentially therefore I am*, which is backed by the whole theory of dualism. This is a more secure than saying, for example, 'I think therefore I am'[101] or 'I doubt therefore I am'. Mere thinking or doubting has no definite starting point whereas self-reference develops out of our interacting dualistically with our environment. It has genetic origins and can be traced back to the interactive origins of the universe, as has been argued already. We interact just like all living beings but we surpass them with the intensity and complexity of our interactions, both personal and social, because we have this notion of self. Thus, we establish and maintain the security of our self and our inner being, not by acts of thinking or doubting, but by constantly scrutinising and criticising our own thinking about things. We understand ourselves better in thinking of ourselves as interacting

---

[101] Descartes, *Discours de la Méthode*, (1637 - Paris: Garnier-Flammarion, 1966, Quartième Partie,) p. 60 - *"je pense, donc je suis."*

entities and not just thinking entities. If I do not respond at all to events in and around me then I am nothing to myself. I am what I find myself to be by examining how I think and feel and whether my thoughts and feelings match up to my expectations of them. When they do not meet my expectations, I can think about doing something about it. When they do meet my expectations, I can move on with my life without further need for introspection.

Self-reference enables us to be ourselves and not be ourselves at the same time whereas animals are generally incapable of differentiating themselves because they lack sufficient self-awareness. Thus, the self is both itself and not itself at the same time while it interacts with itself and its environment. We can do something for ourselves and then disown it as being unworthy of us. We can recognise words spoken by us as being our own but may repudiate them as soon as they are spoken and taken up by others. The self distinguishes itself by providing more than inner being can offer through intuition alone. It loops out from inner being to accomplish this differentiation which forms the content of conscious activity. To be conscious is to make more of inner being by means of conscious activity such as thought, reasoning, verbalising and so on.

The self therefore emerges according to the *Principle of Self-Reference*. This principle involves a palintropy, or turning in, by which the mental process turns in recursively. The 'self' being referred to here is the identity or unity of the inner being by which the self is what it is. There is a physical process involved in the brain in which one aspect of inner being turns into the rest of inner being to change it in a specific way. The 'self' is therefore the name for the unifying process of inner being to which the palintropy refers. The reference is the turning in process and the self is that which is being turned into. Thus, self-reference is essential to the unity of self, and it has a physical basis in the activity of the brain.

At the same time, the self is not a stand-alone aspect of inner being. Without the notion of self, there is no way of unifying the various aspects of inner being in terms of anything other than themselves. The self cannot be related to such aspects as the mind, will, consciousness and so on unless it relates to inner being in the same way that they do. The mind has nothing in common with the body unless it is viewed as being related as much to inner being as to the other aspects. None of these aspects are stand-alone entities; they are processes intimately involved in inner being and its dynamic and purposeful activities. This means that they are not logically definable entities but intimately interrelated processes.

The notion of mind only makes sense as a reference point for subjectivity and for the inner being that makes subjectivity possible. It does not exist as a physical entity but only as a metaphor for the place of thought. As a notion, the mind is that aspect of inner being in which we collectivise and categorise thoughts, feelings and mental acts as being metaphorically 'in the mind'. It is used as a metaphor for the repository or place wherein our thinking said to take place. The reality of mind lies in the purposeful actions that can be undertaken because of neural activity taking place in the brain. Moreover, the mind can only be that aspect of inner being in which turning in and unifying is taking place to make thought possible.

3. The cultural development of self

Before the advent of intelligent beings, the growth of the inner being in individual organisms was strictly limited to what was required to ensure the survival of the species that was best suited to any particular environment. The growth was limited to what evolution required and it was not subject to development by individual behaviour. This is because evolutionary theory applies not so much to the survival or development of individual beings during their lifetimes as to the interaction between whole species over hundreds of thousands of years at the very least. The survival of individuals was arbitrary and uncertain and their internal development was dependent on good fortune, health, wellbeing and the chance avoidance of sudden death. The advent of intelligent beings made it possible to transcend arbitrary evolutionary progress and substitute much more rapid cultural progress, as is outlined in part six on *The Emergence of Complexity by Dualist Interaction*. This complexifying progress was accelerated by the advent of language by which notions of self became possible.

The interactive culture of an intelligent species makes possible the growth and development of inner being in a way that was hitherto not possible. This is because the individual assumes a role in self-development that is not possible in less culturally based species. As a result of our interactive culture, the inner being's growth in complexity has so far reached an apogee with us so that we greatly excel all other known animals in that respect. The prospect of such growth were greatly facilitated by using notions of self, ego or I by which inner being can refer to itself and differentiate itself at the same time. Self-identity or the ability to identify oneself and to be self-aware arises when inner being turns in on itself to acquire self-awareness. Such notions enhance our interactive powers so that we can relate ourselves more constantly and accurately to our environment. In short, the notion of self facilitates inner being's further development.

I can exist all alone and thinking only for myself, but this is a stunted existence for any human being since we are born to be sociable beings. I exist especially in my interacting with other people in a social context. My life acquires more meaning and intensity as a result. My solitary thinking is meaningless unless it is preparatory to interchange with other people through the spoken or written word. I definitely know I exist because of the feedback relationships which I have with friends, relatives, neighbours, colleagues, and so on. In this way, sociability is essential to our humanness. This is an adjunct of the principle: *I interact therefore I exist*. I simply do not fully as a human personality unless I am constantly interacting with other people.

Our place in society also requires us to acquire abstract notions such as truth, beauty, justice, rights, obligations and the rule of law. We interact with these evaluative notions, as they are here called, to arrive at a better understanding of the role we must play in society. They become part of how we view ourselves and what we are as persons. Thus, such evaluative notions play an important role in socialising us.

4. The variations in self-awareness

While self-awareness is important for our survival and for the development of our personalities, the self is not always self-conscious. We have in common with other animals a capacity for *unselfconsciousness* in which we are immersed in our experiences and unaware of our being distinct from these experiences. In this state of mind we concentrate totally on what we are doing at the moment and we are not conscious of ourselves doing what we are doing. Perhaps, we are in this state of mind most of the time. This aspect of the self accompanies the original development of perception by which we interact with our environment to produce our apprehensions of external reality and its contents. We perceive things without necessarily being conscious that we are doing so. In such cases, we are not self-referentially aware of ourselves, though we are interacting with whatever we are doing or concentrating upon.

The importance of the notion of self lies in making *self-identity* possible. Animals lack the language and conceptual ability to be aware of their actions as being their own, at least to the extent that we are. We can predicate things of ourselves because we have a notion of self by which we can identify deeds as being our own. By self-identity we make things our own. We are able to identify ourselves as something that thinks, acts or feels. This personal identity aspect of the self refers to our ability to interact with our own thoughts which we can own or disown as being ideal or not ideal, truthful or not truthful, and so on.

In our social interactions, we learn to identify ourselves with others. A *social self* develops by which we share our experiences with other people whom we believe to have self-consciousness like our own. In understanding what other people think and feel, we begin to understand ourselves better when we see ourselves in the mirror which other people present to us in their attempts to understand or misunderstand us. This aspect takes us beyond mere self-identity and towards being social persons who have their own place in society. It enables us to interact with others in a social setting, that is to say, what is here called the *sociosphere*.

Another important development lies in our ability to contextualise or put things into context. Our ability to place ourselves in different contexts, perspectives and outlooks allows us to see things from different perspectives. In this way, the self avoids being wrapped up entirely in itself. We have no need to humble human beings in relation to a divine perspective which is beyond our ken. We need only to see things from a higher perspective which nevertheless remains entirely our own. Contexts are therefore important in broadening our viewpoints. We also need to contextualise ourselves in the course of our self-development. As we develop our personalities, a *contextual* aspect emerges in which the self operates within contexts and perspectives. We enter into contexts and perspectives when we act as agents who change things for better or for worse in pursuing our goals, aims, ambitions, desires, motivations, and so on

By entering into those contexts and perspectives we are taken beyond mere self-centredness and become more restrained and sociable persons than otherwise. The cultivation of this aspect of the self is important in helping us to be more thoughtful, less selfish, more focused and less narrow-minded. In showing how we get beyond ourselves and our immediate concerns and experiences, this theory counters the view that only religion can take us out of ourselves. Ultimately, this aspect involves ascertaining our place in the overall scheme of things. . Only by operating within these contexts and perspectives can we ascribe meaning to all our activities. For context-free existence is also a meaningless one. Outside all contexts there are no focal points. I cannot make sense of a word or image that occurs to me unless I can put them into context by remembering the experiences to which I can relate them.

In dualist theory, our self-development necessarily includes all three aspects referred to above – unselfconsciousness, personal identity and contextualisation. (1) We often act unselfconsciously without losing touch with whatever ends we are pursuing, for example, in driving a car successfully to one's destination without being entirely conscious of what one is doing while driving. (2) Our personal identity is important in keeping us on track so that our resolve does not weaken. (3) By putting ourselves into different perspectives we can observe ourselves as 'impartial spectators'. As Smith put it: "We endeavour to examine our own conduct as we imagine any other fair and impartial spectator would examine it."[102] This gives us automatic feedback on our social performances. By constant dualist interaction, these three aspects contribute to a unified personality which is required to enable us work out the meaning and purpose of our lives. These three aspects interact to give us self-development. Without the unifying influence of the unified self, these three aspects of the self are potentially incompatible with each other. They are at loggerheads with each other without the unifying ends and purposes towards which only the whole self can aim.

5. The content of subjectivity

We are the subject of our experiences when we are aware of ourselves experiencing them as something distinct from ourselves. Subjectivity consists in the subjective experiences that result from the unified mental and physical processes underlying these experiences. Our self-identity emerges from the flow of these processes feeding back into themselves to form a unity which is ourselves being aware of our experiences and what we do with them. Consciousness in this context involves our being aware of ourselves (1) as a subject experiencing whatever happens to us and (2) as a subject making objects

---

[102] Adam Smith, *The Theory of Moral Sentiments*, (1759 - London: Henry G. Bohn, 1853), Part Iii, Ch. I, p.162.

of these experiences and making more of them than they were originally experienced to be. We experience subjective events, conduct mental acts, and have objective outcomes such as are listed below:

Subjective Events	Mental Acts	Objective Outcomes
sensations	perceiving	perceptions
feelings	judging	conceptions
thoughts	thinking	notions
ideas	teasoning	opinions
insights	deciding	imaginations
intuitions	remembering	decisions
desires	calculating	goals
impulses	predicting	aims
images	imagining	contexts
dreams	contextualising	perspectives
opinions	theorising	theories

Lists of Subjective Events, Mental Acts, and Objective Outcomes

These lists are not intended to be exhaustive or exact. They exemplify what is meant by 'subjective events', 'mental acts', and 'objective outcomes'. But their contents are not hard and fast, and no horizontal correlation is necessarily intended between these words. 'Thoughts' for instance could be the outcome of thinking acts rather than the 'thoughts' which occur to us intuitively without conscious thinking. The purpose of these lists is clarify our thinking about what we do and how inner being brings experiences to our attention and makes them seem to belong to us until we actively objectify them by subsequent mental acts.

This theory of subjectivity implies that subjective events are the immediate product of inner being that unifies the physical events and makes them available to us at a conscious level. The theory shows us how subjectivity relates interactively to objectivity. When subjective events occur, we interact with them by subjecting them to mental acts, which we perform if we so will. For example, one may experience a slight ache and choose either to ignore it or to pay attention to it. Subsequently, mental acts produce objective outcomes of one sort or another and, in this case, one notices where the ache is located in one's body. These outcomes in turn give rise to more subjective events so that there is potentially no end to this cyclical flow of consciousness. Mental acts such as perceiving and theorising themselves provide materials which emerge in our ideas, insights and intuitions, sometimes in *eureka!* fashion. In this way, there is a constant feedback of information from mental acts into the unconscious wherein the information is reprocessed to produce these ongoing subjective events.

This means that there is a movement from one to many and *vice versa*. Subjective events are presented to us as unified experiences by unconscious processes usually inaccessible to us. Each event is a simple unity of things that happens to us all at once, but in our subsequent mental acts we make many things out of that unity in examining the content of these experiences. In this way, we move constantly from the one to the many and *vice versa* in our thoughts and in our thinking of them. Such experiences cannot be reduced to anything physical since they subsist entirely in the mental *milieu*.

These subjective events are more than the sum of their contents. They *supervene* their material substratum to present us, for instance, with a three dimensional image imposed on a two dimensional picture. We see trees standing in the background of a painting even though they are just blotches on the painting's surface. There is nothing corresponding to them in the external world, apart from these blotches. The trees are entirely in the mind. They supervene their physical existence in the way that we subjectively experience them. This process of supervention is the product of inner being which makes the latter seem to be more than just physical events occurring in the brain. They are nevertheless physical events that we experience subjectivity. These holistic experiences cannot be reduced to the physical events in the brain that cause them because they are part of our very being which makes us more than mere material entities. This process of supervention thus forms part of the feedback process described by the *Principle of Self-Reference* because we can identify ourselves with the subjectivity of these experiences while using them at the same time to distinguish ourselves from external reality.

Undoubtedly, our real thinking processes are even more complex and less clear cut than the processes implied by this theory of subjectivity. It cannot be the whole story. But the theory gives us a way of understanding these processes so that we can be more introspectively in touch with ourselves if we so wish. It also shows how a constant build-up of skills, capacities, knowledge and understanding takes place within ourselves to make us what we are as unique personalities. In that respect, this hypothesis forms an important part of this theory because it accounts for the uniqueness of our mental processes as opposed to the materiality of brain processes underlying these processes.

In summary, therefore, the table above helps us to clarify what subjectivity is in relation to objectivity, and it shows how the former cannot be reduced to the latter. Our conscious mental acts also transform immediate experiences into something distinct from any physical antecedents or analogues. The self or 'I' is conscious of its mental acts and of the products of subjective activity but not of the processes by which these products germinate in the unconscious. The original and unpredictable way in which subjective material is put together in the unconscious, gives us our creative thoughts, insights, illuminations and so on.

6. The reality of self

The reality with which the self is confronted is independent of its own existence. Its independence is constantly confirmed by the whole experience of the self. In other words, we are embedded in a reality which is not of our making and of which we are not a permanent part. The reality we experience within ourselves is a function of everything in our lives and nothing in our lives makes any sense unless we acknowledge the fact of reality's ultimate independence no matter what we say or do about it.

Our apprehension of the content of external reality depends on constant dualist interaction with that reality by means of perception, conception and other mental abilities. What really exists is not entirely in the mind when we can confirm its existence by constantly looking, listening, asking, reading, researching, experimenting or other activities required to satisfy ourselves beyond reasonable doubt of the existence of anything. Subjectivity has its objectivity, and objectivity has its subjectivity only in this constant interaction. We eliminate the subjective element only to the extent of reducing the interference of our personal feelings. What we believe to be entirely objective nevertheless involved our feelings at some level, even if it is only our rational passions such as interest and involvement. But the self are still involved in all our experiences of reality because our consciousness of the independence of that reality is always present. Only the self can be conscious or aware of itself.

Such interactions between our subjective experiences and objective responses enable us to build up our mental skills and abilities. Our genius, originality, and uniqueness result from our personalities being complexified in this way. Our slightly different genetic inheritance combined with slightly different experiences and ways of conceptualising these experiences give us a unique and irreplaceable view of things. Thus, the uniqueness of the personality results from such constant interactions. Outstanding geniuses are those who are more developed and integrated in their internal organisation than most of us. They are able to accomplish much more and in greater depth because their subjective experiences are more sublime, transcendent, and all-encompassing.

These interacting feedback processes also describe how we build up our conceptual or notional view of things. By these means we acquire more detail concerning how we built up this view and how we reach truth by interacting with evaluative notions. We use these notions to evaluate things and build up our judgments and opinions of them and their worth to ourselves and others. In that way, by interacting with abstract notions we build up our judging abilities. We then have the conceptual tools to criticise and improve ourselves.

The point is that these mental processes are entirely our own. They reflect our own subjective idiosyncrasies. We don't need external influences to account for our creative activity or our internal development. Deities, demons, angels or aliens have nothing to do with it. Such imaginary entities only give us a false idea of our own capabilities. Being mere human beings, we will always fall short of divine perfection. But on the whole we can keep faith with ourselves if we are genuinely doing the best we can.

7. The processes of personal interactivity

There are four integral processes necessary to this dualist theory of self and these are as follows. *Firstly,* an interactive, dualist process saves subjectivity from a self-serving solipsism. *Secondly,* the self-referential process of subjectivity builds up its content and presents us with ever more complex intuitions which are tried and tested in relation to external reality. *Thirdly,* the universal notions of truth, justice, beauty etc., are used evaluatively to understand how our feelings and attitudes relate to the external world and its contents. We thereby reach out to the world and create a microcosm within ourselves by interacting with it in our own minds. *Fourthly,* we thus enter into all the contexts, perspectives and viewpoints referred to in this book. They take us out of ourselves and ensure that we are not always thinking of ourselves. We learn to place value on things that are above and below our immediate concerns. Thus, these four integral processes of *self-reference, dualist interaction, evaluation by evaluative notions,* and *contextual scene-setting* are the fundamental to this theory because our understanding of them contributes to our enlightenment concerning ourselves and our place in the universe.

These processes help us to develop our *personal integrity* as they are integral to the complexification of our personalities. Without them we cannot integrate our experiences and make them our own. With them we can build ourselves within to cope more effectively with all the challenges of life. We can then be ourselves without relying on outside influences to dictate to us what we should do with our lives or how we should behave. Thus, self-enlightenment results from actively developing ourselves from within. The relationship between the integral processes in achieving self-enlightenment is shown as follows:

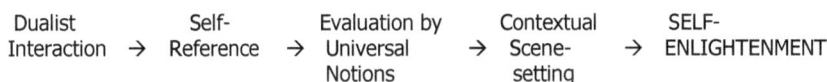

Dualist Interaction		Self-Reference		Evaluation by Universal Notions		Contextual Scene-setting		SELF-ENLIGHTENMENT
	→		→		→		→	

A Procession of Interactive Processes

All the notions of inner identity, such as myself, I or me, mind or even soul, result from the interplay of these integral processes in so far as they are under the control of my will. If they are not under the control of my will, then I am subjected to them rather than controlling them. I must ever strive to be the subject of these notions rather than the object of them. Thus, I cannot be myself unless there is feedback confirming that I am what I am and that I can do what I can do. Who I am to myself is constantly confirmed by my thinking about and doing things with which I can identify myself. Unless these feedback processes refer back to that inner identity, we lose control of them and thus of our very identity. If we fail to use these processes in a purposeful fashion to fulfil our reasoned goals then we are at their mercy. Without these processes our thoughts and actions are products of random chance rather than of integrated thinking. This illustrates the importance of self-control in sustaining our self-identity and the integrity of our personalities.

The purposeful use of these integral processes is reflected in the infinite variability of personality development. The variety of that development is inherently unpredictable. How we develop as persons in relation to our experiences cannot be predicted from a mere examination of genetic or DNA content. The latter contributes to personality development without determining it in absolute terms. As already mentioned, identical twins can develop radically different personalities in spite of being genetically identical. They can develop different sexual orientations, thus disproving the assumption that sexual orientation must be genetically determined.

Thus, understanding such terms as 'subjectivity' and 'objectivity' in this integrative and interactive way, contributes to our introspective powers. We are better able to examine our inner functioning and to become more at one with ourselves. We are concerned particularly with subjectivity since that side of the interaction has been neglected during the twentieth century. The reasons for that neglect are worth discussing in themselves as they throw light on the philosophical mistakes resulting from that neglect.

8. The build-up of the personality

It is clear that we can account for the way that we develop ourselves internally to achieve our highest purposes without resorting to gods, angels, aliens or the rest. We can ask such questions as: "How do we become what we are?" "How do we build ourselves up to become viable human beings?" "What is it to be subjective and unrealistic in our thinking as opposed to being objective and impersonal in our thinking?' But they are all answerable by showing how we move from an internalised subjectivity to an externalised objectivity and *vice versa*, and thereby build up our personalities by interacting with our environment, other people, society, and so on. At least four aspects of the self are relevant to this interactive study of the self and they are outlined as follows:

A. *The Unselfconscious Aspect* in which the self is immersed in its experiences and is unaware of its being distinct from these experiences. In this state of mind we concentrate totally on what we are doing at the moment and are not conscious of ourselves. Perhaps we share this unselfconscious aspect with all living creatures, and most of us are in this state of mind most of the time. It is what Hume means in saying "when I enter most intimately into what I call *myself*, I always stumble on some particular perception or other, of heat or cold, light or shade, love or hatred, pain or pleasure."[103] This aspect of the self accompanies the development of perception by which we interact with our environment to produce our apprehensions of external reality and its contents. In this aspect, self-awareness is identical with what we are doing in external reality. In a sense, we become ourselves in immersing ourselves in this manner.

B. *The Self-Identity Aspect* in which we know ourselves to be thinking, feeling or doing. This is a self-referential aspect which takes us beyond the abilities of other

---

[103] Cf. David Hume, *A Treatise of Human Nature*, 1739 - ed. Nidditch - Oxford: the Clarendon Press, 1978, Book I, Part IV, Section VI, p. 252. Thus, from this analytical, reductionist point of view, the self is "nothing but a bundle or collection of different perceptions . . ."

living beings in so far as we can refer back to ourselves and be self-conscious of what we are thinking or doing. Animals lack the language and conceptual ability to be aware of their actions as being their own, at least to the extent that we are. We can predicate things of ourselves because we have a notion of self by which we can identify deeds as being our own. We are able to identify ourselves as something that thinks, acts or feels. Kant calls this the 'I' that thinks and can become an object to itself.[104] We achieve our 'personal identity' by comparing ourselves at present with our past memories.[105] As Thomas Reid put it:

> I am not thought, I am not action, I am not feeling; I am something that thinks, and acts, and suffers. My thoughts and actions, and feelings, change every moment—they have no continued, but a successive existence; but that *self* or *I*, to which they belong, is permanent, and has the same relation to all the succeeding thoughts, actions, and feelings, which I call mine.[106]

This aspect of the self refers to our ability to interact with our own thoughts which we can own or disown as being ideal or not ideal. But the permanence of the self depends very much on the continuation of interaction which must persist undaunted till we die.

C. *The Social Self Aspect* which we share with other people whom we assume to have self-consciousness like our own. To use Adam Smith's phrase again, this is an 'impartial spectator' aspect by which we learn to see ourselves as others see us.[107] In understanding what other people think and feel, we begin to understand ourselves better when we see ourselves in the mirror which other people present to us in their attempts to understand or misunderstand us. This aspect takes us beyond mere self-identity and towards being social persons who have their own place in society. It enables us to interact with others in a social setting, that is to say, what is here called the sociosphere.

D. *The Contextual Self Aspect* which refers to the operation of the self within contexts and perspectives. We enter into contexts and perspectives when we act as agents who change things for better or for worse by pursuing his or her goals, aims, ambitions, desires, motivations, and so on. Only by operating within these can we ascribe meaning to all our activities. By entering into those contexts and perspectives which take us beyond mere self-centredness, we can become more restrained and sociable persons than otherwise. The cultivation of this aspect of the self is important in helping us to be more thoughtful, less selfish, more focused and less narrow-minded. This aspect is therefore of particular importance to the development of dualist theory because it concerns how we get

---

[104] Cf. Immanuel Kant, *Critique of Pure Reason*, 1787, B155, trans. N. Kemp Smith, (London: Macmillan, 1964), p.167.

[105] Cf. John Locke, *An Essay Concerning Human Understanding*, Book II, ch. XXVII, §18, ed. P. H. Nidditch, (1700 - Oxford: Clarendon Press, 1988), pp. 341-342.

[106] Thomas Reid,p. 345a.

[107] Cf. Adam Smith, *The Theory of Moral Sentiments*, (1759 - London: Henry G. Bohn, 1853), Part III, ch. IV, p.221.

beyond ourselves and our immediate concerns and experiences. Ultimately, this aspect involves ascertaining our place in the overall scheme of things, so that we are interacting within the domain of the cosmos, as herein defined.

The contextual aspect of the self includes all three of the aspects above in the following way: (1) We often act unselfconsciously without losing touch with whatever ends we are pursuing, for example, in driving a car successfully to one's destination without being entirely conscious of what one is doing while driving. (2) Our personal identity is important in keeping us on track so that our resolve does does not weaken. (3) Being able to observe ourselves as 'impartial spectators' gives us automatic feedback on our social performances. But these three aspects are wrapped up into a unified personality by means of the contextual aspect which helps us to work out the meaning and purpose of our lives.

Without this contextual aspect, the other aspects of the self are potentially incompatible with each other. These aspects can be at loggerheads with each other without the unifying ends and purposes towards which the whole self can aim. The contextual nature of the self as agent is discussed in more detail in my unpublished works. Here we are concerned with the dualist interactions by which the self builds itself up in relation to its environment. We don't amount to anything except in our interacting constantly with our environment, other people, ideas and society in general.

My existence doesn't just depend on my thinking or experiencing things - as in Descartes' *cogito ergo sum* - I am thinking therefore I am.[108] As already suggested, *I am interacting therefore I exist* - is more accurate from a dualist point of view, I understand myself better in thinking of myself as an interacting entity and not just a thinking entity. After all, if I do not respond at all to events in and around me then I am nothing to myself. Making an end out of such a 'nirvana' is a life scarcely worth living, though Buddhists seem to think a lot of it. Meditative techniques have their place but, as ends in themselves, they can only enslave us obsessively. Indeed, they may become a head-in-the-sand excuse for not doing positive things in the real world.

In summary, therefore, I exist especially in my interacting with other people in a social context. My life acquires more meaning and intensity as a result. My solitary thinking is meaningless unless it is preparatory to interchange with other people through the spoken or written word. I definitely know I exist because of the feedback relationships which I have with friends, relatives, neighbours, colleagues, and so on. By existing only for myself, I become less than myself.

The emergence of these four aspects of the self is illustrated in a rudimentary way in the following diagram:

---

[108] Descartes, *Discours de la Méthode*, 1637 - Paris: Garnier-Flammarion, 1966, Quartième Partie, p. 60 - *"je pense, donc je suis."* Bernard Williams translates 'cogito' as 'I am thinking': cf. *Descartes: The Project of Pure Enquiry*, London: Penguin, 1978, p.73.

```
┌──────────────────────────────────────────────┐
│  C   o   n   t   e   x   t   u   a   l   S  e  l  f │
│  ↑  ┌────────────────────────────────────┐  ↑  │
│  │  │  S   o   c   i   a   l   S   e   l  f │  │  │
│  │  │  ↑ ┌──────────────────────────┐ ↑ │  │  │
│  │  │  │ │  S e l f - I d e n t i t y │ │ │  │  │
│  │  │  │ │ ↑ ┌──────────────────┐ ↑ │ │ │  │  │
│  │  │  │ │ │ │  Self-Awareness  │ │ │ │ │ │  │  │
│  │  │  │ │ │ │    ↑      ↑      │ │ │ │ │ │  │  │
│  │  │  │ │ │ │    │      │      │ │ │ │ │ │  │  │
│  │  │  │ │ │ │    ↓      ↓      │ │ │ │ │ │  │  │
│  │  │  │ │ │ │ External Reality │ │ │ │ │ │  │  │
│  │  │  │ │ ↓ └──────────────────┘ ↓ │ │ │  │  │
│  │  │  │ │  I   d   e   a   l   i   t  y │ │ │  │  │
│  │  │  ↓ └──────────────────────────┘ ↓ │  │  │
│  │  │  S   o   c   i   o   s   p   h   e  r  e │  │  │
│  │  └────────────────────────────────────┘  │  │
│  ↓  C     o     s     m     o     s  ↓  │
└──────────────────────────────────────────────┘
```

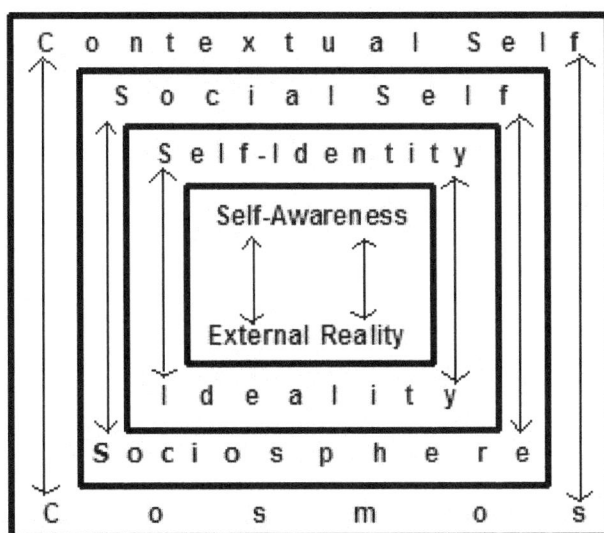

In understanding our own inner battles, it is helpful to imagine each of these four aspects of the self waging war within the contexts of external reality, ideality, sociosphere and cosmos to assert and develop themselves. These contexts are always threatening to overwhelm us since their content originates outwith ourselves.

A. *Self-awareness* is ever in danger of losing itself in externalities, and it is forever battling to maintain itself within the external context. This occurs, for example, when circumstances spiral out of control and we have difficulty keeping on top of them.

B. *Self-identity* does not come peacefully into the world but through a struggle to establish itself within the subjective chaos of ideality. In fearful situations, our imagination can run away with itself and we are liable to lose touch with reality.

C. *Social self* must fight to assert itself amid the competing voices of the sociosphere. If we are not to lose our individuality entirely, we must strive to be true to ourselves and maintain a haven of harmony within us.

D. *Contextual self* has an overall battle of cosmic proportions to establish itself in the broadest possible context. In battling to keep in touch with ourselves as a whole, we become the cosmos at large. Our integrity depends on our encompassing everything in our lives so that we become ourselves and behave ourselves well in all circumstances.

We alternately identify ourselves with and differentiate ourselves from whatever we are interacting with. We have complete control over this process as long as we do not identify ourselves totally with something other than ourselves or differentiate ourselves completely from that thing. Being stuck at the extremes often means lapsing into dogmatism, inflexibility, vagueness, empty-headedness, or whatever.

To reiterate, therefore, the self exists as active agent while it is interacting with itself, its experiences, its surroundings, other people, books, computers, television, iphones, ipods, kindles and so on. In continually looking around us and listening intently, we are interacting with our surroundings. Indeed, all our purposeful and meaningful activity involves our responding to something or other and when we respond to the subsequent response we are interacting. Thus, this interacting is the basis of our consciousness, which ceases to exist when we stop interacting, as in a deep coma or death. Moreover, our will involves an ability to interact by wilfully moving from one activity to its related counterpart. It is the unified effect of the self in carrying out its aims, desires, and aspirations. When we fail to achieve our aims, this supplies us with the feedback to define the limits of our will.

This interactive approach to understanding the self helps us to deal with the illusory nature of the 'I' which so preoccupied Kant.[109] For instead of 'I think', it is '*I interact*' that becomes the basic unit of both rational and empirical psychology. Thinking is only one form of interacting; we interact also through sight, touch, hearing, tasting, and smelling. This bridges the yawning gap between the rational and the empirical. To be thinking about what we are tasting involves a range of interactions that include reason and experience in an unbroken chain of interactions. Thus, in this interpretation, the activities of self can both objectively subjective and objectively subjective at the same time.

The 'I', 'self', 'will', 'soul' and such like notions require no empirical evidence for their existence. Our constant interactions in alternately identifying and distinguishing ourselves with and from that which is other than ourselves, ensures that we get to know ourselves and our limitations. Such notions are not substances as they refer to internal interactive processes by which we constantly stay in touch with ourselves and cope with the complexities of external reality. Thus, we shall see that this interplay of identifying and distinguishing things forms a better basis (1) for the so-called laws of identity and contradiction and (2) for logic, than is laid down, for instance, in Aristotle's *Organon*.[110]

The starting point for all our interactions is always our subjective experiences. We are passive beings in the subjective events such as sensations, pains, ideas and the like. We make objects of them in thinking about them. The subjecting part of the self involves our being distinct, if only momentarily, from that with which we are interacting, for example, when a thought, idea, or impulse strikes us. They are distinct from us in their first occurring to us but they rapidly become at one with us when we make sense of them in relation to our experiences as a whole. Thus, this theory of self enables us to think of ourselves in purely interactive terms and therefore as free agents in that respect.

---

[109] Cf Kant's 'Paralogisms of Pure Reason', *Critique of Pure Reason*, 1787, B399 onward, trans. N. Kemp Smith, London: Macmillan, 1964, p. 328f.

[110] Aristotle's *Organon* of course comprises the six books, *Categoriae, De Interpretatione, Analytica Priora, Analytica Posteriora, Topica,* and *De Sophisticis Elenchis*.

9. Using this theory of the self

Firstly, understanding ourselves helps us to understand others. We can use this theory to understand in general terms what it is to be other people without actually experiencing what it is to be someone else. It gives us common ground by which to compare our subjective experiences and perhaps those of other intelligent beings. We assume that other people are interacting with their thoughts and feelings in roughly the same way as us. We are justified in that assumption because we know how we would interact in the same circumstances. We see people interacting in the same way and judge them to be experiencing similar interactions as ourselves.

But this common ground is strictly limited because we cannot actually *be* the other person and experience what they are experiencing. We are all the same in being different and we are all different in roughly the same ways. This is just as well since the reductionist programme implies that there are no essential differences between the mental events experienced by one person and another, and that everybody's experiences are reducible to elements which are common to everybody. If this were true then we would have no need to communicate with each other but simply work out by logical and mathematical deduction what other people are experiencing. Such machine-like uniformity or 'artificial intelligence' is surely the converse of what life is all about, for example, its spontaneity and diversity, and the pleasure of living from minute to minute.

Secondly, interactive tools enable us to achieve greater self-realisation. The aim of this theory is to provide the interactive tools to evaluate and improve our behaviour so that we can demonstrably do the best we can. Thus, the next level in our quest for self-realisation is to use these tools to arrive at the best possible goals and purposes available to us. These tools include the primary contexts and perspectives, which enable us to broaden our opinions and understanding of things. We thereby rationalise our actions so that they acquire a value and meaning which goes beyond them.

Thirdly, we must also ensure that we face up to realities. Increasing self-knowledge is to no avail if it does not mean clarifying goals and facing realities. In building up one's personality or character the complexity of subjective output grows relative to objective realisation and *vice versa*. The interactivity of the subjective and objective processes means that they may refer to the same things depending on what we are doing with them. In this way, internal confusion is avoided and our personal integrity is preserved. This theory of the self is ultimately all about preserving and promoting personal integrity.

Fourthly, contexts and perspectives also develop the self. Every goal or aspiration aims beyond itself and thus enters a context or perspective which incorporates it. In helping other people, we see things from their perspective which is incorporated into ourselves to feel and think as these people do. Helping other people often means benefiting the human race as a whole, whether we consciously aim to do so or not. In this way our aims and goals are elevated and made sense of instead of merely being our own selfish ambitions and aspirations.

For at each level we must go beyond the current context to judge and evaluate our actions from a more incorporating context. In this way we remain true to ourselves and to the ultimate truths towards which we are all striving, one way or another. In so doing we understand the contexts within which our best choices are arrived at and our most relevant judgments made. Contexts are thus important in taking us out of ourselves and making us less selfish and self-centred, as is exemplified by the attributes mentioned below.

Fifthly, knowing ourselves is essential in a complex society. Understanding ourselves is the key to understanding our place in the universe. If you are not at one with your thought processes, you are out of touch with yourself, even though we need not be complete charge of them from one second to the next. External events are overwhelming instead of interesting and diverting; you have no time to understand what it occurs in the universe at large. Knowing yourself is even more important today than it was in ancient times since our complex world presents us with bewildering choices. It means examining our presuppositions, motivations and inclinations with the aim of becoming a more effective person in the real world.

10. The power of intuition

The self is nothing without intuition. The very uniqueness of the human personality is most displayed most clearly in the eccentric intuitions that can occur to any of us at any time. Intuitive thoughts and ideas come to us and we constantly act intuitively in response to them. It may be a sudden decision to go on holiday; it may involve falling in love at first sight; it may an idea of starting a business. Whatever it is, our intuitions can change our lives though not necessarily for the better. Intuition also means doing things automatically without having to think about them. We know not where these intuitions come from but we assume they are the product of unconscious thinking. They exemplify the power of intuition in enabling us to function effectively and enjoy life to the full.

Intuitions can result from both conscious and unconscious activity. They are the product of inner being or our internal mental activity which can be accessed consciously. Inner being gives rise to the intuitions, thoughts, ideas, feelings and impulses that come to us all of a sudden without any conscious prompting on our part. Intuition is the primary expression of the potential of being and doing. They are generated either consciously or unconsciously. They result consciously when we interact dualistically with our experiences to produce intuitions which are a holistic grasping of our experiences. We become intuitively conscious of them as a whole. They are experienced as one thing or facet that influences our being and doing. When intuitions are generated by unconscious mental activity they come to us all at once as a result of that activity. They are *a priori* products of thought as compared with the *a posteriori* products that make something more of what is given *a priori*.

What is here meant by 'intuition' is variously called by philosophers 'immediate experience', 'intentional object', 'the given', '*a priori*', 'self-evident truth or principle', or 'common sense principle.' Intuition involves what is implied by all of these things depending on the context in which it is used. It also refers to the unconscious, psychological activity underlying these notions. What is given here is a phenomenological account of what it is involved in intuition from the point of view of dualist interaction.

The first intuition experienced by us is that of a goal, aim or end towards which our being and doing is directed. A feeling of hunger strikes us and we then aim to assuage that hunger by eating something. We interact with the feeling and act accordingly. Goals are derived *primarily* from intuitions governed by the inner being and the genetic influences that underlie inner being. These intuitions may take the form of instincts, impulses, whims, inclinations, feelings, habits, routines and similar activities which are not the result of conscious awareness, rational thought or verbal deliberation. They are the product of holistic processes that emerge from inner being. They *mean* something to us so that our inner being has the goal of bringing that meaning to our conscious attention. The meaning is not necessarily verbal but forms an immediate realisation. The intuition is thus the unified product of inspirited activity that makes us aware of what the intuition means to us immediately and without prior notification. A stab of pain makes its presence felt immediately so that we have no doubt of what it means to us. Exclamations such as 'Ouch!' are used to express or communicate our discomfort to others.

Goals originate *secondarily* in the reasoning powers of life-forms of sufficient complexity to be self-aware. Either we decide to do things on a whim and without thinking about them or we do so deliberately by consciously and rationally making up our minds to do them. In this section, we are concerned with goals that are subjectively experienced as intuitions occurring to the living being. The use of reason in forming and executing our goals is dealt with more detail in parts eight and nine of this book.

Our intuitions put us immediate touch with physical reality by means of perception and conception. When these involve images or the sense impressions of hearing, touch and feeling, these are given by genetically inherited processes. We make more of these by the thinking processes that are developed by means language and other abstract symbols. Intuitions produced by these processes are no less immediate since they are produced by habit and routines that have become unconscious and automatic in their functioning. These often considered to be 'rules' but they are generally not hard and fast and can be changed through experience and trial and error.

Other animals are subject to intuition in that they conscious in being aware of what they are doing but not of themselves doing it. Not having a concept of self they cannot identify themselves with whatever they are doing. They may choose to do or not to do something but they lack knowledge of why they are doing it because they have no awareness of themselves doing or not doing it. In short, they do things randomly or instinctively without further thought. Even if an animal seems to recognise itself in a mirror, it cannot understand the process by which its physical form is reflected back to it as it lacks the concepts by which to arrive at such an understanding. It is therefore doubtful whether it could ever experience the reflection in anything like the complexity that we enjoy.

11. The expression of intuition

Intuitions are expressed in a variety of ways. They are first experienced directly and are only subsequently brought before consciousness and expressed in some way. They expressed in a variety of ways of which verbal expression is only one, and it is not necessarily the most important. They are also expressed in our immediate feelings, facial expressions, hand gestures or some such action which is inwardly or outwardly expressed. Intuitions are also expressed in being thought about, concentrated on, felt intensely, undergone or carried out. In expressing intuitions we either do nothing with them or interact with them to make something of them. For instance, we may approve or disapprove of them. Ultimately, everything in life depends on what we make or do not make of our intuitions since by themselves they are not reliable guides to truth and reality.

However, when we express our intuitions verbally, the result is always inexact. We often strive to find the right words but the words may never be enough to express what we feel or think intuitively. We arrive at only approximate descriptions since words and symbols are insufficient to reproduce these intuitions in the immediate way that they are experienced by us. We are cribbed crammed and confined by the ways of expressing ourselves given by the culture we live. Moreover, we are liable often to be misunderstood. In speaking our minds concerning what we think, we must put our intuitions into words and symbols which are communicable to other people. Such assertions are immediately open to analysis, criticism, examination or elaboration of some kind. A command assertion is of course not open in that way as it is meant to be acted upon without question or criticism.

This inaccuracy of verbal expression can also apply to mathematics. The precision of mathematical calculations, proofs and formulae may not be sufficient to overcome the limitations of words and symbols in expressing intuitions. Greater precision does not necessarily represent external reality with any absolute or infallible accuracy. Practical mathematics can be applied with reliable exactitude when it is used in strictly limited circumstances where it is shown to work reliably. But pure mathematics often exists in the world of its own, divorced from complexities of the physical world. Even the science of physics becomes divorced from reality when it seeks aesthetically pleasing formulae regardless of whether they are shown to apply to the real world. For example, the idea of multiple universes may have mathematical appeal but the evidence of their real existence may more difficult to find. Physics then enters the context of mathematics and leaves the context of applied science. Also, the words and symbols of ordinary expressions have more communicable value than the absolute precise value offered by mathematics, since they can convey feelings and nuances that cannot be conveyed in mathematical form.

There is moreover no point in analysing and logic chopping our intuitions just for the sake of doing so. They should be analysed only in accordance with our goals. We may criticise our immediate intuitions by submitting them to rigorous logical analysis. But analysis and criticism should not be done for their own sake but to achieve coherence, clarification or elaboration of our intuitions in relation to our overview or outlook so that our account of things makes sense in itself. Above all, our aims in carrying out analysis must justify the extent to which we engage in it.

Intuitions only acquire meaning within contexts. A context-free intuition would be unconnected to consciousness which can only subsist within a context. Our short-term memory depends on our being conscious of an occurrence which would not be retained otherwise. It would be forgotten as soon as it experienced as we remember things only because the context is required to catalogue the experience in one's memory. Remembering a telephone number depends on the need to do so relative to the context in which it is to be used. Moreover, the truth of intuitions may only be ascertained by reference to different contexts to which they may be compared and judged interactively. They acquire meaning in that way which supplies information used to further our goals. Thus, our aim in giving expression to an intuition is to give it meaning and significance in our thinking about it.

Our developed intuitions are those that are built up through experience and have complex unconscious processes underlying their simple, unified apprehension as immediate intuitions. They may take the form of perceptual, conceptual and metaphysical intuitions. They occur to us immediately as a result of cerebral activity that brings our thoughts together into unified understanding or apprehension of something or other.

12. The durability of intuition

Our immediate experience of things and events is intuitive in so far as we don't have to think about or analyse it. External reality is given to us intuitively and is experienced all at once and undivided at any moment in time. This is because our skills for doing so are unconscious and already well learnt. Thus, we normally don't have to think about what we are seeing and hearing and touching because our perceptual skills are so well honed in early childhood. Such intuitions are habitual and automatic unless they let us down and we have to do more than just look, listen or feel. Thus, perceived reality is reliable or not reliable because of the quality of childhood learning. The more perceptual learning we undergo at an early stage the better perception is in adulthood. We can be mistaken or misled by our perceptual organs when in ill-health, facing optical illusions, or when we don't pay attention to the objects of these organs. We have to constantly monitor perceptual activity if we are to keep in touch with reality. We do this by recursively looping back on what is being perceived by us to ascertain with any certainty just what it is we are perceiving at any point in time.

Our perceptual intuitions are immediately given by means of our inherited sense organs. But the intuitions of inner being are also given immediately. The one gives rise to objectivity and the other to subjectivity. Our apprehension of external reality depends on a constant dualist interaction between the intuitions of the senses and the intuitions of inner being. Such an apprehension is also at the root of our consciousness in general.

As already mentioned, perceptual intuitions involve the formation of conceptions about what exists or does not exist in external reality. Thus, conceptual intuition consists in the intuitive reception of conceptions, thoughts, ideas, or notions which are given as objects before the mind. The thought of an impending catastrophe may occur to one intuitively. Its actuality is or is not confirmed later. The actuality of a conceptual intuition is established by evidence, testimony or critical analysis. The reality of an intuition in a system of thought or a context is established by its coherence within that system or context. The external reality of an intuition is established by correspondence involving trial and error, experiment, investigation and other forms of research.

In short, we need to do things with our intuitions other than simply accept them at face value. The potential in any thought is found in grasping it intuitively; whereas its actuality is realised by subsequent analysis of its contents. Analysis means making an object of the thought whereas an act of intuition puts thoughts together anew so that the resulting intuition becomes a subject in itself. Our thoughts turn into themselves to reach a unity which occurs to us all at once. When an idea occurs to us, its centrality is reached by intuition and the intuiting person identifies entirely with it at the moment of grasping it. It is, as it were, himself *per se*. The thought cannot be distinguished from the object of thought in the intuitive event. This is the beingness or the *Dasein* of the intuition. It durates at the moment of intuition and it exists absolutely at the moment of being intuited. It is not established as representing reality but remains a mental chimera. It requires more to be done to it to ensure its relationship to external reality.

When we identify with our ideas by means of intuition, our thoughts turn into themselves to reach a unity of thought that occurs to us all at once. Thus, in intuition, there is no infinite regress that spirals into infinity. Infinite regresses do not occur when there is a recursion of thoughts. Our thoughts are not stuck in a groove as they move forward through time. They form loops as they move on as is illustrated in part eight on *The Logic of Dualist Interaction*. Bergson calls this interval of time '*la durée*' or 'duration'.[111] This duration gives us time to link the past to the future by using past experience to plan for the future. The notion of duration consists in a combination of past experiences linked with the present. For example, the passing of sixty seconds is experienced as a lasting minute when we think of it as being a whole minute that has elapsed. Thus, the thought that we

---

[111] Cf., for example, Henri Bergson, *Time and Freewill: An Essay on the Immediate Data of Consciousness*, translated by F.L. Pogson (from *Essai sur les Données Immédiates de la Conscience*), 1913 (New York: Dover Publications, 2001), Ch. II, pp. 104-105.

have later differs from the previous thought because it takes account of that thought and adds to or subtracts from it in some way.

Clinging to one intuition is to make a god of it – absolute, *Dasein*, duration in the manner of continental philosophy. When philosophers such as Hegel, Bergson and Heidegger build their philosophies round the absolute, duration and *Dasein* respectively, these notions represent their experience of reality with which they are perpetually interacting. They are constantly testing their ideas and concepts in relation to their respective dominant intuition. These notions are names for their thinking about things.

In conclusion, therefore, intuition in dualist theory can only be provisional since it can only be a product of inner being and it must be tested, in an empirical way, to ascertain how things are in reality. Thus, an interaction between inner being and external reality is an important part of dynamic logic. What is here called 'inner being' is the unconscious source of intuitive reasoning. At every level of consciousness, our 'inner being' provides the given material of our acts of perception, imagination, conception, theory and language. This inner being is contrasted with 'external reality' of which we are constantly conscious if we are conscious of anything at all. The products of inner being are always provisional except in so far as they are shown or known to be directly resonant of reality. A constant interaction with the realities of the outside world is therefore implied in all dynamic accounts of that world and its contents.

While we are awake and alert, our brains are constantly working away and keeping us in touch with external reality through what we see and hear and feel. We are not usually aware of the constancy of this brain activity. It constitutes our inner being, and we attend to its products in apprehending the contents of reality. Thus, the act of attending to what is given in reality involves interactions with that reality and we are not entirely aware of all the interactions that are occurring. What is immediately given to our senses may not be what is actually there as our sensory processes are largely unconscious and are not infallible. Thus, we may make mistakes in not seeing what is really there, as in optical illusions. We constantly seek secure knowledge of what is really there to correct the mistakes and distortions due to the inadequacy of our sensory equipment. This is done by our interrogation of reality which amounts to a constant interaction with it. Such an interrogation may involve a dynamic account which is a subject for the next part on *The Logic of Dualist Interaction*.

Book Three

Exploratory

Part Eight
The Logic of Dualist Interaction

1. The basis of dynamic logic

The logic of dualist interaction is a dynamic logic in which we interact dynamically with the world to arrive at ongoing accounts that are provisional and not absolute. Dynamic logic is holistic in that it takes an overall view that includes inductive as well as deductive reasoning. It is fluid, personal and intuitive compared with formal logic that deals in a fixed way with the form of our arguments. It is therefore dynamic in the sense that it is time-related and moves on from one moment to the next to keep in touch with realities or the way things are. It reflects the constant effort that we must make to face realities and function effectively in the world. It generates dynamic accounts that take account of things as a whole in a constant and unending quest for truth.

Dynamic logic is innovative in its inclusion of both deduction and induction, that is to say, both deductive reasoning from general statements to particular instances, and inductive reasoning from particular instances to generalisations, hypotheses or theories. It gives the lie to the traditional view that deductive logic is somehow more accurate and produces certainties whereas inductive reasoning is less accurate and produces only possibilities. A Great Schism has arisen in western thinking because these two ways of reasoning are treated differently and in comparative isolation from each other. Dynamic logic is a way of bringing them together dualistically and interactively.

The traditional view is that inductive reasoning produces theories and hypotheses by generalising from particular instances. But generalisations of all kinds result from intuition first and foremost. Einstein, for example, thought of the formula $E=mc^2$ before finding out that it applies universally. He did not try out different formula in any systematic way nor did he generalise it from particular experiences of using it. He did not point out any prior instances of energy being converted into matter, from which the formula could have been generalised. He arrived at it intuitively in thinking holistically about relativity and the interrelationship between light and energy.[112] In his original formulation he speculated about the emission of light through radioactive radiation, making the

---

[112] "A famous cartoon shows Einstein at a board, trying out one possibility after another: $E=mc^1$, $E=mc^2$, $E=mc^3$, ... But he didn't really do it that way, arriving at the squaring of 'c' by mere chance." David Bodanis, $E=mc^2$: A Biography of the World's Most Famous Equation, (London: Macmillan, 2000), Part 2, p. 54. Einstein published the formula in one of his papers on Special Relativity in 1905, and in 1907 it suddenly occurred to him that it could be applied more widely to the problem of gravity. "I was sitting on a chair in my patent office in Bern when all of a sudden a thought occurred to me . . . I was startled." Quoted by Bodanis, op. cit., Epilogue, p. 204. This 'happy thought' led eventually to the General Theory of Relativity.

bald statement: *"If a body gives off the energy E in the form of radiation its mass diminishes by E/c²".*[113] The discovery of the formula was simply an act of intuitive insight.

Formulae such as $E=mc^2$ are expressions which can form part of a dynamic account in which they are expanded upon to show their truth and relevance in the world at large. This occurs when they are being applied, say, in a classroom or a research context when they are being used to solve or illuminate a particular problem This applies to all symbolical and verbal expressions as well as propositions, sentences, statements, stories, poems and the like, as long as they make sense. The purpose of such dynamic accounts is to show what is true or false, applicable or inapplicable about these expressions in a broader context than that of their being valid in a formal logical sense. The dynamic account therefore goes beyond the deductive analysis achieved by formal logic.

In this part of the book, the interactive contents of the dynamic account are outlined. It shows how the dynamic account begins with the intuitive grasp of an idea, formula or verbal assertion and is then elaborated interactively. An important distinction is made between intuition and induction. Basically, intuition produces theories and induction confirms the application of theories in the many instances in which they apply or refutes them in the instances where they do not apply. Induction looks beyond the theories to take the broader picture so that connections can be made with instances where the theories apply. It looks at the contexts in which they are applicable. In the part nine on *The Pursuit of Truth by Dualist Interaction,* the build-up of these contents by the various methods of pursuing truth is discussed.

2. The nature of the dynamic account

Dynamic logic uses dynamic accounts that describe the way we reason out things in interacting with our world. Such an account involves a holistic pursuit of truth to establish the reality of things in a specific time frame. The object of a dynamic account is to establish the truth of an expressed intuition, thought, feeling, idea, opinion, hypothesis, theory, or system of thought, in relation to the facts. All of these may be grasped intuitively as a whole when we think about them, but the dynamic account elaborates these thoughts in a systematic way to show the truth or falsity in them. When a thought occurs to us, we invariably put it into words to make sense of it. In formal logic, these words are said to form statements or propositions which are valid or invalid occurring to their internal form or structure. But a dynamic account goes beyond and behind the form of verbal or symbolic expressions to examine and elicit the meaning, motivation, purpose and all aspects relating to the expressions that pertain to their truth. As such a dynamic account is potentially limitless in its content, but it is restricted by the context in which it is made and by the facts to which it relates.

---

[113] As quoted by Jeremy Bernstein, *Einstein*, (London: Wm. Collins & Sons, 1973), ch. 2, vii, p. 84.

The word 'account', as used here, dates back to the *logos* (λóγος) of ancient Greek philosophers. '*Logos*' in Greek means simply 'word' but the philosophers used it variously to refer to reason, a reasoned argument and sometimes to an account or a system of thought expressed in words. Thus, for example, Heracleitus (c.540-480BCE) thought it important to get the 'Word' right:

> Of the Word (*logos*) as I describe it, men always prove to be uncomprehending, both before they have heard it and after they have heard it. For although all things happen according to this Word, men are like people with no experience, even when they experience such words and deeds as I explain, and when I distinguish each thing according to its constitution and show how it is.[114]

Other Greek philosophers used the word in this metaphysical sense of giving a comprehensive account of things.[115] This use of the word by the philosophers explains the beginning of the gospel of John in the New Testament, where 'word' (*logos*) also has the sense of an 'account'.[116] It was intended to give a metaphysical basis for Christianity by identifying Christ with the Word. Thus, this particular use of '*logos*' by the philosophers refers to a holistic view of things expressed in words and conforming to truth. But this view was sidelined by Aristotle's development of a deductive form of logic based on sentences or 'syllogisms'. The lopsided nature of formal logic is discussed below.

There may be future, present and past dynamic accounts. A *future* account aims to get things done by deciding, judging, choosing, planning and the like. A *present* account describes what is happening now from a witness's point of view, in terms of what is being seen or experienced at the moment. A *past* account relies on one's memory or that of others, or on documents, paintings, photos, films and other forms of evidence. A dynamic account may contain all these aspects but still not be necessarily true. Other information or evidence may emerge to change, confirm, detract from or indeed disprove the account. A dynamic account is therefore concerned with what was, is or will be the case in reality in referring to a specific point or period in time. Whether it applies equally to different point or period in time is another matter since that depends on context.

The dynamic account incorporates both induction and deduction. It is built up inductively through dualist interactions to produce a holistic view of an event, situation, idea, system of thought, theory and the like. This includes deductive

---

[114] Translation as in G.S. Kirk and J.E. Raven (1957), *The Presocratic Philosophers*, Cambridge: CUP, 1989, Ch. VI, p.187.

[115] For example, the sophist, Gorgias (c.490-c.380BCE), cf. Jonathan Barnes, *The Presocratic Philosophers*, (London: Routledge, 1989), Ch. XXIII, pp. 528-530; and the stoic, Zeno of Citium, (333-261BCE), cf. W.K.C. Guthrie, *A History of Greek Philosophy*, Vol. I, Ch. I. p. 19.

[116] John ch. 1:1."In the beginning there was the word and the word was with God and God was the word" In Greek: Ἐν ἀρχῇ ἦν ὁ λόγος, καὶ ὁ λόγος ἦν πρὸς τὸν θεόν, καὶ θεὸς ἦν ὁ λόγος.

logic but goes beyond it substantially in its comprehensive and ongoing quests for truth.

In so far as a dynamic account is purposeful and practical it is concerned with effective action and not just the truth of what is said about the action. Effective action is that which is seen or shown to be done. It is not always reasoned out verbally and a dynamic account can rationalise an action on an after-the-event basis. In this way, it begins with an intuitive grasp of the whole truth of the matter. It proceeds by taking account of all relevant factors that serve to make sense of the situation. The dynamic account therefore includes our reasons for deciding, judging, choosing, planning, believing and it is concerned with action and not just words. The following are examples of the dynamic procedure at work:

Example One: The dynamic account of the scene of an accident would include not just a statement of what happened but also the reactions and feelings of the witnesses, what was done, during and after the accident and all the details relating to it that are sufficient to give the most complete possible account of the occurrence of the accident, its beforehand and aftermath, its participants and so on. It is thus built up by dualist interactions conducted over time.

Example Two: The dynamic account of a scientific experiment will refer not only to what was done and what was accomplished. It will also refer to the care taken to avoid bias and contamination that might prejudice the validity of the experiment's outcome. It will include the aims and motivations of the experiment as well as the experience and expertise of the participants.

Example Three: The dynamic account of a book summarises not only its contents but also information about the author, the influences leading up to it and the consequences of its publication, the sales of the book, the reactions of readers and so on.

Clearly, the context is required to limit the amount of information required to make the account satisfactory for the purpose for which it is being performed. Otherwise, the account would stretch to include the whole of society as well as the universe at large. For example, the context of a court of law means that the account must satisfy judge and jury as well as the prosecutors, advocates, accused, and defendants.

Dynamic accounts can be expressed in symbols as well as words. They feature in science and mathematics when their methods are being described critically. Thus, for example, Gödel's incompleteness theorem is such a dynamic account within the limits in which it was conceived. So-called 'meta' sciences are also of this dynamic type. Mathematical proofs and formulae are therefore a form of dynamic account as described herein, when they are performed purposeful and in a realistic context. Through the symbolic language of mathematics we harmonise with outer reality as precisely and accurately as it is humanly possible for us to do.

Mathematics is therefore not derived from logic in the way described by Russell and others. Rather logic is a form of mathematics, especially what is called Boolean algebra. Mathematics provides us with its own forms of dynamic account which are in many instances more in tune with reality than any verbal accounts. Thus, in dualist theory, mathematics embodies dualist interaction *par example*. It is a method of representing dualist interactions in a stable manner so that we can understand and predict the workings of the universe. A mathematical formula such as $x = y$ is dualistic in that the left hand side relates to the right side such that the two things could not be more equal. A dualist interaction between the two sides is performed when mathematical rules are applied equally to both sides in solving equations.

A dynamic account deals with the way we reason about things. It differs from an empirical or descriptive account that describes things and events as they are, without going into greater detail. Such an account may itself be subjected to a dynamic account which examines the reasoning behind the account, namely, why it is only descriptive and overlooks important details. This examination will include the consistency and clarity of the argument as well as the quality of the evidence on which it is based. This applies particularly to news reports whose logical structure and evidential basis may well be questionable, not to mention the motivations, prejudices and inclinations of the reporters and news editors behind the reporting.

By means of dynamic accounts we can make sense of our lives by accounting for fundamental dualist relationships such as the following: (a) There is our existence as human beings and there is our account of that existence; (b) there is external reality and there is our account of that external reality; and (c) there is the universe and there is our account of that universe. In each of these examples, there is something and there is an account which we can make of it using words and symbols to make sense of it. Different accounts of these may differ substantially depending on context and the interests of those making the accounts.

Therefore, there is a dualist interaction between ourselves and whatever we account for in words and symbols. Our words and symbols are not themselves real or factual but refer to what is real or factual. They are fundamentally dualistic. Thus, dynamic logic concerns how we relate dualistically to what is not ourselves to give a true and accurate account of that interrelationship, regardless of personal motivations. It is therefore a form of logic in which we rationalise or make sense of our thoughts or actions by giving an account in speech or writing of the way things are in truth and reality.

3. The relation of the dynamic account to formal logic

Dynamic logic therefore incorporates formal logic which is a deductive logic limited to the form of words that we use in arguing for or against points of view. Our arguments are either valid or invalid depending on the form in which they presented. This means that formal logic is linear in its presentation as it follows the linear pattern of human speech in which one word follows another. Its scope is therefore limited to what can be spoken as being true or false in relation to other words that have been spoken. It does not give the whole truth of the matter unless it forms part of a dynamic account that does strive towards comprehensive truth.

Most sentences in the English language are in the subject/predicate form in which the existence of the subject implies the existence of the predicate when the whole sentence is true. If it is true that the cat sat on the mat then the existence of both cat and mat are implied. Formal arguments are usually put in the general, deductive form of a statement *p* implies *q*, so that if the existence of one implies the existence of the other. Thus, Bertrand Russell sought to derive mathematics from the statement *p* implies *q*. He begins his *Principles of Mathematics* by saying: "Pure mathematics is the class of all propositions of the form '*p* implies *q*'". He considered his method to be philosophical analysis in which "we seek to pass from the complex to the simple, from the demonstrable to its indemonstrable premisses".[117] This is "the general doctrine that all mathematics is deduction by logical principles from logical principles" as advocated by Leibniz.[118] This overlooks completely the role of inductive reasoning in giving rise to the assumptions behind deductive reasoning. It is arguable that a dualist interaction between deduction and induction is required to take account of the flexibility and self-referential nature of our thinking. Therefore, it is not surprising that Russell's logical enterprise floundered on his reducing things to rigid logical classes, giving rise to his well-known 'paradox'. The failure of formal logic to take account of the role of inductive reasoning is the subject of the next section.

In dynamic logic, the logical principles of identity, contradiction and the excluded middle become derivative assumptions rather than unsubstantiated ones that have no empirical basis and are applied uncritically by logicians. The derivations of these assumptions are outlined as follows:

The principle of identity, A is A, is in fact derived from the uniformity of nature, namely, the assumption that things continue uniformly the same unless they are altered by causal means. A thing is identical with itself because everything is of 'one form'. They remain what they are stated to be, rather than things that we interact with on an ongoing basis. In dualist theory, they are not identical with themselves; they only interact with something capable of apprehending and thinking about them. Also, everything varies in relation to context. Thus, 'A is A' means that an object is being identified with the speaker's previously conceived notion of it. Something can both exist and not exist in different contexts but not in the same context unless there is some confusion or misunderstanding about it.

The principle of contradiction - A is not A - is not fundamental to nature. Nothing in nature contradicts itself. When one statement contradicts another, the contradiction is all too readily remedied by qualifying and elaborating one or other statements until the contradiction is overridden. Persuasive speakers and

---

[117] Bertrand Russell, *Principles of Mathematics*, (1st edition 1903, 2nd edition 1937 - London: Routledge, 1992), ch. 1, p. 3.
[118] *Op. cit.*, p. 5.

writers only need to elaborate their arguments sufficiently to avoid contradiction and inconsistency. This makes their arguments logically true but not necessarily ultimately or verifiably true in the above mentioned senses. Thus, the limitations of this principle require the dynamic account to counteract them by setting contextual limits and clarifying the purpose which the account is intended to fulfil.

The principle of the excluded middle - either A or B - divides up the contexts to which different statements refer. It creates two different contexts which in reality may not be strict alternatives or be strictly exclusive the one from the other. For example, 'either the cat exists or it does not exist'. Two different contexts are posited: the one in which the cat exists and the one in which it does not. But to make any sense of this, we need to know the context in which it is being said and that context is not given in or with the sentence. It might make sense to say this when someone hears a noise that sounds like a cat. Then legitimate doubts about its existence arise. Another flaw in this principle is its apparent exclusivity, as it seems to divide the entire world into two exclusive contexts. Thus, Kant gives the following remarkable example of the excluded middle: "The world exists either through blind chance, or through inner necessity, or through an external cause." He says that "When taken together, they constitute the whole content of one given knowledge."[119] The possibility of other alternatives such as quantum physics now gives us is ruled out arbitrarily. These limitations are typical of how the limited view that formal logic imposes on the world. The possibility of alternative views to those three given principles is ruled *a priori*. In this way, deductive thinking closes people's minds by ruling out possibilities without reason or evidence being given.

Dynamic logic goes beyond formal logic in giving an overall, holistic account of a state of affairs that includes both deductive and inductive elements. It includes the processes here called 'contextualisation' and 'conceptualisation'. These aspects of logic are implied in the later philosophy of Wittgenstein in which he criticised the shortcomings in formal logic. Contextualisation is implied in the 'forms of life' and 'language games' distinctions made by him. "Here the term 'language-*game*' (*Sprachspiel*) is meant to bring into prominence the fact that the *speaking* of language is part of an activity, or of a form of life [*Form des Lebens*]."[120] As Wittgenstein was writing in German he had no distinct word for 'context' which is surely more appropriate than these cumbersome terms.[121]

---

[119] Immanuel Kant, *Critique of Pure Reason*, (1787), trans. N. Kemp Smith, (London: Macmillan & Co., 1964), A74, p. 109.

[120] Wittgenstein (1953), *Philosophical Investigations*, trans. by G.E.M. Anscombe, (Oxford: Blackwell, 1968), §23, p. 11.

[121] The nearest German word seems to be '*Zusammenhang*', which means not just 'context' but also 'connection' and 'association' - literally 'hanging together'. The word is translated as 'context' in later works such as *On Certainty*, but in the Tractatus 4.22, it is translated as 'nexus' and is linked with 'concatenation' (*Verkettung*). Thus, we can think in English of a context as being a relatively self-contained unit, whereas it is more difficult to think that way in German.

Conceptualisation refers to the 'family resemblances' (*Familienähnlichkeiten*) between concepts.[122] This draws attention to the interconnectivity of our ideas, which are not as isolated and sacrosanct as the Platonic view would have us believe. Broadly speaking, contextualisation is relevant to inductive reasoning while conceptualisation deals with deductive reasoning. The latter therefore includes formal logic in so far as it is concerned with deductive arguments. There is more about these aspects of the dynamic account in section eight below.

How dynamic logic goes beyond formal logic may be illustrated using the classic syllogistic argument of formal logic as follows:

> All men are mortal
> Socrates is a man
> Therefore, Socrates is mortal

Proof of Socrates' mortality purportedly follows from the truth of the first two propositions. If these propositions are true, the conclusion must be valid. There is no need to look outside the argument as the form is deemed sufficient to validate its conclusion. In dynamic logic, this syllogism is accounted for in a more elaborate way. Its truth does not just depend on its form but, firstly, on the holistic coherence of its contents and, secondly, on the correspondence of these contents to facts that are not implied within the syllogism:

- The words are analysed by a conceptualisation that looks at their definitions and their family relationships with each other. We assume at the outset that the word 'men' is here defined as referring to mortal beings - biological entities that must die. Socrates is the name of a man who actually lived in history. Therefore, the evidence for his actual existence must be examined and considered acceptable or unacceptable as the case may be. This means referring to sources that confirm the fact of his existence.

- The word 'mortal' is defined as being confined to the physical existence of Socrates as opposed to his being immortal in the sense of an important figure in history. It is therefore necessary to see the concepts of the arguments in relation to other concepts not included in the argument itself. In being more broadly defined, the words correspond more exactly to outer reality. It needs to be stated explicitly that the word 'mortal' refers to his physical death in 399BCE, according to the sources.

- Both the words and the whole argument must also be examined by a contextualisation that places it in its proper context so that it coheres together in relation to a particular period in time and place. In the present context, the word 'mortal' is confined to the physical existence of Socrates. From all these facts and arguments, it can be inferred more securely than simply from the given form of words that Socrates lived and died and that he was mortal like the rest of us.

- Moreover, the resulting account may vary in relation to the context in which it is made. If additional information about Socrates becomes available then a new context is created in which a different account of his

---

[122] Cf., for example, *Philosophical Investigations, op. cit.,* §67, p. 32.

mortality may emerge. In this way, dynamic logic responds to environmental changes in a way that formal logic cannot.

4. The limits to dynamic logic

J. S. Mill in his impressive but deeply flawed book, *A System of Logic*, defended syllogistic reasoning as being "from particulars to particulars without passing through generals."[123] A child having burnt its fingers in a fire will refrain from putting them again into the fire without having "thought of the general maxim, Fire burns."[124] But this assumes that inductive reasoning must always be verbalised into a expressible 'maxim' or generalisation. However, the child has clearly formed the idea that fire burns one's fingers. It remembers having had its fingers burnt by the fire. The inference is both intuitive and inductive even though the child may not yet have the words to express the idea. We shall see that the building up of inner, ineffable knowledge of this kind is an important part of dynamic logic.

Dynamic logic describes how we reason by interacting dualistically with our environment to produce an account of some kind for some specific purpose. The dynamic account is built up by acting and reacting to the given evidence and incorporating that evidence to make a coherent account that corresponds to what really happened. The result is an account that is composed of concepts whose meanings depend on the context in which the account is made. The account has to be made anew and may differ in another context, in which it is criticised and amended accordingly. This gives this logic its dynamism: it is not fixed or absolute and the dynamic account must be performed constantly and repeatedly in every situation and at every instance.

One account of the same state of affairs may not be the same when performed in another context. For example, an account of the differences between various species of fish may differ according to the contexts in which it is given by fishermen who have practical experience of different fish, by zoologists who have precise knowledge of the differences between fish, and laypersons who have only knowledge from their buying fish to eat, reading books, watching television, consulting the internet etc. The account given by laypersons will usually be less accurate and limited in scope compared with the accounts given by the former two.

A dynamic account is never the whole truth of the matter. It may contribute towards the truth which always recedes into the distance. The truth must be constantly striven for as that is what our lives are all about. This means that any dynamic account must itself be accounted for, and the account following it, *ad infinitum* (or "to the last syllable of recorded time" as Shakespeare put it.[125])

---

[123] John Stuart Mill, *A System of Logic: Ratiocinative and Inductive*, (1843 - London: Longman, 1970), Book II, Ch. III, §3, pp. 123a.

[124] *Op. cit.*, Book III, Ch. I, §1, p.185a.

[125] Shakespeare, *Macbeth*, Act V, Scene V, line 21.

Literally, we are never done accounting for ourselves, both as individuals and as a species. This is simply because our words and symbols are never sufficient to account for everything; there is always more to be said about anything.

This is where the sceptical *epochē*[126] plays its part. The *epochē* is the break or suspension of judgment that makes us stop thinking and reasoning. It enters the dynamic account at the point where the evidence for the line of reasoning is insufficient to support the premises convincingly. It emerges where reason must falter and stop if it is to avoid exceeding common sense and sound thinking. That *b* follows from *a* must be supported by evidence outside that logical connection, and the *epochē* provides the opportunity for intuition and induction to look for evidence for or against the reasoning involved. However, there is no end to the evidence that is required for absolute conviction. The elaboration of the account is limited by context and by what is intuitively found to be sufficient.

Thus, the problem with a dynamic account of this nature is not consistency. Any contradiction can be eliminated by the elaboration of the account to eliminate it. If a political opinion is not convincing, politicians tend to spin it out and beef it up to make it more convincing. They will do all they can to get their message across. Whether it is true or even workable is another matter altogether. The problem is that there is no potential end to such elaboration. It can go on forever. However, an account may be limited or brought to an end in at least four ways.

1. It is limited by what is sufficient to account for how things really are or to get things done. We think of what is practical enough to accomplish our immediate ends and no further.

2. The judgment as to what is sufficient may have to rely on what is sufficient for the context involved. The context often makes clear how far the account needs to go to achieve its purpose.

3. As already mentioned, the *epochē* or cut off in thinking can be relied upon to bring the shutters down and stop inappropriate, meaningless and useless trains of thought.

4. But intuition is required to bring the *epochē* into play. Hence the emphasis on inner development in dynamic logic, since intuition has to be developed to a high degree to ensure that our intuitions are not random but based of our experience of the way things are and of what will work in practice. Our intuitions are our *familiaris* or companions that keep us on the right track. They impose the *epochē* in much the same intuitive way that Socrates used his *daimon* or spiritual companion that induced him to pause and take account of other factors that were not previously included in his arguments.

---

[126] The Greek, ἐποχή, from which comes our word 'epoch' meaning era or time period. Edmund Husserl (1859-1938) used the word in the technical sense of suspension of judgment in his system of philosophy known as 'phenomenology'. See his book, *Ideas: General Introduction to Pure Phenomenology*, (1913 - London: George Allen & Unwinl, 1969), First Section, Second Chapter, §18, pp. 80-81.

The main thing is that dynamic account is never the last word on the matter. The external world is under constant interrogation and nothing is taken for granted. Assumptions, presuppositions, axioms, definitions and the like are constantly under review and are always being reviewed and rethought. The truth is not a stable entity but an elusive matter that gives us hard work. We can only hope to move very slowly and methodically towards the truth.

5. The importance of including both inductive and deductive reasoning

The dynamic nature of this logic ensures that it includes both inductive and deductive reasoning in the dynamic accounts as outlined above. It uses both kinds of reasoning interactively and successively, unlike formal logic which is usually lop-sided and incomplete because of its emphasis on deductive reasoning. In going beyond a given sentence or proposition, dynamic account generalises and synthesises all the relevant information relating to the sentence in a holistic way. For example, with the sentence 'All dogs are faithful' we want to know not only what this means but also the evidence for saying this, and this means going into biology, sociology and even anthropology to show how this domesticity emerged from man's bonding with wolves. There is a constant interaction with the available information to update and revise the account so that it conforms to reality as much as humanly possible. Thus, the dynamic account is more concerned with completeness than with the strict consistency of its form.

Formal logic is limited in comparison with dynamic logic because it was originally based by Aristotle on the deductive procedure of geometrical proofs. This gave this form of logic a bias towards deductive reasoning. The place of inductive reasoning in formal logic has never been properly worked out. Induction as a subject is often tacked on to the end of logic books without being integrated into the system as a whole. It is usually associated with probability and is compared unfavourably with the alleged exactitude of deductive arguments.

The deductive procedure begins with axioms and definitions, and it proves its propositions by deductive means. Axioms and definitions are simply given by intuitive reasoning (*nous*). Thus, Aristotle's system of logic (as contained in his *Organon*[127]) gives no account of where our axioms and definitions come from apart from intuition. He thought that intuition is as much a source of truth as scientific knowledge (*epistemē*), and it is the starting point for that knowledge.[128] We now know that non-Euclidean geometry is based on different axioms from the geometry that Aristotle assumed to be directly representative of reality. Axioms are no longer regarded as fixed or invariable, nor are first principles

---

[127] Aristotle's collection of books known as the *Organon* (meaning 'instrument') comprises the *Categories, De Interpretatione, Prior Analytics, Posterior Analytics, Topics,* and *On Sophistical Refutations.*

[128] Aristotle, *Posterior Analytics,* II, 19, 100b3, Loeb edition, *Organon II,* p. 261.

assumed to be for all time in the way that he did. They may vary according to context and according to what we are doing with them. In other words, we interact with them and we should not regard them as fixed objects of thought.

Because the axioms and definitions of geometry are arrived at by intuition, Aristotle thought that first principles (*archē*) in general must be apprehended by intuition. But the method by which these principles are apprehended is induction (*epagogē*).[129] However, he never worked out the relationship between intuition and induction because he concentrated on the deductive development of his logic.

The importance of distinguishing them is clear from the following example. Often when politicians say that their policy is 'the right thing to do', they only know *intuitively* that it is the right thing to do. The full reasons for their decision may only come after it is made. Initially, they have looked at the whole situation and reached an intuitive decision that seems right. The correctness of the decision can be justified later by giving a full account of the matter. Only then they have reasoned inductively as they have looked at all the instances in a methodical manner and made a choice from them according to preconceived criteria. The logical consistency of the account can also be assessed according to the validity of the deductions being made in it.

Aristotle had no way of including induction in his deductive system except by arguing that induction is also a form of deductive reasoning. In his only treatment of induction of any length, he explains it in terms of deductive syllogisms. Essentially he argues that all long-lived animals are long-lived because they lack the deficiencies preventing it.[130] The lack of deficiencies is then a property or quality of the animals that are long-lived. The property of being long-lived is only assumed. The procedures by which we discover and confirm long-livedness are left out of the equation. Nothing needs to be done to confirm or deny the assumption. Thus, Aristotle failed to work out what he meant by induction as a distinct way of seeking truth which is of equal value to deduction. This failure stultified human thinking until the 17th century when the scientific movement got underway through Francis Bacon's rival '*Novum Organon*' which was in its turn equally biased in favour of inductive reasoning.

However, it is Aristotle's successors who are to blame for not building on his system of logic in a critical way. He recognised the shortcomings of his system in the last paragraph of his *Organon*, where he says that his system is not to be considered complete or the last word on the matter, but that we should be very grateful for what he has discovered.[131] His successors such as Epicurus simply took his system of logic as given. In his voluminous works, Epicurus 'proves' in an absolute and dogmatic way the 'truth' of his doctrines concerning, for example,

[129] Aristotle, *Posterior Analytics*, II, 19, 100b3-100b17, Loeb edition, *Organon II*, p. 261.

[130] Aristotle, *Prior Analytics*, II, 23, 68b15, Loeb edition, *Organon I*, pp. 513-5.

[131] Aristotle, *On Sophistical Refutations*, xxxiv 184b, Loeb edition, p.155.

the atoms and the void.[132] Not until the late 19th century was atomic theory shown in a scientific way to be correct, and not just a plausible doctrine. The works of the philosophers were later ridiculed by Christian writers such as Lactantius[133] and Eusebius[134] for their apparent vacuity and pointlessness. Logic was used by such Christian writers not only disprove rival doctrines but also to 'prove' the validity of their own doctrines. Similarly, logic is being used nowadays by creationists and anti-scientists to discredit scientific conclusions even when the latter are based on impeccable and exhaustive scientific research by well-meaning people. Dualist studies will show that dynamic logic is not so easily misused.

The over-emphasis on deductive reasoning at the expense of inductive reasoning also made words and sentences more important than what refer to or fail to refer to. Deductive reasoning depends on the definitions of words such as 'men' and 'mortal' being fixed from one context to another. The effect is to fix and limit the definitions of words to suit the argument without referring to anything in the real world. Thus, Plato famously defined 'man' as a 'featherless biped'.[135] Apart from the realms of humour and satire, it is doubtful whether there is any context in which such a definition can be usefully applied. In fact, it was allegedly ridiculed by Diogenes the Cynic. When he heard that Plato was praised for the definition, he plucked a chicken and brought it to Plato's Academy and said "Here is Plato's man." After this incident, we are told that "with broad flat nails" was added to Plato's definition of man.[136]

The emphasis on word definition has given us dictionaries that consolidate language and inhibit its free development as an organic instrument of communication. There is surely no need for words to be defined rigidly for all time to come. It can stultify language, slow communication, and retard cultural and economic progress. The reality is that we benefit from the fluidity and adaptability of language as in the burgeoning of new language to cope with the complexities and novelties of the computer age.

Furthermore, the reliance of formal logic on making deductions from definitions leads to a dogmatic focus on words and sentences as being real in themselves. This obsession with the reality of words and sentences goes back to Aristotle's definition of truth in terms of what is said: "truth consists in saying of

---

[132] See Lucretius, (c.99-55BCE), *On the Nature of Things* (*de Rerum Natura*), in which 'the atoms and the void' theory is expounded in exquisitely exhaustive detail.

[133] Cf. Lactantius, (c.240-c.320CE) *Divine Institutes*, Book III, 'Of The False Wisdom of the Philosophers' where he compares the simple truth of scripture with the contrived eloquence of philosophers..

[134] Also, Eusebius of Caesarea, (264-340CE), *Praeparatio Evangelica*, Book XV, Preface where he expresses contempt for the unprofitable study of the philosophers.

[135] Plato, *The Statesman*, 266e, as in *The Collected Dialogues of Plato*, (Princeton: Princeton University Press, 1961), p. 1031.

[136] Diogenes Laërtius (c. 300 CE), *Lives and Opinions of Eminent Philosophers*, Loeb Classical Library, 1980, Vol. II, Book VI, Ch. 2, Diogenes, §40, p. 43. A likely tale!

that which is that it is or of that which is not that it is not."[137] This implies that what we say is directly representative of reality. In contrast, the dualist view emphasises the interactive relationship between words and sentences and that to which they may or may not refer. In the pursuit of truth, our words and sentences are related interactively with reality so that there is no absolute truth out there waiting for us. They cannot be real in themselves but only what is meant by them in a referential manner. This prevents bigots and extremists, fantasists and conspiracy theorists from making out that their arguments are sacrosanct merely because these arguments make sense logically regardless of how they actually relate to external evidence and experience.

Thus, the effect of Aristotle's view is that ultimately words become indistinguishable from the things to which they refer. Reality thus resides in the words themselves. This turns deductive logic into a 'lingualism' in which linear sentences express the reality of things in themselves.[138] Sentences become the only reality; hence the post-modern proclamation: *il n'y a pas de hors-texte* (literally "there is no outside-text" or "there is nothing outside the text").[139] W. V. O. Quine typically defines the pursuit of truth in terms of words:

> Logic, like any science, has as its business the pursuit of truth. What are true are certain statements; and the pursuit of truth is the endeavour to sort out the true statements from the others, which are false.[140]

Quine acknowledges that logic is not the only way of seeking truth, and he also argues that in a sense scientific method is 'the last arbiter of truth'.[141] Though he likes to think of logic as a 'science', clearly the 'methods of logic' are distinct from 'scientific method', otherwise his book of that title would also be a work on 'scientific method'. Logical methods may be applied to scientific statements but they do not produce true scientific statements themselves, since only scientific methods achieve such 'truths'. It will be seen in the next part on *The Pursuit of Truth by Dualist Interaction*, that truth seeking is a process and that our words may reflect truths though they are not themselves 'the truth'.

The social effect of this lingualism is to give prominence to talking heads and 'sound bites' for whom talking is a substitute for doing things. Bureaucrats reign supreme and produce vast, verbose reports and documents that serve no purpose outside themselves. Rules become more important than people, and the adhesion to rules and regulations means more than the inconvenience meted on the people they are imposed upon.

---

[137] Aristotle, *Metaphysics*, Book IV, Ch. 7, 1011b, 25-30.

[138] Ian Hacking, *Why Does Language Matter to Philosophy?*, (Cambridge: CUP, 1981), p. 183: "The doctrine of lingualism is that only the sentence is real."

[139] Jacques Derrida (1967), *Of Grammatology*, trans. G. C. Spivak, (Baltimore: Johns Hopkins University Press, 1972), Part 2, ch. 2, p.158. [Also, Derrida (1988) *Afterword: Toward An Ethic of Discussion*, published in the English translation of *Limited Inc.*, p. 136]

[140] W. V. O. Quine, *Methods of Logic*, (London, RKP), 3rd ed., 1974, p. 1.

[141] Willard Van Orman.Quine, *Word and Object*, (Massachusetts: MIT Press, 1960), p. 23.

Thus, the consequence of this lingualist view is that unless something is expressed in words in some text or other it cannot be said to exist. Yet much of our reasoning is wordless and not expressed in any grammatical form whatsoever. Thoughts, ideas, images, concepts come to us without necessarily being verbalised. In particular, inductive reasoning tends to be intuitive in origin and is arrived at by unconscious synthesising of experienced material. This accounts for the *eureka!* phenomenon whereby scientists, and creative people generally, arrive at their big ideas without the aid of any prior process of deductive reasoning.

As already mentioned, Francis Bacon in the early 17th century put forward an inductive view of science that heralded the scientific revolution of the later 17th century. However, his view was biased in favour of induction and did not include the deductive aspect of Aristotle's philosophy. It was left to Descartes to put forward a system of philosophy comprehensive enough to challenge the ancients. But his approach to dualism consisted in making the very limited categorical distinction between mind and body. He also revived Plato's ideas and continued to use Aristotle's form of logic as given. In short, he took no account of Bacon's inductive philosophy and gave us a rationalist philosophy based on deductive logic.

The failure of Descartes and other philosophers to account for both induction and deduction in one unified dualist approach ensured that philosophy became divorced from science altogether. It should have taken science under its wing but instead philosophy became for centuries a civil war between an emphasis on induction/deduction and its derivatives rationalism/empiricism as shown in the following table.

Inductive Reasoning	*Deductive Reasoning*
Synthetic	Analytic
Rationalist	Empiricist
Idealist	Realist
Monist	Pluralist
Holist	Reductionist
Absolutist	Relativist

The Dogmatic Separation of the Components of Dualist Interaction

This Great Schism between inductive and deductive reasoning ensured that a system of thought based on dualist interaction was ruled out from the outset. The schism was reinforced by John Locke's empiricist philosophy which derived ideas entirely from perceptual experience. Then David Hume showed that inductive conclusions cannot be drawn from evidence by deductive logic. But he merely compounded scepticism in human reasoning powers as he failed to give us an adequate account of how we arrive at conclusions through inductive reasoning. For example, he pointed out that we cannot deduce from our experience that the sun will necessarily rise tomorrow. We may know it with certainty from our experience but the contrary proposition is equally logical. David Hume put it thus:

> "*That the sun will not rise to-morrow* is no less intelligible a proposition, and implies no more contradiction than the affirmation, *that it will rise*. We should in vain, therefore, attempt to demonstrate its falsehood. Were it demonstratively false, it would imply a contradiction, and could never be distinctly conceived by the mind."[142]

However, in a dynamic account we can take a more holist view and include inductive evidence based on our astronomical knowledge that the sun will indeed rise tomorrow. Such possibilities that the sun might blow up overnight or a comet might obliterate the Earth meantime are highly unlikely events that we can now anticipate beforehand by astronomical observation. This shows how a holistic account can include inductive reasoning and be just as valid as a vehicle of truth as deductive reasoning.

The equivalidity of these methods of reasoning was recognised by Thomas Reid (1711-1796) who reacted against Hume's scepticism and he stated in 1774: "When induction is sufficiently copious, and carried on according to the rules of art, it forces conviction no less than demonstration itself does." Therefore he said that Bacon's "*Novum Organon* ought therefore to be held as a most important addition to the ancient logic."[143] However, Reid himself did nothing to work out the dualist position involved in adopting both these methods of reasoning.

In response to the success of science up to 19th century, J.S. Mill in *A System of Logic* argued that induction is the source of all our knowledge since all inference and proof "consists of inductions, and the interpretations of inductions".[144] This provoked an extreme reaction from the logicians such as Frege and Russell who rejected this view and attempted to build deductive logic on better foundations than hitherto. Thus, the Great Schism between deduction and induction has remained to the present day. Only a dynamic logic such as is outlined here incorporates both these outlooks and offers a way out of this impasse.

---

[142] David Hume (1772), *An Enquiry Concerning Human Understanding*, ed. Selby-Bigge Oxford: Clarendon Press, 1975, Sect. IV, Part I, §21, pp. 25-26. What he says in his *Treatise* is a little more subtle:

> "One wou'd appear ridiculous, who wou'd say, that 'tis only probable the sun will rise to-morrow, or that all men must dye; tho' 'tis plain we have no further assurance of these facts, than what experience affords us."

David Hume (1739), *A Treatise of Human Nature*, ed. Nidditch, Oxford: Clarendon Press, 1980, Book I, Part III, Sect. XI, p. 124.

[143] Thomas Reid, 'A Brief Account of Aristotle's Logic', as in Sir William Hamilton's edition of *The Works of Thomas Reid D.D.* (Edinburgh 1895 - also Georg Ohms 1983), Ch. V, p. 708a. Hamilton informs us: "This treatise originally appeared in the second volume of Lord Kames's *Sketches of the History of Man*, published in 1774", *op. cit.,* p. 681a footnote.

[144] John Stuart Mill, *A System of Logic: Ratiocinative and Inductive*, (1843, London: Longman, 1970), Book III, Ch. I, §1, pp. 185a.

6. Three ways of reasoning: linear, circular and spiral

Dynamic logic is not confined to linear reasoning of the syllogistic kind in which one word or symbol follows another in a linear pattern. The ongoing, interactive nature of dynamic logic means that it moves forward metaphorically in a spiral pattern. It can be compared figuratively with the linearity of formal reasoning and the circular nature of dogmatic reasoning, as depicted in the following simplistic diagram:

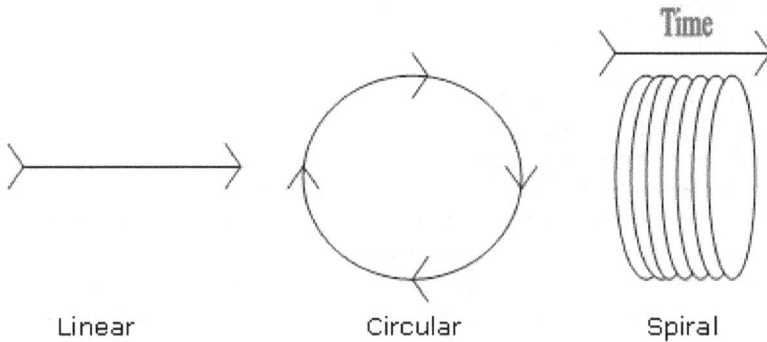

Linear   Circular   Spiral

I. *Linear reasoning* is that of purely deductive, non-interactive logic in so far as it omits the inductive and contextual elements of dynamic logic. It is reasoning in straight subject-predicate sentences in which the words are connected to each other in a linear fashion by their definitions as well as by the syntax and grammar of the sentences. Opinions are thought out in a linear fashion so that ideas are connected in a way that favours the line of thought. There is no way of criticising the ideas because they are necessarily connected in a deductive fashion. Examples of this type of reasoning include novels such as *The Da Vinci Code* and feature films such as *The Bourne Identity* in which events speedily follow events and are justified by a single line of reasoning. In these plots, complex arrays of facts are reduced to one linear way of looking at them.

Linear reasoning also involves categorical thinking which is rigid and unyielding. It depends on clear and unchanging definitions of words so that categories of things can be absolutely distinguished from each other. This is true of the physical world but it leads directly to dogmatic beliefs and opinions in politics and religion. The dynamic account obviously strives to avoid such rigid and unyielding thinking.

2. *Circular reasoning* is that of the close-minded person whose thinking goes round in circles and gets nowhere. It chases its own tail and has no way of breaking out of the circularity of its thinking. This is because closed thinking always returns to fixed axioms and principles which are inviolable to change and impervious to contrary evidence. The end justifies the means because the end is predetermined and inalterable.   In other words, the end of sticking to one's guns

justifies the means of confirming the original conclusion, however contrary to the evidence that means may be. Due to insecurity or other psychological inadequacies the person is not open to other ways of thinking.

Such reasoning may be likened to a computer locked in an unending circuit that can only be broken by shutting it down or resetting it. Dogmatic thinkers are in a similar bind. The circularity of their thinking can only be broken by the *epochē* or break in which we switch off our thoughts and allow them restart in another mode. It involves a suspension of judgment that allows the unconscious to bring out alternative ways of thinking, just as the *daimon* of Socrates made him break off his train of argument and introduce a new line of thought into his argument.

Lack of open-mindedness often leads to an over-rationalisation of positions which are constantly bolstered by arguments instead of being subjected to critical scrutiny. The obvious examples are conspiracy theories that obsessively pursued in spite of convincing evidence refuting them. Clearly, as mentioned above, an *epochē* is needed to break the cycle of thought and allow such monistic obsessives to detach themselves from their precious theories. This includes the unscientific pursuit of goals such as that of Himmler's *Deutsches Ahnenerbe* (German Ancestral Inheritance) organisation which sought to prove Aryan superiority over other races by distorting the relevant facts and evidence. Even scientists themselves may cling to their favourable theories in spite of better explanations becoming available. This includes religious and political extremists who consider their fanatical beliefs to be beyond criticism. They are imprisoned in their line of thought and have no way of escaping from it as they lack the open-mindedness of an *epochē* to help them break the cycle. A conviction of the absolute truth of their outlook entraps them in the narrowness of their respective viewpoints.

3. *Spiral reasoning* depicts the ongoing nature of dynamic logic. Its dualist interactions move forward so that they form a spiral through time. The systematic dualist is always moving forward in his or her thinking. It is time related as compared with linear reasoning that is absolutist. In moving forward in time, every account is reviewed anew so that the thinking is overwhelmingly critical. A constant self-reference occurs in which the spiral returns to itself. Thus, even dualist theory itself is ongoing and can never be finalised in any dogmatic way.

7. The geometrical principles of interactive self-reference.
Here we examine geometrically the nature of dualist interactions as they spiral forth either uniformly, declining or expanding as shown below. Some basic principles follow from these.

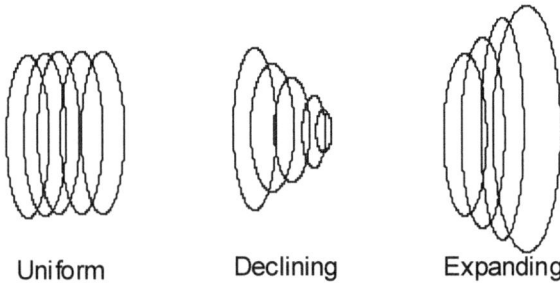

Uniform   Declining   Expanding

As dualist interactions move forwards in time, they can be depicted as spirals. The top and bottom of the spirals are the points or extremes to which a dualist interaction extends. The middle portions represent the areas of moderation. The following principles govern the relationships between linear, cyclical, and spiral interactions, as exemplified by above two diagrams.

1. *Linear and cyclical interactions:* When the midpoints of a linear interaction become identifiable in both directions then the interaction can be expanded into cycle which is either clockwise or anticlockwise in direction. For example, courage may move towards cowardice through a midpoint of dispiritedness, and cowardice towards courage through spiritedness. Thus, a linear interaction between courage and cowardice becomes a clockwise cycle with dispiritedness at the top and spiritedness at the bottom of the cycle. The midpoint point is always a causal factor which fuels the cycle and keeps it going.

2. *Cyclical and spiral interactions:* When a cycle moves forward in time through self-direction, it forms a spiral which may be uniform, declining or expanding in its dimensions.

- A uniform spiral retains the same diameter and continues indefinitely in one direction. This signifies a stable and reliable interaction system in which we remain in touch with both sides of the dualist interaction.
- A declining spiral corkscrews down to one point and ultimately to zero and nonentity. This signifies a spiralling into monistic subjectivity which is increasingly out of touch with realities.
- An expanding spiral widens indefinitely to infinity and chaos. This signifies a diffusion into pluralistic multiplicities in which we increasingly lose touch with ourselves or any unifying principle by which to order our conceptions.

3. *The Progression of Dualist Interactions:* A uniform spiral progresses by spawning further dualist interactions which lend precision to our thinking. When dualist interactions are listed in a connected way as in figure nine, they are open to further development by suggesting more specialised dualist lists which clarify our thinking still further. Dualist relationships are thus developed and become better understood in specialised lists that are implied by more general lists. In the absence of such development, a list of connected dual interactions may collapse, spiral, or diffuse into one single view, which signifies a

dogmatic train of thought which is an inability to appreciate the value of opposing points of view.

The spiral nature of this reasoning means there is a progression of dualistic interactions, each of which corrects the previous one to keep our feet on the ground in facing realities. The succession of cyclical interactions ensures that at each point there is always the possibility of an *epochē*, a break or suspension of judgment which objectifies beliefs, opinions, ideas, theories etc. The latter are put out of one's mind and can be returned to with dispassion and objectivity to assess their reality, truth, validity, reliability, appropriateness, usefulness or other teleological attributes. In this way, a stream of dualist interactions between our inner being and outer reality forms a spiral over a period of time. What is given by our inner being is subjected both to inductive and deductive reasoning in a cyclical fashion so that over time there is constant movement in distinguishing between what is real and what is not real.

8. The interaction between inner being and outer reality

The development of inner being is essential to a healthy and productive interaction with outer reality. It also plays an important role in both intuition and the successful use of the *epochē*. It ensures that we are inwardly strong enough to avoid being enslaved to our ideas, beliefs, opinions or theories. We are able to them at arm's length and not become too involved or obsessed with them. We also learn to take nothing for granted and always assume that there is something more going on than what is first given to us in any situation.

The *epochē* is the product of the holistic self that takes command and, in so doing, constitutes *willpower*, or the ability to make up one's mind and do or not do something. Such willpower builds up inner being and strengthens the character. Inner being is the accumulated content of the brain and central system that is only partially accessible to us by introspection. It is accessed by us to a limited extent by self-reference when we think about what we are thinking or feeling. There is nothing occult, supernatural or immaterial about this concept of inner being. It refers only to the build-up of experiences, memories, habits, and skills that are stored in the brain and central nervous system. This content vanishes at death along with the physical construct within which it occurs. No doubt the workings of inner being will become increasingly accessible to us as the physical processes of the brain and central nervous system are better understood.

The balanced development of our inner being is essential if we are to be productive and purposeful human beings. As we have seen above, we are all too prone to go to extremes and only a developed inner being can give us a modicum of self-control. A well-developed inner being gives us intuitions that relatively reliable compared with those whose inner being is not so well-developed. It produces intuitions such as the *epochē* that breaks the cycle of dogmatic reasoning and enables us to think out things anew (as mentioned in section three above). It is basically the unconscious workings of our brain speaking to us.

The *epochē* comes into its own at a crossover point between two extreme views – a hanging dualism – as it were. This is where we are both moderate monists and systematic dualists. If, at an irresolvable point, we are unable to make up our minds, we may need to suspend judgment and allow intuition to take over and supply the answer over time. This is all very well when we have to time to retract and reconsider before leaping forward – *reculer pour mieux sauter* – as the French say. The immediacy of circumstances may call intuition into play and act on instinct or impulse. This is where the depth of inner being may be the deciding factor in making our gut feelings authentic and reliable. Thus, indecision is an essential feature of dynamic action, but where there is time to deliberate then the dynamic account is useful in ordering our thinking.

In a dynamic account, intuition can only be provisional since it can only be a product of inner being and it must be tested, in an empirical way, to ascertain how things are in reality. Thus, an interaction between inner being and external reality is an important part of dynamic logic. What is here called 'inner being' is the unconscious source of intuitive reasoning. At every level of consciousness, our 'inner being' provides the given material of our acts of perception, imagination, conception, theory and language. This inner being is contrasted with 'external reality' of which we are constantly conscious if we are conscious of anything at all. The products of inner being are always provisional except in so far as they are shown or known to be directly resonant of reality. A constant interaction with the realities of the outside world is therefore implied in all dynamic accounts of that world and its contents.

While we are awake and alert, our brains are constantly working away and keeping us in touch with external reality through what we see and hear and feel. We are not usually aware of the constancy of this brain activity. It constitutes our inner being, and we attend to its products in apprehending the contents of reality. Thus, the act of attending to what is given in reality involves interactions with that reality and we are not entirely aware of all the interactions that are occurring. What is immediately given to our senses may not be what is actually there as our sensory processes are largely unconscious and are not infallible. Thus, we may make mistakes in not seeing what is really there, as in optical illusions. We constantly seek secure knowledge of what is really there to correct the mistakes and distortions due to the inadequacy of our sensory equipment. This is done by our interrogation of reality which amounts to a constant interaction with it.

The dualist view thus enables us to ascertain the truth and reality of our thinking by considering the interactions between our inner being and outer reality. A simple example of this interaction is as follows. When I misplace my spectacles, I think about where I might have placed them. I do this within myself – inner being. I search for them, on the basis of where I think I might have left them – outer reality. An interaction between these positions occurs as I eliminate all the possibilities, and I continue thinking and doing until I find them (or give up out of exasperation!)

We interact with outer reality whenever we perceive, conceive, think, act, move or do anything wilfully in relation to what exists in external reality. The effect of conscious interaction is to create actualities which always exist potentially in the universe. Not everything is possible as we are actualising at each moment of time the only reality which is constantly potential in the universe. This explains the indeterminacy of the universe as seen from the perspective of quantum physics. Until we consciously perceive the room around us, it only exists potentially and not absolutely. Our certainty that it continues to exist when unseen is based on the totality of our past experience which assures us intuitively that the room continues to exist as a potential source of perceptual experience. For all we know for sure the room might suddenly disappear as a result of a fire, a sink hole, a bomb, or a plane landing on it. But such events are rare and our past experience assures us of this rarity.

In this way we explain the relationship of the observer with the universe which is otherwise mysterious at the level of quantum physics. Anything is possible in reality and we as observers are responsible for finding out what is actually the case. The observer's acts of perception ensure that potentialities become actualities because an interaction takes place to bring the actuality into being. Also, each interaction takes time to occur and this accounts for the time lag between a physical event and the subjective awareness of it. Consciousness takes its time and we pay for it in the end with our demise. Thus, it is within time that our actual experience of reality is made possible. The rest is an eternity of possibilities.

In conclusion, therefore, our experience of interacting with reality facilitates the build-up of inner being. In this way, inner being becomes increasingly in tune with the realities of life and living. The aim is to make us more successful decision makers, planners and doers, and not just brilliant thinkers. The components of the interaction between inner being and outer reality may be summarised as follows:

Inner Being	Outer Reality
subjective	objective
synthesis	analysis
induction	deduction

It is fundamental to dynamic logic that there is a constant interaction between inner being and outer reality which keeps us in touch with what really exists or does not exist. The above contrasts are outlined as follows:

Subjective/Objective: In dynamic logic, these go together and are inherently inseparable in the interactive process. Thus, distinguishing between the subjective and objective is our constant irresolvable task which is monitored by dynamic logic. The subjective is centred on the individual's inner being or unconscious processes. But this is not exclusively so since there is always an interaction going on between what is subjective and objective. The interaction does not stop simply because we have ascertained the reality of the scene before us. We have to make sure that we are accurately observing the contents of that scene. We are then being objective about what we are perceiving. What is thought to be totally objective therefore includes the things and events that we experience as not belonging to us in the way that images, ideas and dreams belong to us.

Synthesis/Analysis: Our inner being synthetically brings our thoughts, images, feelings together and presents them as a synthetic whole when they occur to us or come to mind. We analyse them when they are thought about and reduced to their parts or components. The interaction between these means that we are not committed to going in one direction of either synthesis or analysis but pursue together to achieve the best possible dynamic account of the circumstances concerned.

Induction/Deduction: As already stated above, induction draws particulars together into wholes whereas deduction splits wholes into their parts. Induction is related more to inner being than outer reality because of its intuitive source. Deduction is most valid in dealing with the discrete entities of outer reality which are more amenable to definition and analysis.

In this way, the relationship between inner being and outer reality is seen to be constantly interactive. In dualist theory, the mechanism that enables us to continue these interactions from birth to death is the dualist interaction since it is such one-to-one interactions that we stay in touch with reality. In the simplest terms, dualist interactions involve the following: Our inner being gives rise to thoughts concerning what we mean by such and such and refer that meaning to outer reality for confirmation or refutation of the said thought. Thus, the sense of what we are thinking is as important as that to which it refers and *vice versa*. Also, both inner coherence and outer correspondence are involved because truth is constantly striven for by interaction rather than established formally by deduction. In this way, dynamic logic is more compatible with scientific method than formal logic because it reflects more accurately the experimental nature of our thinking. As is argued at length below, conceptualisation concerns the inner coherence of our conceptions and their interrelationships with other conceptions whereas contextualisation deals with how they correspond meaningfully to the contexts within which they are used.

To act purposefully and effectively, we need to be realistic about things. Thus, the logic of dualist interaction also concerns how we stay in touch with reality to remain productive and purposeful persons. It is refers directly to situations in their context more than to the words used to describe these situations. This approach ensures that the words are never mistaken for the situations themselves. For the situations are usually more important than the words used to describe them. This is because what we actually do is usually more important than what we say. Our accounts of these situations relate interactively with the situations and remain true to these situations only in so far as they are constantly revised and updated by what we are doing in respect of them.

For example, in watching a news report on television, it is not enough merely to understand the words being spoken by the reporters. It is also necessary to have our own thoughts and feelings that relate to the situation being reported. By thinking for ourselves we arrive at an opinion about the events, the reportage, the people involved and so on. In that way, we are not enslaved to an uncritical belief in news reports that may be no more than propaganda or highly biased accounts. At the same time, any opinion arrived at can never be the final and absolute one. There are other sources of information that can be consulted such as books, articles, and the internet. Our opinions can always be altered and improved as new facts and information become available. In dualist interaction, our thinking is always on the move and never static. In this way, 'dynamic logic' is distinguished from other forms of logic that are static and analytical in comparison.

9. Contextualisation and conceptualisation

Both of these are essential to dynamic logic and the relationship between needs to be clarified. Conceptualisation is intimately connected with contextualisation and *vice versa*. They interact with each other in the dynamic accounts that we make when we establish the truth and validity of our reasonings, plan our future, justify our beliefs and so on. The relationship between these is important for two reasons. *Firstly*, it overrides the relativism which makes it impossible for us judge between different ways of thinking and behaving. *Secondly*, it goes beyond the categorical thinking that has dominated western thought since Aristotle. The basis of both these is tabulated as follows:

Contextualisation (ct)	Conceptualisation (cc)
Contextualisation involves putting our views, opinions, beliefs, ideas, or theories into context. What is given to us intuitively must be in some context or other if it is to be meaningful to us. When we put our experiences into words, the context provides the limits to what we say about them. Anything that is said acquires its meaning within some context or other. Psychobabble may not make sense in itself but it is useful in the context of people seeming to communicate with each other. There can be no context-free arguments; they must take place in a particular context to acquire any meaning at all. Contexts provide the limits within which our concepts, notions, ideas, images, thoughts must function to be meaningful. Wittgenstein referred to these contextual boundaries obliquely in his treatment of 'languages games' or 'forms of life'.	Conceptualisation is the expression in words and symbols of thoughts, ideas, feelings, opinions, beliefs, theories, plans, projects, plots and the like. It is the process of making conceptual distinctions by relating words and symbols to other words and symbols. This includes the logical analysis of words but goes beyond it in being non-linear and multi-dimensional. It takes account of the fact that concepts have links in all directions with other concepts. They have 'family resemblances' between each other, as in Wittgenstein's later philosophy which recognised the inadequacies of formal logic in that regard. We may say that a car generally has an engine, four wheels, seats, and so on, but there is no end to the details that we might add to a description of any car. This means that any description can only be a limited, linear statement that fails to include

The latter provide the contexts within which concepts derive their meanings. His failure to give a theoretical basis to his terms meant that there is no way of judging between one 'language game' or 'form of life' and another. They are all treated as equally valid; hence the relativism of the 20th century.	everything that can be truthfully said on the subject. Such limits to concepts in relation to other concepts are determined by the contexts in which they are used. Our description of a car need only be full enough to suit the context in which we describe it, *e.g.*, in the context of buying a car.

Contextualisation: The application of contextualisation involves putting things into the context in which they are meant to be used and understood. This process of contextualisation organises our views and opinions within a hierarchy of contexts that range from the most important contexts to the least important contexts. We mentally interact within contexts and focus on their contents when we find meaning and purpose, and particularly when we make choices, decisions and judgments. Thus, for example, in thinking about and discussing historical topics we do so within the context of history within which we make meaningful statements that made sense in that context and perhaps in no other. Religions make sense within their various contexts but not necessarily in the context of humanity's future. What the logicians call 'possible worlds' are merely different contexts within which we think about things or not as the case may be.

By putting our thoughts into context we can resolve contradictions and paradoxes which cannot be made sense of in any other way. For instance, in the context of physics, tables and chairs are not solid objects as they are composed of empty space. However, in the context of everyday life they are undeniably solid objects. Put into that context the understanding that they are solid objects is not fundamentally contradicted by what physics tells us of their ultimate nature. Each context has its own priority depending on what we are doing and how we chose to view our surroundings. We chose the context according to our aims, goals and aspirations. What we conceived to be real or unreal depends on the context in which we choose to view it. This does not make reality any the less real. It only means that our apprehension of it changes according to how and why we are interacting with it.

Contexts are also essential to our inner development. Without a context to orient ourselves, we cannot function as rational beings. If we wander aimlessly about the streets without a thought or care in our heads, there is no context or milieu by which to make sense of that behaviour. It exists for its own sake without reference to anything else. Similarly, dogs are easily distinguished from the foxes that now live in our cities. A dog wanders randomly sniffing around whereas a fox is focused on going from A to B without distraction. It has aims and purposes to fulfil and to that extent it seems to have more inner life than the average dog that lives for the moment. Contexts are therefore essential for our inner development for the following reasons:

- They help us to build up our inner being and project it outwards so as to reduce self-centredness. By putting ourselves into contexts beyond mere self, we become sociable persons instead of isolated individuals.
- They are the medium by which we relate to external reality in using language and symbols. We stay in touch with harsh realities by entering into the most appropriate contexts by which these realities can be made sense of and manipulated for our ends.
- Putting things in context involves the *epochē* or break that makes us see things anew and can break the cycle of bigoted thinking that prevents us from seeing different points of view that might be better and more realistic than the fixed viewpoint that otherwise continues unbroken.
- They enable us to find additional meaning in things and make life and the universe more meaningful and valuable to us. Contexts also provide us with additional perspectives by which we appreciate other points of view and become more rounded personalities.

Religious beliefs are often not meaningful outside the context of the particular religion involved. Indeed, they are often not meaningful in the overall context of humanity, especially when they consist in showing contempt for the rest of humanity. The adherents of any religion will inevitably disagree with the beliefs of other religions. This evidence therefore shows that there is a context outside all religions from which they may be judged and evaluated. If we regard religious beliefs as being human in origin, they must also be viewed in the context of humanity as a whole. Religionists who cannot see beyond their own religion will automatically demonise unbelievers and regard them as less than human because they cannot elevate their thinking to embrace the context of humanity as a whole. If they see their religion in the context of humanity as a whole then their religion becomes one viewpoint among many. Its absolute supremacy can no longer be sustained logically. Thus, the contextualisation of religion is a potential antidote to religious fanaticism and extremism.

Contextualisation is a process of putting ourselves into contexts wider than our narrow selfish contexts of everyday life. We do this quite naturally when we feel guilty at the sight of starving children in the underdeveloped world or when we sympathise with people being killed for demonstrating against oppressive regimes. This contextual view enables us to make philosophical sense of these feelings and thus universalise them. They are made part of our rational thinking about ourselves and our role in this world. The more that we reason out our problems, the more we are able to cope with them and ultimately to solve them. Such reasonings make us more secure about the future, and the humanist consensus depends on the ubiquity of such optimistic thinking. It is also important for humanists to promote the contextualization process because, for example, god-belief tends to de-contextualise people's thinking. God-belief is a form of de-contextualization in which all contextual thinking is reduced to a divine outlook. Any human outlook is subordinated to the divine one. In other words, unless people put their thoughts into wider contexts, such as those exemplified here, they will not see any further than God. The wider contexts need to be seen in relation to each other and not to the exclusion of all the others, as in the case of god-belief. We are nothing compared to that entity therefore there is no point in our doing anything for ourselves.

Contexts differ from notions, concepts or categories in that they are holistic and encompassing rather defining and restricting. When we conceive of contexts as notions or concepts, we are thinking of their language usage. We define notions by showing how distinct they are from each other. But contexts are functions of our thinking about things rather than objects of language. They embrace our thoughts expressed in words but are not expressed themselves in words when they are in use. When we contextualise our thinking, the contexts provide the areas within which we think about things. They transcend language usage and constitute the framework for our thinking in notions and conceptions. Our words and symbols lack lasting meaning and reference unless they are expressed within some context or other. The contents of contexts are shared with each of them and therefore they cannot be usefully separated or logically analyzed as if they were distinct from each other. We interact with and within contexts in such a way that each of them can contain all the rest.

Conceptualisation: As mentioned above, categorical thinking creates rigid and absolute distinctions between concepts based on limited definitions which are universalised by dictionaries and the like. Conceptualisation refers to the family interrelationships that link our concepts together into a complete system of thought. That system of thought becomes the context within which they are thought. It therefore ensures that concepts are defined in relation to their context. It looks at all the interconnections of concepts with other concepts and this process has to be undertaken anew in respect of every context in which they are used.

Thus, the process of conceptualisation brings concepts into relationship with each other. They are treated flexibly in terms of their definitions and content. This imposes limitations on the so-called laws of thought as bequeathed to us by Aristotle, namely, the laws of identity, non-contradiction and the excluded middle. The law of identity assumes the identity of objects and events over time unless causal change occurs. This applies particularly to discrete objects and events but it is less applicable to our ideas, beliefs, opinions, theories and the like. In dynamic logic, our thoughts and feelings are only identical *dualistically*; they are not absolutely or formally identical. The law of non-contradiction ensures the consistency of our arguments. But in dynamic logic, an argument is an account that can be elaborated to overcome apparent inconsistencies in expressing our opinions and beliefs. Thus, politicians will attempt to win the argument by elaborating and developing their viewpoint, regardless of its truth or reality. Contextualisation and the application of the *epochē* are required to limit arguments and prevent over-elaboration. It is then possible to relate the argument to contrary facts and ascertain its truth or falsity on external grounds and not just on grounds of internal consistency in the manner of formal logic.

The law of the excluded middle states that something is either the case or it is not and there is no middle position between these. There is no alternative between something being the case or not being the case. But in dynamic logic, the middle ground between contrasting arguments is often where truth is to be sought. In the physical world, things and events can usually be clearly distinguished on an 'either/or' basis, but they are not so clear-cut as far as our subjective activity is concerned.

The result is that in dynamic logic, the excluded middle may be embraced according to context and circumstances. The law of the excluded middle applies to things and events in the external world. Such discrete objects either exist or they do not. They are treated as if they were stable and unchanging. One thing is deduced from another in a discrete and linear fashion. However, the processes of human thinking are not discrete or linear. They are, as described above, abstract and self-referential. Thus the law of the excluded middle may not apply to the subject-matter of dynamic logic that includes the ebb and flow of human thought processes. Sometimes our minds are crowded with thoughts and images and at other times they can be a complete blank. Our thoughts are only linear and consecutive in the way described by formal logic when we apply that logic in circumstances where it is demonstrably applicable.

The effect of including the middle between extremes is to ensure that we are in charge of our concepts and rather than their being in charge of us. We avoid becoming enslaved to our concepts by not making more of them than is justified in reality. In our fluid and open-minded judgments and evaluations, things are not necessarily either one thing or another. They may be both at the same time as when we bear opposing arguments in mind. Even in our judging of physical events we must have a negative view in mind when we exercise our intuitive judgment about these events. We cannot know that the water in a basin is hot unless we have had experience of cold water with which to contrast it. We distinguish the hotness of water by judging it in relation to the potential coldness of water. Thus, the certainty of our judgment that the water is hot depends on the negative possibility that it might have been cold. Our thinking goes from one side to the other without losing touch with the opposing side. The middle is not excluded but remains implicit in our thinking. We really need to measure the temperature of the water to arrive at an objective judgment concerning its comparative hotness or coldness. Thus, interacting with our environment is more important than making judgments that exclude possibilities *a priori*.

None of our beliefs are totally isolated from other beliefs. They are intimately connected with each other no matter how thoroughly we try to isolate them in our thinking about them. There is no means of measuring objectively our arguments and beliefs while they remain personal to us and are untested evidentially or in arguments with other people. We cannot think them true or false; we have to do something with them. For that reason, it is important not to exclude the middle altogether. When a belief is held to the exclusion to all other contrary beliefs, it is as if believing only hot water exists and that there is no possibility of cold water making its appearance in the real world. Beliefs depend for their existence as much on the presence of opposing beliefs as hot water depends on the existence of cold water with which it can be compared.

10. Composing a dynamic account

This section summarises in a very basic way the components of a dynamic account. A fuller treatment requires a book in itself. The relationship between this kind of logic and formal logic also needs to be more fully worked out and it is only briefly dealt with here and in previous sections.

A dynamic account typically involves successive applications of contextualisation and conceptualisation to maximise coherence of argument and correspondence to reality. Thus, a dynamic account uses both coherence and correspondence as tools in the search for truth. They are usually seen as distinct means of reaching truth. The static nature of formal logic leads to an irreconcilable conflict between correspondence and coherence theories of truth. Generally speaking, an empiricist view involves correspondence with reality, and this conflicts with the rationalist view that deals with the coherence of ideas and how they relate to each other to arrive at truths. Dynamic logic provides a framework whereby these points of view are interactive in the movement forward to truth, insight and enlightenment. It provides a means whereby the intuitive nature of coherence interacts with the referential nature of correspondence:

The means of reaching coherence and correspondence include elements such as the following:

Coherence	*Correspondence*
connotation	denotation
meaning	reference
intension	extension

Coherence/Correspondence: Coherence refers to the internal structure of dynamic accounts and to the way that the contents can be placed in contexts and interrelated by their conceptual connections. Correspondence refers to the relationship of the contents of a dynamic account to outer reality. The coherence of our dynamic accounts must always be balanced with their correspondence to realities in the shape of perceptual experience, memory, facts, evidence, experiments, witnesses, documents and whatever else we require to keep ourselves in touch with realities. Also, both inner coherence and outer correspondence are involved because truth is constantly striven for by interaction rather than established formally by deduction. The interaction proceeds in two directions towards external reality through correspondence and towards inner being through coherence. The alternation between these comprises the bare bones of any dynamic account. In this way, dynamic logic is more compatible with scientific method than formal logic because it reflects more accurately the experimental nature of our thinking in which there is an alternation between internalised theory and externalised experimentation.

Connotation/Denotation: The connotation is the whole idea, thought, image which contains meaning that must be teased out. Denotation is what the meaning refers to in reality or in the context in which the argument is being made. These distinctions are therefore closely related to meaning/reference.

Meaning/Reference: The meaning of a word, symbol, sentence, paragraph, theory or book depends on the context in which that meaning is being sought. The meaning must refer to something substantive in that context. The reference is tied to what is being referred to in that context. For example, the meaning of war depends on the social and political contexts in which a war between opposing enemies is conducted to resolve the differences that are only relevant to these contexts. Outside such contexts, no war can be conceived to be meaningful or rational.

Intension/Extension: Intension and extension in dynamic logic signify the two extremes of intuition on the one hand and physical acts on the other hand. Their interacting together describes in general how creativity goes hand in glove with practicality. Intension comprises the intuitions, inspirations, illuminations and flashes that occur to us in the creative process. Extension is the reaching out into reality to prove the reality or validity of our creative productions. It means doing things such as looking up references, researching, experimenting, going to different places in search of evidence and so on.

The further development of this logic depends perhaps on more research into the interaction between these aspects by incorporating the two extremes of 19th century Hegelian/idealist view of logic and the 20th century analytical/realist view of logic. The main point is that the dynamic account is not just concerned with the relationship between words but also their relationship to things and events such that they involve doing things and not just thinking about things.

11. The paradoxical nature of our thinking

The approach of dynamic logic helps us to make sense of the paradoxical nature of our thinking since paradoxes result from dualist interactions which are ongoing and cannot be pinned down without changing the thoughts and feelings that underlie such interactions. What we think to be the case, immediately becomes something different because a new situation has arisen following these thoughts. Incompatible situations arise as a consequence. How dualist theory deals with such paradoxes is outlined as follows:

Subjective paradoxes. A description of the mind in terms of dualist interactions is required because the mind is not composed of entities, substances or essences. It is not distinct from the subjective processes that are recursive and constantly on the move. What happens subjectively cannot be pinned down without becoming what they are not. A subjective experience, such as pain or a feeling of elation, both exists and does not exist at the same time because it is identifiable both with what it is and what it is not at the same time, and it can be distinguished from what it is and is not at the same time. This is a consequence of its interacting with itself and with what is not itself at the same time. Thus, a feeling of elation is experienced and is interacted with so that it becomes both something we own and something distinct from us at the same time. We can view it both subjectively as something to be indulged in and as something to be wondered at – is it justifiable? Is it taking possession of us? Furthermore, we can never quite pinpoint where this feeling is in the brain. It is somehow everywhere and nowhere at once. This kind of paradox is comparable with the paradox in quantum physics of quanta being both waves and particles at the same time. This is because thinking about a thought immediately alters the nature and content of the thought so that it becomes that which it was not in the first place.

Self-Reference Paradoxes: The study of dualist interaction enables us to deal with diverse thoughts and opinions in a self-referential way instead of excluding them in a logical and analytical way. Such exclusions give rise to the self-reference paradoxes that plague logic and mathematics. These paradoxes result from formal logic's inability to deal with the self-referential and inclusive nature of our thinking. Russell's paradox, the Cretan liar paradox, and Gödel's proof of undecidability arise because linear logic cannot refer back on itself without contradiction, inconsistency or discontinuity. Gödel's proof, for instance, shows that undecidability and incompleteness lie at the heart of mathematics. No mathematical proof can be the final truth of the matter since it always lacks some factor and can never be worked out completely and utterly. This is analogous to the dynamic account that never be completed and never decides anything beyond all doubt. The theory of interactive self-reference can help us to get beyond such paradoxes by introducing circularity into our description of thinking instead of insisting on verbal linearity as is required by formal logic.

Russell's Paradox. This is the self-referential paradox in which the class of all classes is said to contain itself. There is a looping back of our thinking to include the class of all classes within that context. We thereby think ourselves into the class of all classes as being a self-contained context. Hence the importance of contexts in the development of dynamic logic. For the context is more than just a set or class. It is like a notion in that it is an intuitive whole which is more than the sum of its contents. It is not the same as the set or class in logic and mathematics. The class of all classes is a context and not a 'class-concept'. It therefore cannot be a member of itself since it is the context within which all classes function. In Bertrand Russell's original formulation of the term 'class', he envisaged it as the 'many' as compared with the 'one'.[145]   The class is an aggregation of physical objects like a pile of apples or a group of animals. The class of objects differs from the context: for instance, the army as a class of things is nothing but a collection of soldiers; as a context, the army contains much more than just the soldiers comprising it, e.g., its battles, its weapons, its power etc. Dynamic logic is thus concerned with the context as a holistic and dynamic

---

[145] Cf. Bertrand Russell, *The Principles of Mathematics*, (2nd edition, 1937), London: Routledge, 1992, pp. 68ff, 76, and 102.

process rather than with the logically neat collections of things which are the concern of deductive logic.

Extremist paradoxes. To repeat the quotation from Thomas Reid: "Extremes of all kinds ought to be avoided; yet men are prone to run into them; and, to shun one extreme, we often run into the contrary."[146] A good example of this lurching from one extreme to another is *the nice/nasty paradox* in which an exceptionally nice person treats someone whom they regard as 'nasty' in much nastier way than the allegedly nasty person would think of treating them. Who then is the really nasty person? The nice person has seemingly swung to the other extreme in defence of an absolute ideal of niceness which they wish to enforce on others. In their minds everyone ought to be nice, or else suffer the consequences by having nastiness applied to them. They are also unconsciously looking for deference and conformity from everyone. Such a mentality is at the root of all utopian experiments designed to make us better people at the expense of our basic human right not to conform and not to be nice, sweet and smiling all the time. If we are to avoid such behavioural extremes, we need to be more self-aware of these excessive tendencies, and a better understanding of dualist interaction is crucial in that regard.

Boundary paradoxes such as the paradox of the heap exemplify the need to be constantly interacting with our thoughts and external reality to ascertain what is or is not a heap. The paradox says that the grains composing a heap may be taken away one by one until a point is reached where it is no longer a heap but say a group of grains. Conversely, grains may be added one by one until a point is reached where they form a distinct pile. The paradox is that it can be both a heap and not a heap at one point of time when it is indefinite one way or the other. The concept of the heap is therefore a fluid process that differs from one point of time and another. Concepts are not to be regarded as fixed for all time but depend on the application of dualist interaction to clarify when a boundary is or is not being breached.

12. The humanisation of negation.

Metaphysical idealists treat negation or 'nothingness' as having an object which is to be contrasted with existence or 'being' (as in the title of Sartre's book, *Being and Nothingness*[147]). But the act of negating becomes a more human process when it is tied to one context or another. That centaurs do not exist is true in the context of external reality. But it is not true to say that they do not

---

[146] Thomas Reid, *Essays on the Active Powers of the Human Mind*, as in Sir William Hamilton's edition of *The Works of Thomas Reid D.D.* (Edinburgh 1895 - also Georg Ohms 1983), p. 635b.

[147] Jean-Paul Sartre, *Being and Nothingness*, (1943 - London: Methuen, 1972). This book is replete with contextual confusions. For example, 'the Other' is analysed as if everyone were the same, thus betraying an autistic lack of appreciation of the differences between individuals and their points of view (cf. especially p. 361f.)

exist in the context of Greek mythology. Negation originated as a means of delineating our notions of things so that they conform more or less to external realities. Voids, vacancies, and privations help us to fill in the gaps between things. But our reification of abstractions has led to a reification of fictitious and imaginary entities which only exist within specific contexts. The non-existence of things which we expect to be there only impress us when they are relevant to the context of our own experience. They are not necessarily relevant to anyone else's experience.[148] It is in a formal and impersonal context that negation leads to Hempel's Paradox, namely, the uninformative conclusion that the existence of a non-black non-raven confirms the existence of black ravens in general.[149] It implies that the nonexistence of anything is connected in some way with the existence of everything. But this can only be in our thinking about things and it tells us nothing about the content of external reality.

The existence of nothing as privation. In dynamic logic, the notion of 'nothing' is functional and is not complete nonexistence. It is privation rather than a total absence of everything. This follows from the way the laws of identity and contradiction are used in this form of logic. Instead of enforcing these laws absolutely in a formal manner, we make use of sameness and difference in respect of the same and different things. If something is not the same then it is different in specific ways. The 'nothing' always refers to something else and not to nothing whatsoever. It could not exist at all if it were nothing in the sense of complete absence of everything. It would therefore have no meaning as a word if it referred to the total absence of everything whatsoever. Thus, it refers to that which is lacking or absence and not to nothingness as such. It is the same as negation and therefore is opposed to being positive. The need for the notion of nothing arises because consistency means ruling things in and not ruling things out. There is no such thing as nothing whatsoever since whatever is ruled out of existence in an account continues to exist in the original context or a different one. Whatever is ruled out does not disappear but is moved elsewhere in our thinking about it.

'Nothing' is a figure of speech signifying absence or privation. It cannot mean that nothing exists in the same way that entities exist. The act of negating does not concern nothing or nonentity. It is a tool by which conceptions are delimited for the purpose of thinking or talking about things in a logical, consistent and sensible way. There is nothing but the universe and that includes everything in it. This rules out the possibility of our referring to anything outside the context of the universe which contains everything that we can know about it. It limits the

---

[148] Sartre, *op. cit.*, p. 9. Contrary to Sartre's view, the failure of a friend to meet you in a café has no relevance at all to the context of the café in question but everything to do with the context of your personal life.

[149] Carl G. Hempel, *Aspects of Scientific Explanation*, (New York: The Free Press, 1965), p.15: "Any non-raven represents confirming evidence for the hypothesis that all ravens are black."

concept by making it the only possible context in which anything can exist or take place. Similarly, computers are based on Boolean algebra which is about alternatives that are switched on or off. It does not concern the existence or non-existence of anything in particular.

Negation is thus ruled out in so far as it attempts to make something non-existent which is anything but non-existent. In dynamic logic, negation is only functional in relation to opposites. Everything exists in relation to its opposite. That opposite consists not only of its complete negation and also of that with which it is contrasted. Thus, the fact that opposites cannot be ruled out means that nothing can be negated completely. It will pop up somewhere no matter how hard we try to rule it out.

To posit something without taking account of its opposite is unrealistic idealism. Idealism is a one-sided monism which seeks to eliminate dualist contrasts. It relies on the excluded middle to make a reasoned choice between alternatives impossible. The alternative is always unthinkable and therefore thought to be 'nothing'. In this thinking, belief is absolute and non-believers are nothing but expendable nonentities.

The non-existence of nothing supports the non-existence of God since there is nowhere for it to exist in or outside the universe since there is nothing but the universe. There are no gaps in the universe that are not potentially identifiable and distinguishable in some way. Therefore, there are no gaps for any creator to exist or make its effect on the universe or its contents.

13. Some more features of the dynamic account

Holism: Dynamic logic takes a holistic, overall view that includes contradictions and paradoxes. For example, my pen belongs to me in a sense but it does not belong to me in so far as it tells no one about what I am as a person. I am much more than my possessions, my internal organs and even my experiences. I am both my experiences and not my experiences at the same time. They belong to me but they do not define me. I may even think of them, rightly or wrongly, as dreams that never really happened. I am the activity that involves my experiences but I am not myself the experiences. In interacting with them I define myself during that activity but I am nothing outside that activity.

Paradoxes and contradictions are resolved into the holistic picture in which they make sense in relation to each other even though they make no sense in themselves. This is why contextualisation is so important in its relationship to conceptualisation. It provides the limits to which our holist views are taken in embracing everything about any subject matter.

The holistic nature of dynamic logic means that it embraces the passage of time. In comparison, the relative timelessness of formal logic makes it unsuited to deal with ongoing mental events that seemingly conflict with each other. Dynamic logic takes its time and therefore has time enough in which to make sense of everything since everything fits together in the overall scale of things. If they did not fit together in that way, then events could not happen consecutively or predictably. There would be universal chaos and demonstrably there is not. We are able to make sense of most of what is happening around in spite of our ignorance about so many things in the universe. Moreover, in dynamic logic, we interact dualistically with this overall view of reality and do not treat it as a static form of absolute being in the Hegelian way which is a monist rather than a dualist view.

Questioning: Our dynamic accounts are built up by our interrogations and the asking of questions. Questioning therefore brings an additional dimension to dualist interaction. The acquisition of language has given us the ability to use questions by which we interact with our own thinking and with other people. The relationship between question and answer are important forms of dualist interaction. In posing a question we invite an interaction on a one-to-one basis with whomever we are conversing, and even with ourselves on occasion. *A question is therefore an interactive prompt.* It invariably invites a response whether it is an answer to the question or not. Even when we are wondering or pondering about things we are in a sense questioning what we have in mind. For example, we may ask ourselves, "I wonder whether she will be at home or not?" before doing something to find out. Questioning therefore has functions such as the following:

- Questions help us to understand and clarify our thinking about things that we have only vague and incomplete thoughts about.
- Questions arise when we seek information and the answers create data which may not have existed before.
- Questioning enables us to know each other's minds. We generally know we are dealing with a person rather than a computer when the answers are unexpected or unpredictable.

Indeed, every human interaction may be expressed in a question/answer form. When observing someone doing something, we may first ask ourselves: 'What are they doing?' and then ask them 'What are you doing?' We are interacting firstly with ourselves and secondly with the other person by posing these questions. Such is the importance of questioning that human society ceases to be open and free whenever we fear to question anyone or anything.

Time: As time moves forward, so each dynamic account is open to revision and restatement. Each moment of time is potentially a new context that has to be taken account of if there is any possibility of significant change having taken place. Such changes confirm the reality of time. There is the relentless passing of time – second by second, minute by minute, day by day and so on – over which we change, deteriorate, decay and eventually cease to exist as unified entities. In common with all other entities in the universe, we endure as identifiable and distinguishable beings only for a limited period of time, and in defiance of the ravages inflicted on us through the passage of time. The processes that preserve our unity, sooner or later, run out of time as nothing lasts forever. Our existence is maintained over a period of time because our bodies constantly reinforce the atomic, chemical and metabolic processes that are necessary for the body's continued unity. Eventually, their ability to maintain these interactive processes is diminished, thus heralding our eventual demise. We therefore *persist* through time, *subsist* through the unifying processes, and *exist* as identifiable and distinguishable entities in our own right. We have only a brief spell of time within which to persist, subsist and exist. Our time is finite because the interactive processes that preserve our unity do not last forever. Every unified entity only lasts as long as its internal processes are capable of maintaining its unity.

If we all lasted forever, we would run out of space in which to exist, and there would be no time available to get anything done since there would be no room in which to do it. All we can do is contribute in our own small way towards the possible immortality of a future universe which is complex and well-developed enough to maintain its existence forever. Perhaps this is the ultimate purpose of intelligent beings in the universe. We are here to make sense of the universe and thus contribute to the eventual conquest of time.

Similarly, dynamic accounts have their day, and their relevance is limited because of the passing of time. Changing events make all dynamic accounts questionable in terms of their relevance and usefulness. They are entities that have their beginning and end like all entities. No matter how much time we take to make the most of our accounts of life and love, we must run out of time sooner or later. And even the timeliness of the account of logic given in this book is necessarily questionable.

14. The further development of dynamic logic

There are at least eight aspects of dynamic logic that may be developed and put into practice. The development of each of them in relation to each other would also contribute towards rendering dynamic logic into a systematic science:

The Planned Pillars of Dynamic Logic

- *Dualistics* – dualist interaction and the avoidance of extremism. Constant interaction with ourselves, our environment and other people is necessary for thoughtfulness and open-mindedness

- *Cyclitics* – self-reference and self-criticism. It concerns how our thinking loops back to examine what went before. As we move forward in time, dualist interactions become cyclical.

- *Deterministics* – uncertainty, choices and decision-making, goals and aims. All our thinking is not to be made for its own sake but to get things done and achieve our aims as human beings.

- *Significatics* – meaning, sense, value and significance. Unless what we say or do has meaning and significance, it has no value and connection with our lives as a whole.

- *Ideatics* – ideas, notions, concepts and their interrelationships. In any system of thought we need to ascertain the interrelationships between our ideas and notions to achieve clarity and highlight the significance of our words.

- *Contextics* – contexts, perspectives and viewpoints. Only by putting our thoughts, feelings and actions into context can we assess their value and meaning.
- *Holistics* – wholeness and completeness. The integrity of our personalities depend on our getting things together as a whole in order to make sense of our lives as a whole.
- *Teleologics* – the ends towards which we direct our actions. All our lives have potential ends which we must thrive to establish and then fulfil.

Dynamic logic uses all these functions in carrying out the aims mentioned above. It thereby enables us to make sense of the reasoning behind these functions. *Dualistics* describes the nature of dualist interaction as it moves between extremes and avoids being polarised to the extremes. This requires us to criticise ourselves and so refer back into ourselves as *cyclitics* shows. This may give rise to uncertainty in our decision-making and goal-setting and we can use *deterministics* that uses dynamic logic to explore the means by which arrive at decisions by correcting imbalances and distortions in our thinking. Our choices, decisions and goals gain meaning and significance by relating them to ourselves as a whole and hence *significatics* moves into play as we establish the value or lack of value to things in that way. The notions and concepts that we use are interrelated in the way described by *ideatics*. All our concepts get their meaning from the contexts and perspectives in which they are used and so *contextics* is involved here. In our attempt to make all our thoughts into a unified, meaningful whole requires *holistics*, and the ends to which we devote ourselves involves *teleologics*.

Part Nine
The Pursuit of Truth by Dualist Interaction

1. Truth is about deeds not words

The logic of dualist interaction consists in using truth to build up dynamic accounts and to constantly revise and update them. Here we examine the ways in which truth is pursued as a continuously self-critical process. In dualist theory, truth is not an end itself but a means to getting things done that are worthwhile doing. The dynamic account is not the whole truth of the matter since it is limited to what is practical and expedient in specific circumstances. For example, the facts as presented to a jury are limited to what is relevant to the crime; they are not exhaustive of every conceivable detail concerning the case. Personal details of defendants, prosecutors, judges, jury members are omitted. The total life stories of accused persons are not included, and so on. Similarly, a dynamic account is limited according to the context in which it is used.

We can never get at the whole truth; it is always relative to context or the situation in which it is being sought. We are constantly faced with error, falsehood, distortion, half-truths, lies and deceptions. Thus, we are always seeking and re-affirming whatever truth we find or establish. What is false or erroneous usually consists in the misuse of words and symbols in referring to the facts but it may also be a mistake, misinterpretation, a misreading of the facts, a deliberate lie to fool or exploit people, or an invention or fantasy in which the facts are changed or distorted for some purpose or other. Thus, words are not always reliable vehicles of truth. But current views of truth begin and end with words and this has retarded our efforts in getting to the bottom of it.

Instead of grappling with the complexities of truth, 20th century philosophers generally took the easy way and proclaimed it to be practically indefinable. They sought a minimalist, deflated truth when it is in fact a complex and unwieldy process that needs exposition more definition. Making sense of this minimalist approach has led to a veritable 'Burgess Shale' burgeoning of exotic truth theories, including minimalist, deflationist, disquotationist, redundancy, prosentential, and super-assertible theories.[150] This is scholastic pedantry run riot. In all these cases, truth and falsity are assumed to be about words rather than deeds.

For example, Tarski's reduction of truth to a useless tautology such as "the sentence 'snow is white' is true if, and only if, snow is white" does not advance our understanding of truth.[151] It merely trivialises it. It changes nothing since the truth of the matter really concerns whether it is a fact that snow is white in the

---

[150] Cf. Simon Blackburn and Keith Simmons, (eds), *Truth*, (1999 - Oxford: OUP, 2003), where these minimalist theories are discussed in depth.

[151] Alfred Tarski, 'The Semantic Conception of Truth', *Philosophy and Phenomenological Research*, 4 (1944). Reprinted in Blackburn and Simmons, *op. cit.,* ch. VIII, pp. 115-143. The 'snow is white' quotation is on page 141.

context in which it is being said. The words 'snow is white' cannot be universally true since snow gets dirty and can be coloured with chemicals. Also, it doesn't look white under a microscope. This unnaturally narrow minimalist approach arose because truth and falsity were rendered *ad hoc* instruments of formal logic by the likes of Frege[152] and by Wittgenstein in his *Tractatus*.[153] They both made thoughts and facts a matter of words expressed in propositions. As a result, an overall view of truth has proved elusive as it has been hi-jacked by the logicians and enslaved by their wordplay.

Focusing on words means that truth is often contrasted with falsity or falsehood. But falsity does not exist in the external world any more than evil exists in it. It is a function of our putting limits to our definitions of words or symbols in pursuit of our ends and purposes. Thus, falsehood belongs to our words and symbols and the way that we use them in communicating our thoughts, expressing our feelings, and in stating facts. If you say something that is manifestly wrong or false, you have chosen the wrong words to express the truth of the matter. Our words are meant to relate to reality and they are false in so far as they fail to do so. If you misstate how you feel, you are saying something false that does not relate to the reality of how you feel.

When we use words to express our apprehension of reality, we socialise our thinking since words are social artefacts. Words relate to the society in which we communicate our thoughts and feelings. While words can relate to reality in some way, they cannot themselves be real. Taking words too seriously makes them seem more real than they really are. They must always be taken 'with a pinch of salt' and we must constantly work hard to ensure that our words refer as accurately as possible to reality. This may seem to be an obvious and trivial point but religious writers and philosophers have consistently made too much of words. Fanatics, demagogues and ideologues are typically obsessed with words and reify them to excess. They think that by out-arguing people *ab nauseum* they must be *ipso facto* in the right and everyone else in the wrong. Thus, the arguments are never themselves the truth but only the extent to which the words composing the arguments relate directly to reality and are shown to be so. It is argued below that formal logic is largely responsible for the unspoken assumption that words to be more real than they really are.

The very existence of things depends on context and not on the form of the words. The fact that there is no hippopotamus in the room is only makes sense in the context in which someone is speaking of the possibility of such a creature being in the room. Such a ridiculous context arose in an early argument between

---

[152] Cf. Gottlob Frege, 'The Thought: A Logical Inquiry', *Mind*, 65 (1956), pp. 289-311. Reprinted in Blackburn and Simmons, *op. cit.*, ch. V, pp. 85-105. See p. 89 of the latter where thoughts are treated as being inseparable from sentences.

[153] Ludwig Wittgenstein, *Tractatus Logico-Philosophicus*, trans. D.F. Pears & B.F. McGuiness, (1921 – London: Routledge & Kegan Paul, 1969), for example, (1) p. 21, §3.14: "A propositional sign is a fact" (*Das Satzzeichen ist eine Tatsache*); (2) p. 35, §4: "A thought is a proposition with a sense" (*Der Gedanke ist der sinnvolle Satz*); and so on.

Wittgenstein and his mentor Bertrand Russell. When Wittgenstein doubted the meaningfulness of existential propositions, Russell responded: "I invited him to consider the proposition: 'There is no hippopotamus in this room at present.'" Russell searched the room accordingly to confirm this.[154] Thus, the truth of what is said depends on whatever is done to confirm the nonexistence of the hippopotamus. It does not depend on the form or analysis of the words being used.

Human beings have made too much of words from the time they first learnt to use words to express their emotions and to refer to things in the external world. They thought that their words had a mystical or magical power to change things, just as the cave paintings of Palaeolithic peoples were presumably used to invoke the animals they depict. Thus, the ancient Egyptians used words as spells and incantations in their 'books of the dead' scrolls that they buried with their dead to invoke gods and goddesses in favour of their deceased relatives. Words became sacred things with a life of their own. Thus, the ancient Greek poets were said to be inspired by the muses. Their words were divinely inspired instead of being the product of their unique creativity. Finally, the Jews turned their sacred book into a vehicle of worship and veneration as the words were thought to be inspired by God. This paved the way for all the word bound religions that have followed. In that way, the truth is perverted by being identified with words alone, regardless of the evidence or indeed the reality to which they may or not be related. Unhappily, this kind of untruthfulness is still rampant among religious people even today.

Aristotle perpetuated this adulation of words by making truth a matter of saying what is or is not the case (see pp. 161-2). The result is the lingualism already referred to (on p. 160). In a lingualist society: politicians are trained to say the right thing rather than what they really think or believe; political correctness makes totems and taboos of words no matter the true intention behind them; the words, images and fashions of the mass media are made to represent the whole culture though they may have little to do with the lives and lifestyles of the silent majority; actors become superstars though they do little more than speak the words written for them; and so on.

2. The world is made of facts not words

The dynamic account depends on facts more than words to establish and review its truth. Words don't do anything on their own whereas facts imply that something is being done in relation to them. Words are only factual when they involve doing or not doing things in relation to reality. A fact is an interactive unit of truth which relates to external reality. Facts are therefore important units of any account that purports to be real and truthful. Thus, a truthful account is composed of facts that may be verified or falsified in relation to external reality. The word 'fact' comes from the Latin *factum* which is the past participle of *facere*

---

[154] Cf. Bertrand Russell, 'Ludwig Wittgenstein', *Mind*, Vol. LX, 1951, p. 297.

meaning 'to do'. Strictly speaking, 'fact' signifies something which is done, an act or deed. A fact only becomes an object of truth when it is possible to do something regarding it in relation to reality. A working fact is therefore is a process that applies at a particular point in time rather than a fixed, determined object. It is only stable in so far as it refers to past events. Even then, they may not represent the whole truth of the matter and are subject to further revision, rethinking and updating.

It is important to clarify the role that facts play as our agreement concerning what is or is not to be done depends on our agreeing what the facts are. We must reach general agreement about the facts concerning the plight of the human race; otherwise we will do nothing together to ensure our future. No such agreement will be reached while our apprehension of reality depends on words spoken and not on hard, cold facts concerning what really exists.

The fact that external reality is totally independent of us has been argued for elsewhere in this book (e.g. pp. 80-3). It is also confirmed by our being totally superfluous to the world in that our deaths will not bring the world to an end; it will carry on regardless. If external reality were not totally independent of us, then our dreams could be just as real as external reality. But we emerge from our dreams into a palpable and undeniable reality. It is only fanciful to suppose that our lives are themselves a dream out of which we will emerge at death or even before death. There is simply no evidence to refute in any conclusive way this primary assumption of the total independence of external reality. Thus, the universe and its physical contents, including ourselves, exist completely independent of any words or symbols that we use with regard to them.

The universe and its contents constitute the facts of external reality. We establish these facts by doing things such as looking, listening, handling, experimenting and so on. The dualist view of truth involves interacting with these given facts to arrive at the truth. In interacting with the given facts we keep in touch with reality. In our thinking and speaking about the facts about the universe we necessarily put these facts into contexts to make sense of them in words and symbols. The contexts are the go-betweens that enable us to think and speak about these facts meaningfully and purposefully. The truth is arrived at by a process of interacting with the facts and by expressing the known facts in words and symbols. Thus, the words and symbols used to express are not the facts themselves since they can be differently expressed and are open to constant revision to make the words and symbols represent more exactly the given facts.

3. The importance of facts

Facts are sturdy things. As Robert Burns pithily put it: "Facts are chiels that winna ding, and downa be disputed."[155] In plain English: "Facts are fellows that

---

[155] Robert Burns, *A Dream*, verse 4, as in *Poems and Songs of Robert Burns*, ed. by James Barke, (London and Glasgow: Collins, 1955), p. 82. In this poem, written in 1786, he imagines himself at the Birthday Levée of George III, wherein Burns is unable to dispute the fact that the king, his bed and his clothing are in a poor state.

won't be beaten and are not to be disputed." But what kinds of fact are indisputable? The dualist answer is that complex facts are only indisputable after being subject to complex truth processes that are detailed in the sections below. However, indisputable facts may be (a) given by direct intuition, (b) reached by truthful reasoning. These give us indisputable facts only in limited contexts such as the following:

(a) Direct intuition gives us facts that are accurate by virtue of perception. Our instinctive reactions are intuitive in that sense. We see a car coming towards us and we instinctively step aside to avoid it. A footballer heading a ball towards the goal is reacting immediately without conscious reasoning. In these intuitions there is direct interaction with external reality.

(b) The most truthful forms of reasoning involve mathematics and science. If there are five apples in a fruit bowl and later there are only four apples, it is a fact of arithmetic that there is one less apple in the bowl. It has presumably been taken from the bowl. Gleaning that fact requires a perceptual interaction with the contents of the bowl that consists in looking at them and counting the number of apples accordingly.

The doubts and uncertainties about facts arise when they are remote from possible verification or refutation. Reasoning by induction does not always give us conclusive facts. Induction synthesises or brings together our thoughts and it presents us with an idea, feeling, opinion, hypothesis, theory or something that makes sense of things as a whole. For example, in watching a murder mystery film or play, we may arrive at an inductive conclusion as to the identity of the murderer given the evidence presented to us. However, a further twist in the plot may alter the evidence and we find that our conclusion has been drawn over hastily.

There are three principal types of fact that may need verification in complex situations: (1) perceptual facts that may be confirmed or denied by using such senses as sight, hearing, touch, and feeling; (2) scientific facts that are subject to appropriate scientific methods; and (3) social facts that apply to meaningful human activity. *Perceptual facts* are those dependent on the direct perception of objects and events. On hearing the reports of others about what has happened we know that we can verify these reports by seeing or hearing them for ourselves. *Scientific facts* depend for their truth or falsity on the particular scientific methods by which they are obtained. The most problematic and relevant are *social facts* since our future depends on our agreeing about them. Though these types are interrelated, we are largely concerned here with the status of the last two.

The facts themselves are never adequately represented by the words or symbols that we use to express them or make sense of them. There is always more going on than the words or symbols can express or encompass. The extent of our emotional attachment to the facts is usually omitted in any account of them. The same facts may be differently expressed by using different words or symbols. It is a fact that water is H_2O, and that salt is sodium chloride. These facts remain the same, however they are expressed. The fact that the sun is shining may mean: (1) that sun is constantly emitting its energy upon the Earth; (2) that the clouds have parted to allow it to shine; (3) the Sun King is smiling; or some such. Its meaning varies according to context and the intention of the speaker or writer.

Most of the facts we deal with in daily life are arrived at intuitively by means of perception and conception. Perceptual intuitions are true when we see, feel, smell or taste what is really there. This is regardless of whether we put these intuitions into words or not. However, the facts are not always what we intuitively believe them to be, especially when we examine them in retrospect. When an intuition occurs to us we may regard it instantaneously as being factual and as representing realities directly and immediately. This tendency must be overcome by mental discipline.

When facts are expressed in words or symbols they acquire values that are subjective to one degree or another. Expressed facts cannot lack value when we express them intentionally and communicatively since it is in their value to us that they are meaningful and useful. We would say nothing at all if we had nothing of value to say. However, the facts lose something of the pristine reality that they have when not so expressed to anyone in particular. Thus, for example, I may look up at the night sky and say to myself 'Look at these stars!'. This expresses my feelings in gazing at the stars so that it is little more than an internal expression of my feelings which is of value to me alone. But if I say to someone else 'Look at these stars!' I am stating a fact but also communicating my emotions in the expectation that the hearer will also experience these emotions. Similarly, if I tell someone that water boils at one hundred degrees centigrade, this is a fact that I think may be of value to the listener, otherwise I wouldn't bother saying it. The person may or may not be able to do something with this fact and the value of the expression will lie or not lie in that.

When we are seeking the truth we are usually trying to eliminate emotional and subjective factors to reach a more real expression of what exists or what is or was happening. The most important way of reaching objectivity is by expressing the facts in their most appropriate context. Scientific facts are value free only to the extent that they are purely mathematical and free of practical application. But in forming part of theories, these facts acquire value in these theories because of the value that their advocates put on the theories in possessing and propagating them. Scientists typically are excited about their theories and only their professional discipline prevents them from advocating their theories dogmatically against any evidence that threatens or refutes them. It is in their professional interests to get at the root of matters regardless of their personal predilections

The accuracy and reliability of expressed facts depends, first and foremost, on the context in which they are used. We need effort and perseverance to put facts in the appropriate contexts in which they apply. Thus, the fact that two plus two makes four does not apply when one is adding two glasses of water to another two glasses of water by pouring them into a jug. Two plus two makes one in that case. In mathematics we learn to contextualise the facts very precisely so that the formulae and proofs referring to them are as accurate and reliable as is humanly possible.

We often put facts in the wrong context, for example, when we treat fictionalised characters in books, cinema or television as if they were real. Thus, the falsity of our expressions arises when we carelessly or maliciously misuse the facts in that acontextual way. A fact becomes fictional when it is expressed in a fictional context, but an overenthusiastic person may treat it as being representative of reality. For example, the depiction of zombie pandemics destroying civilisation may be thought to be a factual possibility instead of being an improbable invention. A viral infection cannot possibly turn people into zombies instantaneously or indeed sustain them after death. The pathological liar is always expressing facts in made-up contexts which can be shown to be non-existent, inaccurate or distorted. The conspiracy theorist is often taking facts out of context to prove some improbable myth or other.

Nevertheless, every assertion bears some truth in so far as it has meaning, and every assertion is factual in so far as it refers to something else beyond itself. Therefore, neither truth-bearing nor factuality is sufficient for us to rely absolutely on words and symbols for our decisions. We must ultimately evaluate the extent of fact and truth in any assertion by reference to context and perspective. Thus, facts are established not simply by the form of words and sentences or by their definitions. Their relationship to the sociosphere and what is happening therein must also be taken into account.

Facts are those assertions in which there are sociospheric relationships between the words and symbols we use in these assertions and the meanings inherent in them. These words and symbols have no meaning outside the context of sociospheric activity. This includes even facts stored in libraries and in digital form. Their meaningfulness depends on their being brought out of storage and used in a social context. Social facts therefore exist *sociospherically* rather than actually, unlike those events and states of affairs which are not facts in so far as they actually happened regardless of whether they were expressed in words or symbols. Thus, we have no idea what was said by early primitive peoples though we can be sure that they were communicating with each other. Facts exist *cosmically* when they have been established in science, history or some settled science, field of knowledge or subject of study. They then have the potential to exist for posterity and hence for all time thereafter. Short term facts are those current in the sociosphere of intercommunication whereas long term facts form part of the cosmos over and above any sociospheric context in which they are used.

This interactive view of the expression of facts is vindicated by the scientific method. The build-up of scientific knowledge is essentially interactive. It is constantly being refined and perfected to get at the truth. Similarly, in the dualist view, we use words and symbols in interacting with things and events. Their truth therefore depends on the quality and frequency of our interactions with things and events. The truth depends on all things being equal and all conditions being fulfilled pertaining to the truth. The truth of the fact that the water boils at 100° C at sea level depends on the conditions in which it is being boiled. For example, there may be impurities in the water that alter the temperature at which it boils. Moreover, we cannot be sure that we know all the conditions required to make water boil at that temperature. The truth of any scientific theory depends on possible limitations, qualifications, refinements, or revisions in the light of further knowledge and understanding. Thus, scientists are constantly refining the contexts in which their researches and experiments are being conducted. The ultimate context at this time is CERN's Large Hadron Collider which is colossal and powerful enough to provide the best possible conditions for exploring the world of quantum physics. Theoretical facts are never established absolutely but only as interactive processes which we may correct and update according to future events. The reality of such facts may not be doubted while they enable us to deal directly and effectively with reality.

Thus, scientific truth increases our knowledge and understanding through science, mathematics and the social sciences including history and archaeology. But when we are trying to get things done in the world we must constantly delve for the truth as a means to practical ends. Thus, truth-seeking in dualist theory is a constant interchange between ourselves and an external reality that is independent of our apprehension of it. We interact with external reality on the one-to-one dualist fashion. Moreover, the pursuit of truth by dualist interaction is a way of thinking that can be learnt and cultivated. It is a multi-faceted notion that has many meanings according to the context in which it is used. It is an extremely abstract notion that needs constantly to be brought down to earth by constant revision and updating. Facts are therefore the building blocks of the dynamic account. Establishing them with any certainty involves more than one way to truth.

4. The limits to truth

Truth is not important enough to be deified or made more important than we are. It is only as important as we choose to make it. In other words, its importance lies in our use of it. Make too much of it, and we end up as dogmatists, fanatics, or extremists. Make too little of it, and we end up as sceptics, nihilists or cynics. Truth is no greater than our quest for it. At its best, the truth is an unending search that helps us to face up to and deal with the facts and realities of life. As André Gide put it: "Believe those who seek the truth. Doubt those who have it. Doubt everything but not yourself."[156]

---

[156] Or "Believe those who are seeking the truth. Doubt those who find it." This is perhaps a more accurate translation of the French: "Croyez, ceux qui cherchent la vérité, doutez de ceux qui la trouvent; doutez de tout, mais ne doutez pas de vous-même." André Gide, *Journal 1939-1949 Souvenirs*, (Paris: Gallimart, 1954), "Ainsi Soit-il ou Les Jeux Sont Faits" – à ma fille Catherine Jean Lambert, p. 1233.

It is clear therefore that truth is not a simple monolithic attribute which consists in saying or asserting something truthful. It is not found simply in sentences or propositions as the logicians assume. It concerns what we mean by the thoughts and feelings which we may or may not express in words, exclamations, exhortations, phrases, sentences, paragraphs, calculations, formulae, theories, novels, and so on.

Truth is intimately connected with other abstract notions, and it involves innumerable mental processes. If truth is treated simply as notion or concept then it is impossibly complex to unravel since it is intimately connected to thought, belief, knowledge, fact, reality, existence, being, possibility and necessity, for a start. A thought can be either true or false; a belief is believed to be true or is found to be false; having knowledge of something is to know it is true; a fact can make an opinion true or false; reality is what our true thoughts, opinions, and theories are about; existence or being refer to what truly exists; possibility awaits actuality in truth; necessity follows from something being true.[157] The complex interconnections between all these notions makes truth an intractable notion that cannot be pinned down by any simple definition.

We may assume that the truth, in the sense of the ultimate reality of life and existence, is 'out there' and that it exists as something we can strive to understand and comprehend. But all our efforts to reach it are inevitably limited and circumscribed. We can only reach truths that are conclusive in limited ways. This is because conclusive truth only exists as a context within which facts, states of affair, events, and external objects are assessed, evaluated, ultimatised, and verified from a higher perspective than what is directly perceived or thought as being factual, actual, or real. We imagine what the conclusive truth could be like and compare our present knowledge and understanding with that. We then evaluate that knowledge and understanding within that context and establish the extent to which it is wanting. In this way, dualist theory deals with truth, not as an end in itself, but as an *interactivity* between ourselves and the world.

Though the truth of the matter is the way things really are, no truth counts for anything unless a person or persons is facing up to that truth or failing to do so. Truth is relative to person, time and place, or else it is being proclaimed a timeless dogma that is inhuman and untouchable (such as God or holy scripture). Even scientific laws are relative to time and place; they makes sense to humans but not necessarily to alien beings having a different physical constitution and different faculties from ours. An assertion is true or false for somebody somewhere or it is nowhere or nothing as far as we are concerned. Truth-seeking is an interactive process in which we relate to something other than ourselves to make it a part of ourselves, or not as the case may be. Even the truths of mathematics have to be true for someone. Falsity and negation come into play when we fail to identify things or relate to them in positive terms. As we shall see, logic operates at this level.

---

[157] Cf. Pascal Engel, *Truth*, (Acumen Publishing Ltd., 2002), p. 1.

5. Truth as an activity

In dualist theory, truth is a process and not a property or predicate of words or sentences. There is no such thing as a statement which is absolutely true or false. There is only a statement expressing the facts which is can be shown to be true or untrue by doing things in relation to the facts. The truth of the fact that I have left my glasses next door depends not on the statement of that fact but on the reliability of my memory of having left them there. I find out whether my memory is reliable or not by going next door to find them. When I find them there, I confirm the fact that I did indeed leave them there. Thus, I have confirmed the fact by dualist interaction, and that action confirms the fact and the statement of fact is merely ancillary to that action.

In dualist theory, there is no 'determinate relation' between our expression of the facts and the facts themselves. There is a constant fluid interaction by which the expression of facts are improved or corrected when necessary. The facts of science may be mathematically determined but our apprehension of them depends on what we can make of them. The mathematics only lends precision and accuracy to the facts of science. Expressing them mathematically is not sufficient to make them absolutely true in all conceivable circumstances.

There are at least six ways in viewing truth as an activity, and these can be divided into practical and rigorous pursuits. All these methods can be used in the making of a dynamic account depending on the context and purposes for which it is being used. When we pursue truth in practice we are doing so as individuals facing specific tasks, social demands, work place requirements and so on. When truth is pursued rigorously, this involves the use of specific methods to establish truth or falsity in retrospect.

Truth pursued in practice

Truth-Telling: This is the social and personal use of truth we are all supposedly familiar with. It is telling it the way it is, was or will be. It can't be the truth unless high standards of honesty and sincerity are being applied.

Truth-Seeking: This is when we are seeking the truth by doing something or using a technique or method to find it. Scientific methods are the most thorough means by which we seek truth.

Truth-Applying: This is when we apply what we believe to be true to practical situations. We arrive at a thought which we think is true or false and then do things to ascertain which the thought relates truly or falsely to the facts.

Truth pursued rigorously

Truth-Validating: This is the use of logic to ascertain valid ways of stating things. This is used in the analysis of words and sentences within the framework of linguistic definitions.

Truth-Proving: This is proving truths by the use of mathematical methods. For example, the solving a quadratic equation would be an application of truth-proving.

Truth-Accounting: This is about accounting for the truth of a state of affairs or what has really happened in a particular time and place. It is the most general of all the quests for truth as it includes all the other means of getting at the truth.

The Practical Pursuit of Truth

Aspect	TRUTH-TELLING	TRUTH-SEEKING	TRUTH-APPLYING
Application	Using universal notions such as honesty and sincerity to adhere to high standards of truthfulness. Also demanding high standards of truth-telling from other people	Using a trial-and-error process using questions and methods of inquiry to seek practical and ultimate truths of optimal use to us and humanity in our everyday life	Using truths themselves in practical situations, and establishing that they are useful and satisfactory. Also recognising that the truth may be socially harmful.
Activity	Keeping an open mind	Pursuing a specific view of truth	Applying truths
Attitude	Facing Facts	Positing Truths	Appreciating Truths
Aim	Truthfulness and sincerity	Understanding and insight	Illumination and Practicality

The Rigorous Pursuit of Truth

Aspect	TRUTH-VALIDATING	TRUTH-PROVING	TRUTH-ACCOUNTING
Application	Using formal logic to validate statements and arguments to establish what is true or false by formal and generally accepted modes of logical argument	Using mathematics to prove formulae, theorems, scientific theories. Using experiments and tests to confirm or deny truths.	Using dynamic accounts to arrive at truth as a whole, and also correspondence and coherence to assess would-be truths and detect the limitations of their respective justifications
Activity	Making logical distinctions	Applying mathematical rules	Confirming or denying truths by referring to facts
Attitude	Dissecting arguments	Enforcing consistency	Criticising Truths
Aim	Validity and Consistency	Proof and verification	Accuracy and predictability

The Six Activities of Truth

6. The practical pursuit of Truth

Truth-Telling: Truth is the oil that lubricates the mechanisms of an open society. If we can't depend on people telling truth most of the time, trust and reliability goes out the door. Without trustworthiness to keep us on track, the entire fabric of society must grind to a halt through a lack of purpose and direction.   When we spurn the truth, our everyday lives become impossibly irksome. We would be wary of buying anything in a supermarket or on the internet if we could not rely on the truth of what we are being told about the products we are buying. We rely on the mass media uncovering the truth about current events and laying that truth before the public. Unless we are truthful to ourselves and others we cannot communicate effectively with our fellows.

Trust and sincerity involve truthfulness. We may establish the meaning and value of things from our own point of view, but unless we are genuinely convinced that our conclusions are true we are guilty of insincerity and untrustworthiness in sharing them with other people. If we are not truthful with ourselves, we can't be truthful with others. If we want our working relationships to be smooth, then we must remain true to ourselves in spite of our personal feelings about those we are working with. We don't allow these feelings to tarnish the truth about what we are and why we are there. Truthfulness is therefore important as an interpersonal facilitator which makes our relationships work regardless of personal animosities.

Truth-telling is about disclosure and openness as truth itself is independent of what we seek for ourselves. Truth-seeking goes one stage further in using methods to uncover the truth. Thus, truth-seeking is what we do in sustaining and furthering our lives. Truth-applying is constantly required to keep us on track and make sure that we have not inadvertently strayed from truth. Truthfulness in the sense of telling the truth and of being true to oneself is important prerequisites to truth-seeking. There is no point in seeking truth unless one is disposed from the outset to be truthful and true to oneself.

The authentic person is true to himself in wanting nothing hidden or devious about themselves. It involves honesty, sincerity and "a courageous confrontation with the truth" according to Bernard Williams.[158] But the process is more complex than that. We begin by establishing the values in our lives that are true of ourselves. We exercise judgment in evaluating our behaviour, and when we reach a certain level of self-criticism, we become truthful persons and are ready to be honest and sincere in our truth-seeking. In being truthful we interact with our thoughts and feelings to get in touch with ourselves as a whole. The constant search for the goodness in ourselves, other people and things in general leads us to be sincere and truthful persons, and we can embark on truth-seeking as lovers of truth for its own sake. Truth-telling ensures a respect for the truth which goes along with a respect for ourselves, other people and the value of life in general.

But "the demand for truthfulness and the rejection of truth can go together" as Bernard Williams tells us.[159] There may be doubts as to whether the truth ever can be reached since we can never be absolutely sure that we have reached it. The fact that a person says that they are telling the truth does not mean that they value truth sufficiently to be able to tell the truth. Truthfulness is not enough by itself as it can breed complacency and naivety. If we are used to being truthful and to others being equally truthful to us then we can accept too readily an alleged

[158] Bernard Williams, *Truth and Truthfulness: An Essay in Genealogy*, (Princeton and Oxford: Princeton University Press, 2002), ch. 8, p. 185.
[159] Bernard Williams, *op. cit.*, ch. 1, p. 2.

truth which is in fact not the case. If everything appears to be going well, we lapse all too readily into lethargy and accept the surface appearance of things. Besides external criticism, we need constantly to reach back into ourselves and criticise ourselves, and reach outwards to interact with that which is distinct from us. This is done by getting outside ourselves contextually as referred to above.

There is also the fear that if everyone told the truth all the time, human society would collapse because most people don't want to face the truth all the time. We all have a limited capacity for facing up to realities. But even the bitterest of truths must be told. For example, in telling a person that a loved one has died, you may try to talk the person round to facing the reality of the situation. Their loved one has had an accident, was immediately taken to hospital, the surgeons have been working hard on their injuries, and so on. You spin out the story but you feel that it is not going down well. Inevitably you reach the point when the ghastly truth must be uttered, that their loved one is dead. The reality and finality of the event strikes home, and the adverse reaction is so extreme, you feel no pleasure or satisfaction having done your duty.

When we deceive people or lie to them, we invariably do so out of weakness. We need strength of mind and resolve to tell the truth when we feel disinclined to do so. Dualist theory aims to strengthen that resolve but not to the point of making people tell the truth naively and thoughtlessly all the time. We must tell the truth because we are fully aware of all the benefits and necessities of doing so. Blurting out the truth all the time is not of sign of strength but of insensitivity, thoughtlessness, lack of tact, understanding or whatever.

If we value truth as involving honesty and sincerity then we should aim both to reduce people's fear of it and to increase their respect for it. Either fear of truth or lack of respect for it underlie most of the lies and deceits in which people indulge. Some people fear telling the truth because of the possible harmful consequences of doing so. Others lack respect for the truth because they think that lies and deceit are the best way to get their way in life. This account of truth aims to show the benefits of truth for those who are fearful or disrespectful of it.

Being truthful is insufficient in itself to keep us on the path to truth and enlightenment because our prized beliefs are only true to ourselves. Being sincere and honest about what we believe in, does not make these beliefs true. We need not only to tell the truth but also to step outside our beliefs, to actively seek the truth within them, and then to assess our conclusions in equal measure. In short, we need the truth-seeking and truth-applying aspects of truth to criticise ourselves and our beliefs, and to take us forward.

Truth-Seeking: This involves any trial-and-error process by which we establish factual truth. It therefore includes the various scientific methods by which truth is sought to add to our knowledge and understanding of the world, life and society. Truth-seeking requires truth-telling to discipline it and truth-applying to try it out. We cannot achieve the ends of truth unless we are doing our best to tell the truth sincerely and also assess its value and validity at the same time. Truth-seeking is the purposeful aspect which draws together the truth-telling and truth-assessing aspects in tandem.

Successful truth-seeking must always take place in some context which gives meaning and value to whatever is said to be true or untrue. If there is no context to what is said, then it can be neither true nor false but merely meaningless. The schizoid person, babbling a stream of disconnected words and sentences, finds no audience, even when he speaks at Speakers' Corner in Hyde Park, London because no one can find a context within which his words make sense to them. The sounds do not refer to anything in particular. In contrast, the conspiracy theorist may also be talking nonsense in concocting a farfetched theory out of a disparate set of facts. But he finds a ready audience because the context is clear whether people believe him or not. They know what he is referring to and the novelty of his view is captivating and challenging. But he is not seeking truth because he already knows what the truth is, and he is merely collecting and distorting the facts to 'prove' what he already believes to be true. He does not have an open mind as far as truth-seeking is concerned.

We seek truth particularly in five important contexts, namely, external reality, ideality, sociosphere, cosmos, and posterity. These five contexts are not exhaustive of the possibilities but are only the most important ones from a dualist point of view. We establish truth or falsity within these contexts by interacting with their contents. Thus, in dualist theory, truth-seeking is a trial-and-error process in which we interact with what we believe is true or not true (1) to discover what is really the case or not the case (external reality), (2) to reveal what we are or are not (ideality), (3) to find out what has to be done or not to be done (sociosphere), (4) to establish what our place in the universe is or is not (cosmos), (5) to speculate about future possibilities (posterity), and such like, though not all at the same time.

This contextual approach enables the dualist theory of truth to incorporate previously incompatible views of truth, such as the correspondence, coherence, and pragmatic theories of truth. The dualist theory of truth covers all these ways of seeking truth performed by us both in everyday life and in the academic and scientific spheres of activity. They are described within an overall system which does not impinge on what anyone is already doing, unless they are using truth for ends which are demonstrably untruthful. The simplest ways to seek the truth of the matter are to ask someone, consult a book, a search engine or whatever. But dualist truth-seeking particularly concerns the truth of an eye witness account, how true to life a novel is, what is true about a historical account, whether scientific theories or hypotheses can be truly relied upon, and not least the alleged truth of religious dogmas and doctrines. But the search for truth is incomplete unless there are modes of assessing in an objective way the truth or falsity of what is claimed to be true or false.

Truth-applying: This is the special activity of applying the truths at which we have arrived both by experience and by learning. It includes the intuitive use of truths by which we use them without thinking about them. It is the dualist counterpart of truth-telling in that we can't always be telling the truth and we have to be careful about what we say. It is a matter of personal choice whether or not we apply the truths that we have learnt. Indeed, it is only by applying them that we find out how practical and applicable these truths are or are not. We often find that it is counterproductive to be utterly open and honest about things. People may resent being told how things really are, for example, when they are dying from cancer. In practice it may be necessary to be less than truthful. As George Steiner put it:

> Ambiguity, polysemy [many meanings], opaqueness, the violation of grammatical and logical sequences, reciprocal incomprehensions, the capacity to lie – these are not pathologies of language but the roots of its genius. Without them the individual and the species would have withered.[160]

Politicians in particular are well-known for their ambiguities, half-truths and downright lies. Yet the situations they find themselves in may make this necessary and unavoidable. We are all imperfect in the discipline of applying truth in everyday life. The use of white lies, evasions, or half truths may well be required by the circumstances in which we find ourselves. But then it becomes a question of whether we can believe anything anyone ever tells. We may cease to rely on anyone's word for it and trust goes out the door.

How do we know when we have reached the truth or whether we are being told the truth? Well, we either accept their alleged truth on face value or we react in some way to what we think may be true or untrue in a number of ways, such as thinking about them, speaking of them, having feelings, attitudes or opinions about them, or imagining them as they could be in the future. In applying truth, we usually interact with that which is not ourselves to relate it to ourselves as a whole. As a result, we make sense or fail to make sense of whatever is said, thought, done, felt or imagined. In short, we discover by a complex trial-and-error process what is the right or wrong thing to do or to say about alleged truths.

7. The rigorous pursuit of truth

Truth-validating: The use of traditional logic is not ruled out by the logic of dualist interaction. It has its place but it is not the ultimate arbiter of truth that the logicians often assume it to be. A dynamic account must conform to logical rules in its internal consistency at any moment in time. But as such an account is subject to constant revision and up-dating, it can change over time. The same account at one point in time will not be consistent with the same account in a previous point in time. The validation of a dynamic account can only be pursued internally. It concerns what is said and what it means in the particular context of the account. It cannot apply outside the account without changing it and adding to or subtracting from it. Thus, truth-validating is only one link in the chain of truth discovery and application.

---

[160] George Steiner, *After Babel: Aspects of Language and Translation.* 3rd ed. (Oxford: OUP, 1998), ch. 3, p. 246.

Truth-proving: This is the use of mathematical proofs to arrive at truths by applying the rules of mathematics, which is used to prove or disprove formulae, theorems, and ultimately scientific theories. Mathematics is successful in so far as it calibrates human thinking to represent external realities with greater precision than is possible with ordinary language or indeed logic. The exactitude of mathematical measurement and formulation imposes discipline on our thinking. The use of mathematical proofs is similarly limited to context as with logical validation. This means using formal modes of assessing alternative statements, hypotheses, beliefs, opinions or the like. These modes include mathematics, scientific research and experimentation as well our own personal endeavours to confirm or deny truths by using our own mental faculties and abilities. By using these modes of judging, we move *from* personal opinion, hypothesis, or conjecture *to* objective facts that can be categorically stated to be true within those contexts in which they appropriately used. To be really thorough in our assessments, we should use all of these modes when appropriate and practical to do so.

In a formal mode, we use positive/negative words such as true/false, confirmed/denied, and conjectured/refuted, to designate the use of these formal modes. For example, 'It is true that electrons exist' does not mean the same as 'electrons exist'. It means that a mode of assessment, namely, scientific research may be used to confirm the existence of electrons. The mere assertion that electrons exist is insufficient, peremptory and dogmatic whereas saying that the assertion is true reassures the listener that their existence can be confirmed in a specific way. The assertion does not acquire the property of truth but is interacted with differently. It implies that scientists are doing things with electrons to show their existence, whereas merely saying they exist gives us no such assurance.

Truth-accounting: This includes the procedure of the overall dynamic account which details everything relevant to the assertion of truth or falsity within a particular context. To be truthful, an account must not only have an internal coherence in its contents but also a correspondence to the facts in external reality. Generally speaking, coherence is associated with the ultimate and all-inclusive aspect of truth, whereas correspondence is associated with acts of assessment, confirmation, or denial and refutation. Coherence may or may not bear truth but correspondence is necessary to make truth.

We use both coherence and correspondence in everyday circumstances. On seeing a clock in a strange town, we immediately assume that it is telling us the correct time. But we do so on grounds of coherence because we see it in the context of a reliable town clock. We have no reason to think outside that context unless we are told or discover that the clock is unreliable. That the true time is on the clock is confirmed because 3.27 pm, or whatever, is roundabout the time we expect to see on it. It fits in with our expectations because it makes sense in that context. If a doubt enters our minds, we would do something more to satisfy ourselves that the time on the clock corresponds to the real time. We might ask passers by whether the clock is accurate, or we could wait and see whether or not the minute hand moves.

When we account for a truth we use meaningful expressions that refer or do not refer to reality. Thus, meaning and reference leads us to make coherent statements that correspond or do not correspond to reality. The result is a consolidation of the facts making up the dynamic account. The following diagram gives a very rough indication of the truth accounting processes involved.

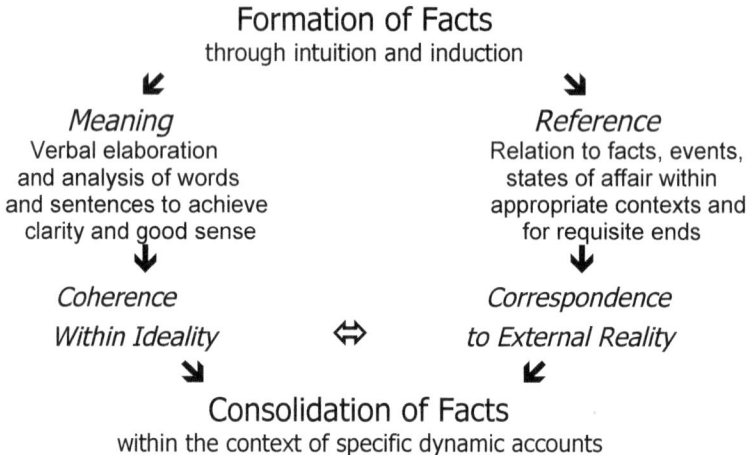

Formation of Facts
through intuition and induction

↙   ↘

Meaning	*Reference*
Verbal elaboration and analysis of words and sentences to achieve clarity and good sense	Relation to facts, events, states of affair within appropriate contexts and for requisite ends

↓   ↓

Coherence		*Correspondence*
Within Ideality	⇔	*to External Reality*

↘   ↙

Consolidation of Facts
within the context of specific dynamic accounts

The Meaning and Reference Aspects of Truth-Accounting

We may arrive at facts by intuition and induction but they then need to be consolidated by working out in detail what they mean and what they refer to. For example, in giving an account of a historical event, the facts are arrived at by consulting the sources, witnesses, documents, photographs and whatever lends itself to giving an accurate account of the said event. The facts based on these sources are arrived at by intuition and induction. They are elaborated verbally to make sense of the event and the words must cohere together as a narrative based on logical consistency. The way that the facts correspond to external events must also be clarified by putting into one's own words the testimony of witnesses and the reliable summary of events by trustworthy contemporary writers. There is moreover endless scope for revision and restatement in all such accounts so that the consolidation of facts is always relative to the particular contexts in which they are being used.

8. The personal pursuit of truth

The future of civilisation depends on everyone pursuing truth in their own way. It has no future if preconceived truths are forced on people without allowing them to think them through for themselves. Its future is assured when there is constant criticism of past truths followed by a constant reinvigoration of culture with new truths and insights, which only relatively isolated truth-seeking individuals can provide. When people are not allowed to think for themselves, they abrogate responsibility for their own lives to truths that overshadow them. This has happened time and again in history when religious, political and scientific dogmas have been used by power-mongers, demagogues, religious fanatics, gurus, and intellectual tyrants to captivate people's minds and enslave them to truths instead to allowing them to be liberated by a personal pursuit of truth.

The importance of truth lies in the overall activity of pursuing truth, and not in any single proclamation of truth. When each of us seeks truth in our own way, we make our personal contributions to truth as a whole, and all of us together seeking truth help the human race move towards the ultimate truth concerning what life and the universe are really all about, however far off that ultimate truth may be. But this ideal can only be fulfilled when we are being sincere and honest in our personal searches for truth and when we reach out to others to share our truths and take on board the criticisms of other people.

When truth-telling is connected to truth-seeking and truth-applying then we have *personal* truth-seeking which belongs to us and is expressive of our own beliefs and convictions. *Impersonal* truth-seeking arises when truth-seeking and truth-applying are disconnected from truth-telling. A notion of absolute truth takes over and rules the person rather the person making use of the truth for the best possible reasons. Truth thus becomes an end in itself instead of a means to bettering ourselves and humanity.

Above all, truth is a human thing which expresses what we are as the unique and indispensable human beings. Once it stops being personal to us and a part of ourselves as a whole then we are in trouble. It is then being imposed from without by some person or organisation pursuing its own agenda and in total disregard of our interests. Ironically, the more personal truth is, the more chance it has of being common to us all, instead of being peculiar to a sect, religion, or group of persons who believe that they have reached absolute, eternal truth. They no longer strive to get to the bottom of things and have given up on personal truth-seeking which alone keeps us on the right path of finding truths that are common to all humanity and can be put into practice by everyone.

The interactive pursuit of truth is what we do when we follow our own interests and enthusiasms to discover things for ourselves. Its personal nature helps us to complete ourselves, find our place in the universe, and give meaning and direction to our lives. We achieve these goals when the pursuit adds to our knowledge and understanding of ourselves, other people, society, and the universe at large. In so far as our talents and abilities allow, the pursuit may also contribute impersonally to the sum-total of human knowledge and understanding. But that is a bonus rather than an end in itself. It is therefore worth examining the importance of personal truth-seeking for the individual and how that personal pursuit benefits civilisation in the process.

If your search for truth is not personal to you then it is forced on you without your having the opportunity to think things through for yourself. When truths have to be accepted without question or criticism then this impedes personal truth-seeking. They are accepted because they are based on superior and unassailable authority, and not because they have been thought through by the person accepting them. This often happens in the case of dogmas which are protected from criticism to suit the purposes of persons pursuing their own idiolectic or idealistic ends. Ideologues, dictators, and religious fanatics are expert at stopping people from thinking for themselves so their own views are forced on people by emotional, authoritarian or fear inducing means.

It is also harmful to disconnect truth from our personal and social involvement in it, as theoreticians such as logicians, scientists, political theorists, and theologians are apt to do. Such disconnections have fostered inhumanity and enmity all too readily in the past, as in the case of religious and ideological truths which are held to be more important than the lives of those disagreeing with such truths.

Such a pursuit of truth demands openness combined with honour, honesty and sincerity so that it can rise above mere idealistic reasoning and be the reliable arbiter of the correctness and justice of our reasonings. Ulterior motives impede our truthful reasonings as they mean withholding or suppressing information which we wish to keep to ourselves. The free expression of all our motives contributes to our openness and to our giving a full and fair account of what makes us what we are. We are not sincerely seeking truth unless we are also being true to ourselves and transparent about our motivations. Thus, 'true' in this context means true by virtue of the methods and processes used to reach it, whether personal, logical, mathematical, scientific, ultimately, dualist. This omnibus view of truth is discussed further in the last section below.

This personal element in truth-seeking involves constant self-reference in which we make ourselves consciously aware of what we are doing and thinking. The process of self-reference is an important source of our moral consciousness. In being moral persons, our internal monitor should always be at the ready to tell us when we have gone too far or not far enough in achieving our goals or fulfilling our motivations.

Going beyond self-reference, the sociosphere is important in providing the ambience in which all our motivations are taken account of. Being answerable for our actions to other people means that the connections between our conflicting motivations are constantly reviewed, and our reasonings are scrutinised from all possible points of view, and conform to reality and the facts. The transactional interconnections of the sociosphere bring isolated individuals, groups, sects, cliques, companies, nations, and international organisations into the common forum within which all truths are ultimately decided in the light of history and posterity. The search for truth is sociospheric activity at its highest and best when it contributes to the future of humanity.

The social value of all truth-seeking activities depends on our interacting with others. We add to our knowledge of things by not settling for truths arrived at entirely by ourselves. In not cleaving absolutely to heartfelt truths, we keep our minds open, and we freely reach out to people, books, mass media, internet and all the other sociospheric sources of knowledge and understanding. Seeking truth also involves being truthful to other people as well as to oneself. We rely on other people's trust for our self-esteem, and we gain more by being honest with people than being dishonest and distrusted. Even the most certain truths of physics and astronomy are only provisional in the end. The laws of physics may have been different billions of years ago for all we know at present. With time and greater knowledge, we may eventually ascertain if and how they were different.

We can also be too personal and individualist in our truth-seeking. This is an idiolectic mode of seeking truth which needs to be corrected by the use of all the other truth-seeking modes, that is to say, the logical, mathematical, scientific, and dualist modes. The idiolectic mode means taking an entirely egocentric and selfish view of things is also called solipsistic as it means behaving as if only oneself and one's experiences really exist. A solipsist interprets everything within the context. We escape the sterile circularity of solipsism by opening our minds to truths and values in contexts beyond ourselves. Even our use of universal moral notions can lead to a sterile solipsism unless they are used in social contexts. Only within these contexts can we develop our notions so that our opinions and beliefs become more truthful and realistic. The idiolectic mode of seeking truth is typically used in religion to justify the alleged veracity of religious insights and revelations. All our personal insights can be selfishly regarded as god-given if we wish to fool others into believing this for own evil ends.

The process of truth-seeking is important in dualist theory because we need it to distinguish fact from fiction, and theoretical constructs from mere story-telling. Otherwise, any story, such as those from holy scripture, can be proclaimed as fact which is beyond criticism. We need also to counter the power of authority which can make up its own truths and enforce them by means of propaganda or emotional blackmail. As Fernández-Armesto shows in his historical survey of truth, all kinds of bizarre methods have been employed in the past to discover alleged 'truths'.[161] It is now necessary to consolidate truth, especially that of the scientific variety, as against (1) the pressures to re-introduce authority as a major source of truth, and (2) the submission to endoxical influences by which mass culture tyrannises and demeans us all. The resurgence of religious fundamentalism and the persistence of political correctness exemplify these two threats to truth, and the both of them need to be opposed by us all as free-thinking individuals.

In this way, personal truth-seeking, using the principles of dualist theory, can contribute to the unity of humanity in its overall pursuit of truth. Instead of people falling out with each other because they cannot agree what is or is not true, dualist principles make agreement more feasible because of the morality of acknowledging differing viewpoints and because of the broadening of contextual horizons which the dualist view encourages. These procedures help us to narrow down all our personal options until we reach those which fit in with everyone

---

[161] Felipe Fernández-Armesto, *Truth: A History*, (London: Bantam Books, 1997).

else's options. Thus, truth-seeking has to be personal to us to ensure that truth is humanised and not rendered more important than the human beings pursuing it. When truths become more important than us, then we are apt to sacrifice our lives or the lives of others in their name.

Logical truth-seeking involves the application of logical principles, mathematical truth-seeking involves measurement and demonstration, and scientific truth-seeking the use of scientific methods. Thus, logical, mathematical and scientific truth-seeking are relatively impersonal, objective methods, whereas personal truth-seeking is conducted within ourselves. It is made personal to us because of our personal involvement in it. Its importance lies in humanising logical and scientific truths which are nothing to us in the abstract and need to be made personal to us (what Polanyi calls a "passionate participation in the act of knowing.")[162] Truth without passionate involvement can never be lasting.

9. The pursuit of ultimate truth

Hitherto ultimate truth has been considered monistically as one thing above all else. In dualist theory, ultimate truth is inclusive of everything whatsoever. As religion is inherently monistic and inward-looking, no religion has ever successfully converted everyone on the planet. None of them ever can do so while they are founded on exclusive and limited beliefs that purport to be the whole truth of the matter. By contrast, dualist view is holistic and all-inclusive. It endeavours to include everything as a whole without excluding anything in particular. It is not destructive of beliefs as it finds a place for all of them, that place is not free of scrutiny and criticism. Only everything about us as a whole can be true of the whole human race. Science has been successful in appealing to every nation and every creed because it possesses this ultimacy of appealing to the whole of humanity. However, the content of science is limited by its severe specialisation and compartmentalisation. Even science cannot give us the ultimate truth of things, and it rightly does not claim to do so.

Thus, the dualist quest for truth can be contrasted with a monist quest in which there is only one way to reach ultimate truth. This ignores all the other ways by which truth may be reached. The single minded pursuit of truth by scientists, artists and other creative people may often be beneficial to humanity. But a single minded belief in one ultimate truth, whether ideological or religious, can be equally inimical to humanity.

The monist view is a static one that views the world as it is. It is a quest for ultimate truth in which people settle for one point of view above all others. They find their ultimate resting place in some religion or ideology whether it be in the Bible, Torah, Koran, Buddhist scriptures, *Das Kapital*, *Mein Kampf*, the works of Sigmund Freud, the works of Carl Gustav Jung, or some philosophy such as analytical philosophy, post-modernism or whatever.

The dualist view takes account of all these viewpoints and finds a place for

---

[162] Michael Polanyi, *Personal Knowledge*, (London: RKP, 1962), p. 17.

them by virtue of its comprehensive conceptual structure. The most obscure religious belief or political viewpoint has its place in the same way that zoology and botany can incorporate every animal and plant that can be identified and categorised. Thus, dualism leads us ultimately to a holism which is an overall appreciation of all viewpoints whatsoever. As holists we can see the value in all religions, ideologies, philosophies and indeed science in general, however critical we may be of them in detail. The whole truth therefore includes everything concerning the human race, life and the universe at large. This comprehensive view is the aim of *Sautonic Wisdom* (the word 'sautonic' being derived from the Greek *gnothi sauton* 'know thyself') as outlined in my book of that name.[163]   In other words, we are all little worlds forever getting to know ourselves in relation to the world at large; each of us is a microcosm with macrocosmic ambitions.

These little worlds are entirely physical and in the brain. There is nothing occult about them. They are the product of our inner interactivity and they are all our own. Our task is to constantly enlarge our little worlds to incorporate the world at large. In so far as we constantly fail in that task, the ultimate truth must and will elude us. Nevertheless, it is the Golden Goal, the Heavenly Kingdom, the Edenic Paradise in which all is sweetness and light. While we can imagine it, we can strive for it. In interacting with it, we may find ways of bringing it at least partially into the real world. To make real what was only ideal is surely the true purpose of our existence. But this must be done carefully, critically and not hot-headedly. It need not be self-damaging and self-defeating like the monist ideals of religion and ideology but rather self-fulfilling like the holist ideals of *Sautonic Wisdom*.

Thus, the ultimate truth for human beings lies not in settling for one viewpoint but in incorporating all viewpoints by interacting constantly with them to make as much of them as humanly possible. This is clearly the opposite of religious or ideological viewpoints that see only one way forward. It accords with the ongoing dualist view that is constantly interacting with the world and its contents. This whole-hearted position provides us with the open-minded outlook to work out for ourselves what we are to do with our lives. In other words, our safety, security and internal well-being lies in constant interaction, in striving to better ourselves, and in taking account of everything in a spirit of open-minded curiosity and vitality. Being open to all things promotes optimism whereas confining ourselves to one point of view or mindset depresses and stunts us as human beings. Dualism can be all things to all men but only by bringing all views into its omniscient fold. This is no easy task but we can all learn to work at it if we have the will to do so. Thus, the task of dualist theory is to supply the reasons and rationale for doing so – a task that is only begun with this book.

---

[163] Alistair J. Sinclair, *Sautonic Wisdom: What We Are Here To Do*, (Almostic Publications, 2015).

Bibliography
Of Works Cited in the Text

Addison, J. (1711), *The Spectator*, nos.122, 117, (London: J.M. Dent, 1909)　　47

Anscombe, (1957), *Intention*, (Oxford: Blackwell)　　88

Aristotle, *Metaphysics*　　22, 162

　Nicomachean Ethics　　42, 64

　Organon (*Categoriae, De Interpretatione, Analytica Priora, Analytica Posteriora,*

　Topica, and *De Sophisticis Elenchis*)　　138, 159, 160

Armstrong, D.M. (1968), *A Materialist Theory of the Mind*, (London: Routledge)　　4, 6, 88

Bacon, F. (1620) *Novum Organon or True Suggestions of the Interpretation of Nature*　　164

Barnes, J. (1989), *The Presocratic Philosophers*, (London: Routledge)　　151

Bergson, H. (1913), *Time and Freewill: An Essay on the Immediate Data of Consciousness,*

　trans. by F.L. Pogson (from *Essai sur les Données Immédiates de la Conscience*), (New

　York: Dover Publications, 2001)　　144

Berlin, Sir I. (1953), 'The Hedgehog and the Fox' in *Russian Thinkers*, (London: Penguin,

　1979)　　92

Bernstein, J. (1973), *Einstein*, (London: Wm. Collins & Sons)　　150

Blackburn S. & Simmons, K. (eds), (1999), *Truth*, (Oxford: OUP, 2003),　　186

Bodanis, D. (2001), *E=mc²: A Biography of the World's Most Famous Equation*, (London:

　Macmillan)　　149

Boswell, (1799), *The Life of Dr. Johnson*, (London: Oxford University Press, 1966)　　30

Buber, M. (1922), *I and Thou*, trans. by R. G. Smith, second edition, (Edinburgh: T. & T.

　Clark, 1959)　　28, 29

Buffon, Comte de, (1749-1767), *Natural History, General and Particular*, (Edinburgh:

　William Creech, 1780), Vol. III.　　26

Burnet, J. (1930), *Early Greek Philosophy*, (London: Adam & Charles Black, 1975)　　21

Robert Burns, (1786), *A Dream, Poems and Songs of Robert Burns*, ed. by James Barke,

　(London and Glasgow: Collins, 1955)　　189

Clark, R. W. (1975), *The Life of Bertrand Russell*, (Harmondsworth: Penguin Books)　　51

Cornford, F.M. (1912) *From Religion to Philosophy: A Study in the Origins of Western*

　Speculation, (Princeton: Princeton University Press,1991)　　22

Dennett, D.C. (1993), *Consciousness Explained*, (London: Penguin Books)　　4, 5

Derrida (1967), *Of Grammatology*, trans. G. C. Spivak, (Baltimore: Johns Hopkins

　University Press, 1972)　　162

　(1988) *Afterword: Toward An Ethic of Discussion* in *Limited Inc.*　　162

Descartes, R. (1637), *Discours de la Méthode*, (Paris: Garnier-Flammarion, 1966,

　Quartième Partie)　　125, 136

　(1641), *Meditations on First Philosophy*, trans. J. Cottingham, (Cambridge, UK:

　Cambridge University Press, 1986)　　3

　(1647), 'Notes Directed Against a Certain Programme', in *Key Philosophical*

　Writings, trans. E. S. Haldane and G.R.T. Ross, ed. by E. Chávez-Arvizo,

　(Ware, Herts: Wordsworth Editions Ltd., 1997)　　3

Dickens, C. (1854), *Hard Times*, (New York: New American Library, 1961)　　42, 43

Diogenes Laertius (c. 300 CE), *Lives and Opinions of Eminent Philosophers*, (Loeb

　Classical Library, 1980)　　22, 161

Donne, J. (1624), 'Devotions upon Emergent Occasions - Meditation XVII'. *Selected*

　Prose, (London: Penguin Books, 1987)　　55

Durkheim, E. (1915), *The Elementary Forms of Religious Life* trans. J.W. Swain, (London: Allen and Unwin, 1976)   26
Eagleton, T. (2005), *The English novel: An Introduction*, (London: Wiley-Blackwell)   52
Engel, P. (2002),*Truth*, (Acumen Publishing Ltd., 2002)   194
Eusebius of Caesarea, (264-340CE), *Praeparatio Evangelica* (available online)   161
Fernández-Armesto, F. (1997), *Truth: A History*, (London: Bantam Books)   205
Feuerbach, L.A. (1854), *The Essence of Christianity*, trans by Marian Evans (aka George Eliot), (London: John Chapman)   120
Frege, G. (1956), 'The Thought: A Logical Inquiry', *Mind*, 65 (1956). Reprinted in Blackburn and Simmons, *op. cit.,* ch. V,   187
Gibbon, E. (1776), *The History of the Decline and Fall of the Roman Empire*, (London: Allen Lane, 1994)   31
Gibbons, M., *et al*, (1994), The *New Production of Knowledge*, (London: Sage)   59
Gide, A. (1954), *Journal 1939-1949 Souvenirs*, (Paris: Gallimart)   193
Guthrie, W.K. (1962), *A History of Greek Philosophy*, (Cambridge: Cambridge University Press, 1980)   22, 151
Hacking, I. (1981), *Why Does Language Matter to Philosophy?*, (Cambridge: CUP)   162
Haidt, J. (2012), *The Righteous Mind: Why Good People Are Dividedby Politics and Religion*, (London: Allen Lane, Penguin Books)   30
Hempel, C.G. (1965), *Aspects of Scientific Explanation*, (New York: The Free Press)   181
Hofstadter, D.R. (1979), *Gödel, Escher Bach: An Eternal Golden Braid*, (London: Penguin Books)   29
(2007), *I am a Strange Loop*, (New York: Basic Books)   29
Hume, D. (1739), *A Treatise of Human Nature* (ed. Nidditch - Oxford: the Clarendon Press)   6, 35, 86, 134, 164
(1777), *An Enquiry Concerning Human Understanding*, (ed. P.H. Nidditch - Oxford: the Clarendon Press, 1975)   87, 164
Husserl, E. (1913), *Ideas: General Introduction to Pure Phenomenology*, (London: George Allen & Unwinl, 1969)   158
James, W. (1907), *Pragmatism*, (New York: Washington Square Press, 1963)   92
Jeans, Sir J. (1930), *The Mysterious Universe*, (London: Penguin books, 1937)   122
Jung, C.G. (1935), 'The Relations Between the Ego and the Unconscious', *Two Essays on Analytical Psychology. Collected Works*, Vol. 7. As in reproduced in *The Portable Jung*, (London: Penguin, 1978)   28
Psychological Types, in *Collected Works*, Vol. 6, Part II.   28, 92
Aion: Researches into the Phenomenology of the Self, in *Collected Works*, Vol. 9   28
Kant, I. (1787), *A Critique of Pure Reason*, trans. N. Kemp Smith, (London: Macmillan & Co.,1964)   35, 135, 138, 155
Kirk G.S. and Raven J.E., (1957), *The Presocratic Philosophers: A Critical History with a Selection of Texts*, (Cambridge: Cambridge University Press, 1969)   23, 151
Lactantius, (c.240-c.320CE) *Divine Institutes*   161
Lawrence, D.H. (1925), *Kangaroo*. (London: Penguin Books, 1980)   50
(1915), *The Rainbow*, (London: Penguin, 1980)   50
Leibniz, (1714), *Monadology, Philosophical* Writings, (London: J.M. Dent, 1990)   10
Liddell and Scott, (1871), *Greek-English Lexicon*, Abridged Edition, (Oxford: OUP, 1983) 23
Locke, (1700), *An Essay Concerning Human Understanding*, ed. P. H. Nidditch, (Oxford: Clarendon Press, 1988)   135
Lucretius, (1st cent. BCE), *De Rerum Natura*, trans. by R.E. Latham, *On the Nature of the Universe*, (London: Penguin Books, 1994)   23, 161

McGinn, C. (1982) *The Character of Mind*, (Oxford: OUP)   4
Mascaró, J. (ed.) (1962), *The Bhavagad Gita*, (London: Penguin)   21
Mazzini, *The Duties of Man*, (London: J.M. Dent & Co., 1955)   55
Mill, J.S. (1843), *A System of Logic: Ratiocinative and Inductive*, (London: Longman, 1970) 155
   (1859), *On Liberty*, (London: Oxford University Press, 1971)   31, 54, 164
Moore, H.T. (1974), *The Priest of Love: A Life of D.H. Lawrence*. Revised edition,
   (Harmondsworth: Penguin Books, 1976)   51
Nagel, T. (1979), 'What is it like to be a bat?', *Mortal Questions*, (Cambridge: CUP)   89
Pinker, S. (1995), *The Language Instinct*, (London: Penguin Books)   121
   (1998), *How the Mind Works*, (London: Penguin Books)   121
Plato, *The Statesman, Collected Dialogues of Plato*, (Princeton University Press, 1961) 161
Polanyi, M. (1962), *Personal Knowledge*, (London: RKP)   206
Pope, A.(1733), *An Essay on Man*   25
Popper, K. (1945), *The Open Society and its Enemies*, (London: RKP, 1969)   42
Paul, St. *New Testament*, Epistle to the Romans   27
Popper, K and Eccles, J.C., (1977), *The Self and its Brain*, (London: Routledge, Kegan
   & Paul, 1986)   5
Quine, (1960), *Word and Object*, (Massachusetts: MIT Press)   162
   (1974), *Methods of Logic*, (London, RKP)   162
Reid, T. (1774), 'A Brief Account of Aristotle's Logic', in Sir William Hamilton's edition
   of *The Works of Thomas Reid D.D.* (Edinburgh 1895 - also Georg Ohms 1983)   164
   (1785), *Essays on the Intellectual Powers of Man*, Essay III, ch. IV., in *The
   Works of Thomas Reid*, ed. Sir W. Hamilton, (Edinburgh: James Thin, 1895)   135
   (1788), *Essays on the Active Powers of the Human Mind*, Sir William Hamilton's
   edition of *The Works of Thomas Reid D.D.* (Edinburgh 1895 - also Georg
   Ohms 1983)   24, 46, 180
Russell, B. (1903, 1937), *Principles of Mathematics*, (London: Routledge, 1992)   154, 179
   (1916) *Principles of Social Reconstruction*   51
   (1951) 'Ludwig Wittgenstein', *Mind*, Vol.LX   188
   (1967) *The Autobiography of Bertrand Russell*. (London: Allen & Unwin, 1975)   51
Sartre, J-P. (1943), *Being and Nothingness*, (London: Methuen, 1972)   180
Scott, Sir W. (1826), *Woodstock, or The Cavalier*, (Edinburgh: T.Nelson, 1926)   46
Searle, J. "Why I Am Not a Property Dualist", Berkeley University site:
   http://ist-socrates.berkeley.edu/~jsearle/132/PropertydualismFNL.doc   7
Shakespeare, *Macbeth*   24, 158
   Hamlet, Othello, Coriolanus, Timon of Athens   24
   King Lear   25
Shannon C.E. and Weaver W. (1949), *The Mathematical Theory of Communication*,
   (Urbana: The University of Illinois Press, 1964)   75
Sinclair, A.J. (2008), *What is Philosophy?* (Edinburgh: Dunedin Academic Press)   41
   (2010), "The Role of Dualist Thinking in Management" Seventh International
   Philosophy of Management Conference, at St. Anne's College, Oxford   59
   (2011a), "Dualism and Humanism," *Essays in the Philosophy of Humanism*,
   Vol. 19 (1), Spring-Summer   ix
   (2011b), "World War One and the Loss of the Humanist Consensus," *Essays in
   the Philosophy of Humanism*, Vol. 19 (2), Fall-Winter, pp. 43-60   ix
   (2013), *From Time to Eternity: An Essay on the Meaning of Time*, published
   as an e-book on Amazon Kindle   107
   (2014), *Punish the Person, not the Crime! Proposing a Social Treatment System*

to *Punish Lawbreakers*, published as an e-book on Amazon Kindle   59
  (2015), *Sautonic Wisdom: What We Are Here To Do*, (Almostic Publications) 26, 68, 207
Smith, A. (1759), *The Theory of Moral Sentiments*, (London: Henry G. Bohn, 1853) 129, 135
Steiner, G. (1998), *After Babel: Aspects of Language and Translation*. 3rd ed. (Oxford:
  OUP)   200
Stevenson, R.L. (1886), *The Strange Case of Dr. Jekyll and Mr. Hyde*, (London &
  Glasgow: Collins)   27
Tallentyre, S.G. (*alias* Evelyn Beatrice Hall), (1906), *Friends of Voltaire*, (London:
  Smith, Elder, & Co.)   53
Tarski, A. (1944), 'The Semantic Conception of Truth', *Philosophy and
  Phenomenological Research*, 4. Reprinted in Blackburn and Simmons, *op. cit.*, 186
Turing, A.M. "Computing Machinery and Intelligence," *Mind*, 1950   40
Vico, G. (1744), *New Science*. (London: Penguin, 1999)   55
Whitehead, A.N. (1925), *Science and the Modern World*, (New York: Mentor, 1958) 92
Wilde, Oscar, (1891), *The Portrait of Dorian Gray*, (London: Minster Classics, 1968) 27
Williams B. (1978), *Descartes: The Project of Pure Enquiry*, (London: Penguin Books) 3, 135
  (2002), *Truth and Truthfulness: An Essay in Genealogy*, (Princeton University
  Press)   197, 198
Wittgenstein, L. (1921), *Tractatus Logico-Philosophicus*, trans. D.F. Pears &
  B.F. McGuiness, (London: Routledge & Kegan Paul, 1969)   187
  (1953), *Philosophical Investigations*, trans. by G.E.M. Anscombe, (Oxford:
  Blackwell, 1968)   155, 156

Name Index

Subject Index